This Distant and Unsurveyed Country
A Woman's Winter at Baffin Island, 1857–1858

In 1857 Margaret Penny set off from Aberdeen, Scotland, with her husband, Captain William Penny, aboard the whaler *Lady Franklin* on a wintering voyage to what is now the eastern Canadian Arctic. Wives of British captains rarely sailed with their husbands and Margaret Penny was one of the few women to break with tradition, becoming the first European woman to winter at Baffin Island. Incorporating the journal she kept during the expedition with commentary by W. Gillies Ross, *This Distant and Unsurveyed Country* recreates nineteenth-century Baffin Island for the modern reader and provides a unique perspective on arctic whaling, the Canadian Arctic, and the interaction between Inuit and European culture at the time of the voyage.

Bringing together thirty years' work on arctic whaling, Ross's invaluable text supplements Margaret Penny's journal to present a complete picture not only of this particular expedition but of arctic whaling in general. Ross provides illuminating insights into the principal characters, the mechanics and strategy of whaling, life aboard ship, the climate and geography of the Arctic, the struggle for survival in the North, and the relationship between the Inuit and Europeans.

The unique combination of Margaret Penny's unabridged journal and Ross's extensive knowledge of whaling makes *This Distant and Unsurveyed Country* an invaluable resource and an unforgettable tale of adventure.

W. GILLIES ROSS is professor emeritus of geography at Bishop's University.

McGill-Queen's Native and Northern Series
Bruce G. Trigger, Editor

1   When the Whalers Were Up North
Inuit Memories from the Eastern Arctic
Dorothy Harley Eber

2   The Challenge of Arctic Shipping
Science, Environmental Assessment, and Human Values
David L. VanderZwaag and Cynthia Lamson, Editors

3   Lost Harvests
Prairie Indian Reserve Farmers and Government Policy
Sarah Carter

4   Native Liberty, Crown Sovereignty
The Existing Aboriginal Right of Self-Government in Canada
Bruce Clark

5   Unravelling the Franklin Mystery
Inuit Testimony
David C. Woodman

6 - Otter Skins, Boston Ships, and China Goods
The Maritime Fur Trade of the Northwest Coast, 1785–1841
James R. Gibson

7   From Wooden Ploughs to Welfare
The Story of the Western Reserves
Helen Buckley

8   In Business for Ourselves
Northern Entrepreneurs
Wanda A. Wuttunee

9   For an Amerindian Autohistory
An Essay on the Foundations of a Social Ethic
George E. Sioui

10   Strangers Among Us
David Woodman

11   When the North Was Red
Aboriginal Education in Soviet Siberia
Dennis A. Bartels and Alice L. Bartels

12 From Talking Chiefs to a Native Corporate Elite
The Birth of Class and Nationalism among Canadian Inuit
Marybelle Mitchell

13 Cold Comfort
My Love Affair with the Arctic
Graham W. Rowley

14 The True Spirit and Original Intent of Treaty 7
Treaty 7 Elders and Tribal Council with
Walter Hildebrandt, Dorothy First Rider, and Sarah Carter

15 This Distant and Unsurveyed Country
A Woman's Winter at Baffin Island, 1857–1858
W. Gillies Ross

Margaret Penny in later life (private collection)

This Distant and Unsurveyed Country

A Woman's Winter at Baffin Island, 1857–1858

W. Gillies Ross

McGill-Queen's University Press

Montreal & Kingston · London · Buffalo

© McGill-Queen's University Press 1997
ISBN 0-7735-1674-3

Legal deposit third quarter 1997
Bibliothèque nationale du Québec

Printed in Canada on acid-free paper

This book has been published with the help of
a grant from the Humanities and Social Sciences
Federation of Canada, using funds provided
by the Social Sciences and Humanities Research
Council of Canada.

McGill-Queen's University Press acknowledges
the support received for its publishing
program from the Canada Council's Block
Grants program.

Canadian Cataloguing in Publication Data

Ross, W. Gillies (William Gillies), 1931–
This distant and unsurveyed country: a woman's
winter at Baffin Island, 1857–1858
(McGill-Queen's native and northern series; 15)
Includes the text of Margaret Penny's journal.
Includes bibliographical references and index.
ISBN 0-7735-1674-3
1. Baffin Island (N.W.T.) – Description and
travel. 2. Whaling–Northwest Territories–Baffin
Island. I. Penny, Margaret II. Title. III. Series.
FC4195.B3Z49 1997   917.19′5   C97-900595-7
F1105.B3R68 1997

All maps drawn by the author.

This book was typeset by Typo Litho
Composition Inc. in 10/13 Baskerville.

Contents

Illustrations   ix

Acknowledgments   xiii

Introduction   xv

Maps   xlii

Icebergs and Bergy Bits   3
5–29 July 1857

The Kind-Hearted Esquimaux   18
30 July – 14 August

Tackritow, My Old Acquaintance   36
15 August – 2 September

All Belonged to One Company   60
3–27 September

What a Size of an Animal!   77
28 September – 28 October

On Terra Firma   97
29 October – 25 November

Ill Supplied with Food   114
26 November – 31 December

I Had My Usual Tea Party   131
1 January – 1 February 1858

The Scourge of the Sea   144

Fish in Every Direction   167
13 May – 30 June

Made All Sail for Aberdeen   184
1–7 July

Epilogue   199

APPENDICES

1   Crew Lists   229

2   Instructions to Missionary   231

3   Whales Killed   234

4   Native Place-Names   235

5   Margaret's Eskimo Glossary   238

References   241

Index   251

Illustrations

Margaret Penny in later life   *frontispiece*

Captain William Penny in 1846   xxviii

Eenoolooapik, who accompanied Captain Penny
to Aberdeen in 1839   xxx

The Moravian mission at Lichtenfels, Greenland   xxxvi

Victoria Dock, Aberdeen, about 1870   9

The *Lady Franklin* and *Sophia* off northwest Greenland in 1850
during the search for Sir John Franklin   11

The coast of Baffin Island south of Cumberland Sound   28

The harbour of Niantilik, where the whaler *Alibi* lost five men
to scurvy 1856–57   31

The whalemen's graveyard at Niantilik   32

Kingmiksok (now Imigen Island), the birthplace of Eenoolooapik and
site of the first intentional wintering, by the *McLellan,* 1851–52   33

Captain John Parker, commander of the Hull whaler *Emma*   38

A steam-auxiliary whaler, the *Diana* of Hull   44

The whalers *Gipsy, Undaunted,* and *Emma* beset
in Melville Bay, 1857   45

Life mask of Uckaluk   53

"The Esquimaux Family" in London after their appearance before
Queen Victoria at Windsor Castle   56

Whalers and boats off Cape Searle, Baffin Island   67

Eskimo whaleboats in Cumberland Sound   68

Whaling with hand harpoon   70

Whaling with gun harpoon   71

Lancing a harpooned whale   71

Towing a whale back to the ship   84

Captain Parker's ship *Emma* flensing a whale   86

The harbour of Kekerten, looking southeastward   93

Kekerten Harbour. A panoramic mosaic   94

The *Lady Franklin* and *Sophia* wintering in Lancaster Sound during
the Franklin search expedition of 1850–51   103

Eskimos of Foxe Basin wearing traditional winter clothing   105

Tookoolitoo (Tackritow)   139

Eskimos hunting seals at breathing holes   142

Eskimo seal hunter in Cumberland Sound   143

Headboard at the grave of a young Scotsman who died of scurvy
at Niantilik a few years after Margaret Penny's visit   151

Sand-blasted headboard at the grave of a man who died of scurvy
at Niantilik in April 1861   156

Part of a headboard at Niantilik commemorating the death
of a man from Shetland   161

Covered whaleboats near the floe edge ready for spring whaling   179

An Eskimo dog team in Foxe Basin   180

Entrance to the port of Aberdeen in 1840   196

Silver teaset presented to Margaret Penny by the shareholders
of the Aberdeen Arctic Company   198

Kekerten Harbour twenty-five years after Captain Penny established
the whaling station   202

Forty years after Captain Penny's men erected a house at Kekerten,
Aberdeen interests still operated a whaling station there   203

Kekerten Harbour. Ships' try-pots for rendering blubber into oil   204

The Reverend E.J. Peck, who established a mission at Blacklead Island
almost four decades after Brother Warmow's visit   208

William Penny, Jr   210

Acknowledgments

I wish to thank the staffs of all the libraries and archives whose resources have contributed to this book, but in particular those of Aberdeen Central Library, Indian and Northern Affairs Canada (Ottawa), the manuscript and newspaper sections of the British Library (London), the Public Record Office (London), the Scottish Record Office (Edinburgh), the Royal Geographical Society (London), and the Scott Polar Research Institute (Cambridge).

Among many helpful individuals who provided useful information are the following: Greg Allen, Mrs B.R. Cluer (Grampian Regional Council, Aberdeen), Arthur Credland (Town Docks Museum, Hull), Miss J.A. Cripps (Aberdeen City Archivist), Mrs Barbara Derbyshire (Moravian Church, Fairfield, England), Joan Druett, John Edwards (Aberdeen Maritime Museum), David Henderson (Dundee Museums), Gordon Junner (Family History Society, Aberdeen), the Reverend John H. McOwat (Moravian Church, Fulneck, England), Dr Ludger Müller-Wille (McGill University), Dr Susan Rowley, Dr Marc Stevenson (Canadian Circumpolar Institute), and Mrs Margaret Yule.

I owe special thanks to archivists I. Bauldauf and Gudrid Hickel (Archiv der Brüder Unität, Herrnhut, Germany), who provided biographical information about Brother Warmow; to Drs Karl Kuepper and Dieter Riegel (Bishop's University), who translated German text; to Dr Louis-Jacques Dorais (l'Université Laval), who examined the orthography and translations of Margaret Penny's glossary of Inuktitut words; and to Dr Julie Cruikshank (University of British Columbia),

Dr Philip Goldring (Parks Canada, Ottawa), and Dr Robert Forrest (Bishop's University), who read parts of the manuscript and made helpful suggestions. I am also grateful to the anonymous readers who diligently reviewed the manuscript for McGill-Queen's University Press and the Aid to Scholarly Publications Program.

Correspondence with descendants of Captain and Mrs Penny and their relatives has been invaluable. I am greatly indebted to Mrs Lorraine Arthur, Mrs June Knox, the late Mrs Kathleen O'Connor, Mrs Rita Penny, Mr and Mrs Richard E. Ross, the late Mrs Helen Ruane, and Mrs P. Elizabeth Whitton. I extend special thanks to Mrs Liz Tregonning, a descendant of one of Captain Penny's uncles, who generously shared the results of her genealogical and biographical research on the Penny family, helped to decipher illegible words, and read part of the manuscript. Emma Birkett kindly allowed me access to the original journal of the 1857–58 voyage and has generously consented to its publication.

The quotation from Queen Victoria's diary in the Royal Archives at Windsor Castle is published with the gracious permission of Her Majesty the Queen.

The idea for the book was conceived in 1989 while I was holding a Killam Research Fellowship. By providing release time from undergraduate teaching, the fellowship enabled me to work full-time on the history of arctic whaling, and it therefore contributed – indirectly but significantly – to this book. I therefore extend sincere thanks to the Killam Foundation and the Canada Council. Research for the project has been supported by grants from the Senate Research Committee of Bishop's University and the Humanities and Social Sciences Federation of Canada. I am thankful for the assistance of these institutions.

Finally, I extend my sincere thanks to the staff of McGill-Queen's University Press and to my editor, Carlotta Lemieux.

Introduction

This book is built around a journal written during the 1857–58 voyage of the Aberdeen whaler *Lady Franklin,* with her consort *Sophia.* It was written mainly by Margaret Penny but partly by her husband, Captain William Penny, one of the most enterprising arctic navigators of his time. Because Margaret wrote more than nine-tenths of the journal, I refer to it throughout as "Margaret's journal." It is almost certainly the only extant diary kept by a whaling wife in the eastern Canadian Arctic, where the very presence of a non-native woman was exceedingly rare. The unabridged journal forms the core of the book.

Diarists who write with a view to publication usually maintain a regular schedule of entries and present enough background information for the reader to understand the significance of their experiences and impressions. Evidently, Margaret Penny had no such idea in mind. She simply described what she saw when she felt like it. Although the gaps in her personal record and the lack of contextual explanation reduce its importance as a historical document, the journal merits publication because it is a unique woman's firsthand view of part of arctic Canada, its indigenous people, and their interaction with British whalemen in the mid-nineteenth century. By itself, the journal would raise many unanswered questions and frustrate the reader, so I have divided it arbitrarily into chapters, and within each chapter I have followed Margaret's entry with a text that explains or elaborates on some of the events, topics, places, ships, and people she has mentioned.

All the journal entries are presented in the usual day-by-day format of a diary and are set differently from my text, so anyone wishing to read the journal by itself as an unadorned personal narrative can easily do so. Each entry written by William is identified by a double dagger at the beginning and end.

"This distant and unsurveyed country" is how a clerk in the British Colonial Office referred to the southeastern part of Baffin Island in 1853, when considering the request of the whaling captain William Penny for a grant of land on which to establish a whaling settlement in what is now known as Cumberland Sound (Great Britain 1853, 24). Penny's application stirred up a lively discussion between the Admiralty, Foreign Office, and Colonial Office, because the political status of the region in question was not clear. No one was quite sure who owned the land. The seaward flank of Baffin Island was outside the limits of the immense territory administered by the Hudson's Bay Company, and although a few British explorers had erected flags and proclaimed sovereignty here and there, no European nation had formally claimed the lands. In the presumptuous logic of an imperialistic age, the Inuit – or Eskimos as they were then known – were not considered to have any sovereign rights over the land they and their predecessors had inhabited for four thousand years.

From the vantage point of a civil servant in London, England, the southeastern flank of Baffin Island could justifiably be described as "distant." Although only a month's sea travel away – far less than British possessions in the antipodes – it was accessible for only a few months in summer. For three-quarters of the year its coasts were blockaded by ice. And in comparison with England, the region was certainly "unsurveyed." This is not to say that there were no charts or maps, but the cartography was rough and superficial. Because Europeans could only reach Baffin Island by ship in summer, their knowledge of its geography was limited to the coasts; they knew virtually nothing about the interior. Even the coastal demarcation was tentative, and a fundamental question could not be answered. Did fiords penetrate from Baffin Bay and Davis Strait westward to Foxe Basin, dividing the region between Hudson Strait and Lancaster Sound into several islands, or was it all one land mass? The uncertainty on this issue had led to various vague regional names being placed on the charts, including Meta

Incognita bordering Hudson Strait, Cumberland Island farther north, and Cockburn Island near Lancaster Sound. On some charts these regions were separated by conjectural, dotted sea passages, but in fact they were all part of what came to be known as Baffin Island later in the century.

It was often asserted – in Great Britain, at least – that the east and north coasts of Baffin Island were British because British explorers and whalemen had often sailed there and because Martin Frobisher and John Ross had erected flags and claimed possession at a few scattered locations, two and a half centuries apart in time. But there had not been any official government claim to the territory, any occupation of the land, or any administration of the inhabitants. The vagueness about sovereignty persisted until 1880, a dozen years after the birth of the Canadian Confederation, when Britain transferred the arctic islands (which it had never formally annexed) and, by implication, its native inhabitants (whom it had never governed or even consulted) to Canada. Even after that, doubts about Canada's title to the arctic islands lingered (King 1905).

At the time of Margaret Penny's voyage to Cumberland Sound in 1857, the absence of European institutions on Baffin Island was in sharp contrast to the opposite shores of Davis Strait and Baffin Bay, where Danish trading posts, missions, schools, and administrators had existed for more than a century. Cumberland Sound was, in effect, a sort of no man's land as far as British and American whalemen were concerned, a region in which they felt they could do whatever they wished – pursue whales, hunt polar bears, walrus, seals, and caribou, introduce trade goods, and employ Eskimos. The activities of the men who pursued the Greenland or bowhead whale exerted a powerful influence on the original inhabitants and their environment during the nineteenth century. Whaling was an ecological and socio-economic force analogous to the fur trade in subarctic regions, but it has rarely been given due recognition as a vital part of the history of Canada or of the maritime history of Great Britain and the United States – whose ports sent hundreds of whaleships into the arctic seas – or even of the largely unwritten history of the Eskimo people within whose homeland it operated as an alien system of resource exploitation for a century.

Most readers are likely to know something about the Eskimo people and about the search for the missing expedition of Sir John Franklin, which was still under way at the time of Margaret's voyage, a dozen years after HMS *Erebus* and *Terror* had sailed from England. But readers are far less likely to be familiar with the activities of European and

American whalers, simply because comparatively little has been written about them. The writing of history is always selective, and although certain arctic themes have been brilliantly illuminated through research and publication, others equally deserving have been left in darkness – overlooked, ignored. The admirable qualities of pre-industrial Eskimo culture in a harsh environment are known throughout the world. The sad episode of Franklin's disappearance in the vast archipelago lying between North America and the Pole, and the many bold attempts by one expedition after another to find the vanished ships and men – adventures accompanied by sensational elements of danger, heroism, and tragedy – have been the subjects of countless articles and books. On the other hand, the achievements of the European and American whalers who sailed within sight of Greenland and Baffin Island year after year – just as boldly and heroically as the explorers and usually with fewer resources – have received little attention. During the period 1845–57, whaling voyages outnumbered Franklin search voyages by ten to one, yet in a standard compilation of arctic expeditions (Cooke and Holland 1968) there are ten times as many references to publications about the search expeditions.

My search for basic information about the thousands of whaling voyages into the Canadian Arctic during the nineteenth century (including answers to simple questions such as where? when? why? and how?) has taken me to thirty-five archives in seven countries. Scavenging for scraps of information in ships' logbooks, private journals, letters, and old newspapers is, to say the least, time consuming. I have been at it for more than thirty years! Happily, my long voyage of discovery has not been totally confined to archives, libraries, and museums. Covering hundreds of miles with hunters by dogsled, whaleboat, and freighter canoe, I have come to appreciate the relationship between Inuit and the land and sea. On low-level flights over Davis Strait, Hudson Strait, and Hudson Bay I have seen modern versions of the formidable icebergs and ice floes with which whalers had to contend in their wind-driven wooden ships long ago. Interviewing native elders who were alive in the last years of whaling, I have partly bridged the deep chasm of understanding between now and then. Camping on the island of Kekerten for several days, I have trodden the very ground on which Margaret Penny strolled a century and a half ago, picking flowers and berries, and delighting in the company of her "Esquimaux friends."

The remainder of this introduction contains background information on arctic whaling, Margaret and William Penny, the missionary

Matthäus Warmow (who also was present on the voyage), the journal itself, and my editorial conventions. By using the headings, the reader can select only what seems most important or can simply advance directly to the narrative.

WHALING

Before the petroleum era, oil rendered from the blubber of whales was widely used for illumination and lubrication in Europe and North America. Ships cruised the world's tropical and temperate oceans in search of sperm whales, grey whales, and humpback whales, and penetrated subpolar and polar seas seeking right whales and Greenland whales. All species provided oil from their blubber. In addition, all but the sperm whale possessed springy slabs of baleen (popularly called whalebone, or simply bone) with which they trapped planktonic food in their mouths. The baleen could be used to make dozens of useful articles, including umbrella ribs and corset stays, but only in the right and Greenland whales was the baleen long enough to exploit commercially. Today, whaling is no longer necessary (although some still goes on) because we have resources and technologies that were not available more than a century ago, when whaling provided one of the principal means of replacing darkness by light – and almost the only means of producing among fashionable women the coveted "hourglass" figure.

In the middle of the nineteenth century whaling was a far-reaching economic activity, almost global in extent. Ships from European and American ports often made voyages lasting three or four years, during which they circumnavigated the world, criss-crossing the Atlantic, Indian, and Pacific oceans during their peregrinations, probing into remote seas and bays, discovering isolated atolls and harbours, sounding depths and charting coasts, laying down place-names, and frequently making the first contact with native peoples. By today's standards, whaling seems a tough way to have earned a living. There were no eight-hour days or forty-hour weeks, no paid holidays or social security, and precious little of what we understand as family life. A long journey accompanied by plenty of hard work and danger, with mediocre food, cramped accommodation, and no privacy comprised the normal working conditions.

Like many economic activities based on biological resources and motivated by profit seeking, the whaling industry experienced successive periods of growth towards a peak and then decline towards stagnation.

By the time of Margaret Penny's voyage, the peak had been passed. British whaling interests had withdrawn from the South Seas sperm whale fishery (Jackson 1978, 142) and had reduced the size of their arctic fleet to half of what it had been thirty years earlier (Lubbock 1955, 270, 364). The American whaling fleet had fallen from an all-time high of 736 ships in the year 1846 to 655 vessels by 1857 (Tower 1907, 121). The downward trend would continue.

Whalemen usually concentrated their efforts on particular regions where whales were numerous in one season or another. The Davis Strait "whale fishery" occurred from April to September in the waters between Greenland and the Canadian Arctic, including Davis Strait itself, Baffin Bay, Lancaster Sound, and adjacent fiords, bays, and straits. In this vast region, roughly a thousand miles from south to north, the quarry was the Greenland or bowhead whale (*Balaena mysticetus*), a large plankton-feeding cetacean, generously insulated with blubber and equipped with slabs of baleen that were sometimes more than twelve feet long. The whalemen's basic strategy was to keep their vessels close to the whales for as long as possible during the annual migration to and from summer feeding grounds in the northern part of the region. To pursue the whales in winter was, of course, out of the question. Arctic whaling thus differed from whaling in warmer ice-free waters because it was seasonal, strictly limited to a few summer months. The whaling grounds were relatively close to ports in western Europe and the northeastern United States, however, so ships could sail to the Davis Strait fishery, carry out whaling, and return within six or eight months. Voyages of several years, which were common in the tropics, were neither feasible nor necessary. Consequently, arctic whaling enabled a man to enjoy far more in the way of family life, because he could expect to be home during each winter (although he might ship out on short merchant voyages). On the other hand, the advantage of a relatively short whaling season and more time at home was offset by the more severe environmental hazards and risks that arctic whalemen had to face. The casualty rate for ships was extraordinarily high.

European whalers began sailing to the Davis Strait fishery before 1700. In the eighteenth century, vessels from several nations made more than 3,500 voyages to the region and secured more than 8,000 whales (W.G. Ross 1979, 100–2). During this initial period, whaling was concentrated on the "East Side," that is to say, along the west Greenland coast; but after 1820, whaling masters adopted the practice of ascending the Greenland coast in May and June, crossing to the "West Side," or Baffin Island coast, in July, and then returning south to Davis Strait in time to take their departure homeward in September, in order to avoid being trapped by winter ice. This fundamental alteration in the geographical pattern of whale hunting around 1820 brought Europeans into contact with the indigenous people of Baffin Island and led within a few decades to the Eskimos' involvement in the whaling activities. After whaling expanded in 1840 into Cumberland Sound, the largest indentation along the coast of Baffin Island, British and American whaling captains began hiring Eskimo men to complete their whaleboat crews, and they were soon employing entire boat crews of Eskimos who operated their own whaleboats, obtained second-hand from the whaling ships. The successful overwintering ashore by part of the crew of an American whaler in 1851–52 led to a new approach in 1853, when four crews – two American and two Scottish – wintered in Cumberland Sound on board their ships in order to be on hand for the productive ice-edge whaling of May and June.

The Arctic in winter was a hostile environment quite beyond the experience of Europeans and Americans. Aside from the sea mammal resources that attracted whalemen to the area, the region appeared to them as a desolate and unfriendly place. But most whaling masters had the good sense to recognize that the native inhabitants had succeeded in developing extensive knowledge, sophisticated equipment, and innovative techniques in order to obtain food, shelter, and other things required for life. Having already employed some of the natives in whale hunting, the captains soon made them part of the wintering process as well. Eskimo men hunted to obtain fresh meat for the ships' crews, and sledded blubber and whalebone over the ice to the ships in spring. The women sometimes made the crews winter clothes from furs and skins. In return for their various services, the Eskimos received useful material goods, including whaleboats, whaling gear, tools, guns, ammunition, telescopes, pots, kettles, wood, metal, and cloth. To the whalemen, Eskimo labour was essential for a successful wintering. And to the Eskimos, Euro-American goods quickly became indispensable to hunter and housewife alike. The basis of a strong and continuing economic interdependence between Eskimos and whites was firmly established in the 1850s.

By 1857, when Margaret Penny sailed from Scotland on the whaler *Lady Franklin*, commanded by her husband William Penny, wintering on the arctic whaling grounds was no longer considered an experiment. It had become an acceptable option. Most of the Davis Strait whalers continued to make their one-season voyages around Baffin Bay, but each year a few ships would sail into Cumberland Sound with the intention of spending the winter. Since the autumn of 1853, when the first four ship captains had committed their vessels and crews to an arctic hibernation, there had been more than a dozen ship winterings, all in Cumberland Sound. In 1857 twenty-nine ships set sail for the Davis Strait fishery – twenty-four from Scotland, three from England, and two from the United States. Of these, six vessels, five Scottish and one American, intended to overwinter.

The Royal Navy in the Age of Sail has been called a "wooden world" (Rodger 1988, 14; Keegan 1990, 1). It is a good metaphor, and it would apply equally well to the fleet of whalers that sailed the seas, because it too was "a society in miniature, a floating world with its own customs and way of life." Each whaleship was a self-contained unit, which carried within its wooden walls everything required for the operation, maintenance, and repair of its gear, for the capture and processing of whales, for the storage of blubber, oil, and baleen, and for the sustenance of its crew. It was a floating island, inhabited by a few dozen men, whose lives were organized, regulated, and governed according to traditiional shipboard systems of command, incentive, reward, and punishment. Cooperating in the business of securing whale oil and bone, the crew worked according to prescribed roles and procedures, within an established chain of command.

In one important respect, however, whaleships were not microcosms of the world or replicas of society on land. They were usually communities of men only. Their crews must have had plenty of opportunity to wish that this was not so – like the American sailors in the Broadway musical *South Pacific*, who complained, "We got volley ball and ping pong and a lot of dandy games. What ain't we got? We ain't got dames!" On board whalers, of necessity, men carried out some of the essential tasks that a woman might normally perform at home. They scrubbed decks, cleaned cabins, cooked food, waited on table, washed dishes, did laundry, and patched clothes (with small sewing kits called "housewives"). But it was nonetheless a male society, lacking the beneficial influence of women and the uplifting nature of family life. A whaler's crew was a fraternity dedicated to a common cause, pulling together for a common objective, and kept in line by rigorous discipline while at sea, but given to boisterous and often licentious behaviour when authority was relaxed, as it usually was in port.

MARGARET PENNY (NÉE IRVINE)

Margaret Irvine was born in Aberdeen on 12 December 1812, the second of three children of George Irvine and Helen Colvile (also spelled Colville, Colvin, or Collie), who had married on 6 August 1808 when both were about twenty-six years old. In the genealogical records, George Irvine's occupation is given sometimes as "weaver" or "winsey weaver, journeyman" but in other places as "farmer." These are not trades that would normally be combined, so the information is puzzling. But it is certainly the same man. George Irvine, "weaver," and his spouse Helen Collie produced a daughter Margaret in 1812; George Irvine, "farmer," attended the wedding of his daughter Margaret to William Penny in 1840; George Irvine, "weaver," was left a widower in 1857 when his wife Helen Colvile predeceased him. The apparently contradictory information about his occupation permits the following interpretation, which is necessarily speculative.

George Irvine's father was a linen weaver, so it is reasonable to suppose that he took up the trade himself, probably under the direction of his father but possibly as an apprentice to another craftsman. The term "journeyman" suggests that after he became qualified as a weaver, he did not set himself up in business but worked for someone else; again, his father is the most likely person. His parents lived in the parish of Old Machar, immediately north of the central part of Aberdeen, and after George married in 1808, he and his wife Helen remained in that part of town, living in the Gilcomston area, on Skene Street, which is situated west of the angle formed by the intersection of the principal thoroughfares of George and Union streets. At some time during the next two decades, George and his family moved from central Aberdeen to the outskirts of the town to take up farming. The Aberdeen voters' list for 1832 includes the name of George Irvine, farmer, at "Hayfield, Hilton," living as tenant of a house. On the modern map, Hayfield Crescent, Hayfield Place, Hilton Avenue, Hilton Drive, Hilton Place, Hilton Road, Hilton Street, Hilton Terrace, and Hilton Walk are all located about two miles northwest of Gilcomston Street and Skene Street. In the first half of the nineteenth century, this area was still open countryside in which farming would have been an appropriate occupation. When his daughter Margaret married William Penny in 1840, George was still described as a farmer, but his place of residence had changed to Balbredie in the parish of Banchory Ternan, southwest of Aberdeen, where he was still living in 1844. After 1855, he was again referred to in several documents as a weaver, and his last place of residence, where he died on 16 April 1868, aged eighty-six, was 7 Saint Andrew's Street, once more in downtown Aberdeen. After starting out as a weaver and then trying farming for a decade or two, he may have returned to weaving in later life; or perhaps he retired from farming but preferred to be known by his first occupation of weaver.

When Margaret was born, her parents were living on Skene Street She was baptized by the Reverend Dr Kidd in nearby Gilcomston Church. Six years later, when she might have been enrolled in a school, the family appears to have been living in the same place, for her younger sister Catharine was baptized in the same church and by the same minister. Presumably, Margaret remained with her family when they shifted to the Hilton area, where they were living in 1832 when Margaret was nineteen years old. Three years later, her future husband William Penny moved to Aberdeen from Peterhead to take up his first whaling command.

On 4 February 1840 Margaret Irvine and William Penny were married in his residence at 46 Marischal Street, Aberdeen, by the Reverend Alexander D. Davidson. Margaret was then twenty-seven years of age and William thirty-one. Their first child, William Kennedy, who was baptized on 28 November 1840, died within six months. He was succeeded by four other children: Helen Eliza in 1842, a second son named William in 1844 (who sailed to Cumberland Sound with his parents in 1857), Janet Robertson in 1846, and Margaret Irvine in 1848. To accommodate the growing family and possibly a domestic servant, Captain and Mrs Penny had moved to a cottage at Polmuir House by 1845, and after a succession of moves within the part of Aberdeen known as Ferryhill, only a few blocks from the harbour, they spent their last years in a small house at 22 Springbank Terrace.

During the seventeen years of married life that preceded the arctic voyage of 1857, William Penny's time at home with Margaret and the children was usually limited to autumn and early winter. In other seasons he was sailing to the sealing and whaling grounds. Beginning in 1850, his wintering voyages took him away from the family for twelve to nineteen months at a time. The prolonged separations must have been hard on everyone but particularily on Margaret, who was left with the responsibility of managing the household and raising the children. It was a situation faced by whaling wives everywhere.

The problem of divided families was especially serious on South Seas whalers because the voyages were so long. Husbands could be separated from their wives and children for years at a stretch – years in which reliable written communication was impossible. A Nantucket woman, Azubah Cash, spent a total of only half a year in the company of her husband during the first eleven years of their marriage, and she finally decided to go to sea with him (Druett 1991, 25). Just three years before Margaret Penny's voyage, an American wife, Harriet Gifford of Falmouth, Massachusetts, complained, "We have been married five years and lived together ten months. It is *too bad, too bad*" (Garner 1966, xvi). Few expressed the sadness and longing of women left at home as effectively as the wife of Parker Smith, captain of a New London whaler, in 1827. She enjoyed the company of a few friends, she admitted to him, "but this, my dear Parker, does not make up for the loss I sustain in being deprived of your agreeable company and when I consider the distance we are apart and the length of time we must be separated and the innumerable trials and dangers to which we are exposed, my heart faints within me and I am ready to exclaim, 'Why is it thus?'" She continued, "I will use all my influence in deterring you from ever going again unless you take me with you" (Colby 1936, 6).

Indeed, a few bold whaling masters and wives did break with tradition and sail together, but the idea was not quickly accepted. The captains had to convince the shipowners that having a wife on board would be feasible and not too costly (they would consume food, some niggardly owners objected). For their part, the wives had to mollify parents, siblings, and friends, who nearly always disapproved. But the advantages gradually became clear, and the practice expanded steadily; in time, even the owners had to reluctantly admit that the "petticoat whalers" exerted a beneficial influence on the crews. By 1853, only four years before Margaret's voyage, a newspaper in Honolulu, the most popular port of call for Pacific whalers, estimated that one out of every six whaling captains had his wife on board. The arrangement was a good one for all concerned, even the newspaper itself: "The enterprising ladies not only preserve unbroken the ties of domestic life that otherwise would be sundered; not only cheer by their presence the monotony and discomforts of long and perilous voyages; not only exercise a good influence in the discipline of the ship, but they make capital correspondents, and through the female love of letter-writing, keep us well posted up in the catch and prospects of the season" (*Whalemen's Shipping List* 1853).

For the period 1820–1920, Joan Druett (1992, 417) has identified 433 whaling voyages on which women were present. Almost all of the women on the ships were captains' wives, but a few were daughters, passengers, mistresses, and occasionally women disguised as men. Some wives took their children along, and not a few managed to produce additional family members during the voyage. Most of the women were American; the practice never became popular on British ships. Although Mary Russell Hayden sailed to the Indian and Pacific oceans on her husband's whaler *Emily* of London as early as 1823 (Druett 1991, 19), only a dozen British women are known to have sailed on whalers during the next hundred years. Margaret Penny was part of a small, exclusive sisterhood.

The image of idyllic tropical islands, white beaches, quaint ports of call, fresh vegetables and fruit, and easy sailing in balmy trade winds may have helped to attract some whaling wives away from their long, lonely vigils at home. Arctic voyages, however, did not offer comparable incentives. There were more than 2,400 whaling voyages to the Davis Strait whale fishery after British whalers began exploiting the east coast of Baffin Island in 1820 (W.G. Ross 1979). If each vessel carried, on average, thirty men – probably a conservative figure – the total number of man-voyages must have exceeded 72,000. Yet the women known to have sailed to the Davis Strait whaling grounds can be counted on one hand.

The naturalist Robert Brown, who sailed as surgeon on the steam whaler *Narwhal* of Dundee under Captain G. Deuchars in 1861, wrote: "Speaking of Captns wives – Mrs Parker & Mrs Penny have both wintered in Davis St! The latter is coming back this year – Mrs Sturrock was one year there – Mrs Deuchars is always bothering the Captn to take her" (*Narwhal* 1861, 1:219–20). Margaret Penny did in fact return to Davis Strait but not until 1863. As for Mrs Sturrock, the year in which she accompanied her husband is not known; the presence of a woman was never noted in the annual whaling reports. Members of the Sturrock family commanded whalers in every year except two from 1830 to 1860, but as none of their voyages involved wintering, the words "was one year there" appear to mean "one season." Mrs Parker may have been on the Hull whaler *Emma*, commanded by Captain John Parker, when it wintered at Godhavn, Greenland, in 1855–56 after failing to reach Baffin Island (*Hull Advertiser* 1856a, b). If Mrs Sturrock made only a summer voyage and Mrs Parker wintered at Greenland, then Margaret Penny was probably the first European woman to winter anywhere among the arctic islands north of Canada. How fortunate that she wrote a diary and that it still exists in family hands a century and a half later!

Whether the idea of accompanying the *Lady Franklin* to Cumberland Sound originated with Margaret or with Captain Penny is not known. Lady Franklin's niece Sophia Cracroft once remarked on Mrs Penny's "ascendancy" over her husband (Woodward 1953, 811), and it may well be that after seeing him depart so often, Margaret simply declared, "I have kept the home fires burning long enough. This time I am going along too." Young William, who at twelve was the same age as his father had been on his first whaling voyage, also went along, but his three sisters remained in Aberdeen. What arrangements were made to take care of them during the next fourteen months are not recorded, but much of the responsibility must have fallen on the shoulders of Helen, aged fifteen. The other girls, Janet and Margaret, were ten and eight, respectively. Helen may have been assisted by a resident domestic servant. The census of 1851 records the presence of Fanny Hurd, a nineteen-year-old servant, in the Penny home, and in 1861 Margaret Low, aged twenty, was listed in the same capacity. Whether any of Margaret's or William's relatives helped look after the children is not known.

Margaret had come close to going on whaling voyages before. In 1853, when Penny was preparing for his first winter trip to Cumberland Sound, he received a letter from Joseph-René Bellot, the French naval officer who had sailed in search of Franklin on the *Prince Albert* under William Kennedy two years earlier and who would die in the Arctic less than six months after writing to Penny. Bellot wished Penny success in founding a settlement and improving the lot of the Eskimos, and he closed with the question, "Is Mrs. Penny going with you, and the family too?" (Bellot 1853). In late May, less than three months before the ship's departure from Aberdeen, a local newspaper reported, "Mrs. Penny goes out with her husband, as it is their intention to have a permanent residence in the Arctic Regions" (*Aberdeen Free Press* 1853). Evidently, she changed her mind at the last minute. Two years later, when her husband left on a second wintering voyage to Cumberland Sound, Margaret again came close to going with him, as she admitted in a letter to Sophia Cracroft in May 1856: "I intended to go out with my husband but when it came near the time of leaveing, the children were in such distress that I considered it my duty to remain altho I would have liked very much to have gone" (Margaret Penny 1856). In 1857, however, she allowed nothing to stand in her way.

WILLIAM PENNY

William Penny was the second of the nine children (and eldest of the three boys) of William and Janet (née Robertson) Penny of Peterhead. He was born on 12 July 1808 or 1809. The inscription on his headstone in the cemetery of St Nicholas Church in Aberdeen records that he "died at Aberdeen on 1st Feby 1892 aged 82 years," and census records for April 1881 and April 1891 give his age as seventy-one and eighty-one, respectively, all of which would make the year of his birth

Captain William Penny in 1846, from the painting by Stephen Pearce
(National Portrait Gallery)

1809, the year cited in almost all biographical sketches and obituaries. On the other hand, old parish records state that he was baptized on 24 July 1808, which would make his age eighty-three at death rather than the eighty-two shown on the cemetery monument. The date of his birth thus remains open to question, though 1808 is gaining favour.

On his paternal side, William's two uncles John and James, his grandfather Charles, and his great-grandfather William had all been tenant farmers, but his father (also named William Penny) broke the mould and chose a career at sea. The elder Penny was born in 1775, and by the time he married Janet Robertson thirty years later he was sailing as a ship's carpenter in either whaling or merchant vessels. In the whaling trade, capable men usually rose through the ranks, beginning as apprentices, ships' boys, or ordinary seamen, then serving as harpooners and boatsteerers, later advancing to the ranks of second and first mate, and sometimes obtaining overall command. The specialists, or "trades people" – cooper, carpenter, cook, and so on – were usually outside this path of promotion, but Penny's father appears to have been an exception. He had qualified as master by 1808, and in 1813 he embarked on his first voyage as captain of the Peterhead whaler *Perseverance*. He continued to command arctic whalers almost every year after that: the *Perseverance* until 1816, the *Alert* from 1817 to at least 1825, and the *Eclipse* from 1828 to 1831. Although his usual destination was the "Greenland whale fishery" (between Greenland and Spitsbergen), he took his last vessel, the *Eclipse*, to the Davis Strait grounds (west of Greenland). He retired in Peterhead and died there in 1853.

His son – the Captain William Penny of this book – first accompanied his father on a Greenland whaling voyage in 1821, at twelve years of age, and sailed with him for several seasons, rising to the position of mate by 1829 (Tillotson 1869, 111), when he was probably on his father's ship *Eclipse* sailing to Davis Strait, the region he would continue to visit almost every year for the next third of a century. He served as mate on the Peterhead whaler *Traveller* in 1832 and 1833, but when he was given command of the whaler *Neptune* in 1835 he moved to Aberdeen.

In the five years between his arrival at Aberdeen and his marriage to Margaret Irvine, Captain Penny sailed regularly to the Arctic on board the *Neptune*. A common routine of Scottish vessels at this time was to depart in late February for the Greenland Sea in search of harp seals (and whales if any were sighted), then return to home port, unload the cargo, take on supplies and some crew replacements, and begin a whaling voyage to Davis Strait in March or April. In this pattern of late-winter sealing and summer whaling, Penny steadily established a reputation as a successful master who explored new territory, tried new methods, and obtained good catches.

A few months after marrying Margaret, William Penny departed again for Baffin Island, commanding the *Bon Accord*. With the help of Eenoolooapik, a young Eskimo he had brought to Scotland the previous season, he found a large inlet called Tenudiakbeek and explored

Eenoolooapik, who accompanied Captain Penny to Aberdeen, Scotland,
in 1839 and returned with him to Cumberland Sound in 1840
(M'Donald 1841, frontispiece)

it with several other whalers. Penny named it Hogarth Sound after
William Hogarth, an Aberdeen merchant and shipowner (later, part
owner of the *Lady Franklin*). Captain Wareham (or Warham) of the
Lord Gambier from Newcastle, however, decided to call it Northumberland Inlet. It turned out to be the Cumberland Strait into which John
Davis had sailed two and a half centuries earlier and had named in
honour of his sponsor, the Earl of Cumberland, and which had not
subsequently been visited by Europeans. Historian Philip Goldring

(1985, 31) has suggested that Elizabethan navigators liked to call bays "straits" or "sounds" (narrow passages connecting two seas) in order "to express their optimism that each break in the Arctic coast might lead to China." After the specific name Cumberland returned to favour in the mid-nineteenth century, whalemen usually called the region Cumberland Inlet or Cumberland Gulf, recognizing that it was simply an arm of the sea, not a potential Northwest Passage. The official Canadian name, Cumberland Sound (which is used in my text), is a curious reversion to the hopeful but inaccurate nomenclature of the Elizabethan era.

After 1840 the number of British arctic whaling voyages fell off temporarily, and although William Penny had taken considerable initiative in opening Cumberland Sound to whalers, he found himself without a command for the next three years while rival captains exploited the region. But in 1844, with a resurgence of the industry, he began a series of successful voyages with the Aberdeen whaler *Saint Andrew*, and in 1849 he assumed command of the Dundee whaler *Advice*. These were years in which British discovery expeditions seemed on the brink of completing a Northwest Passage between Baffin Bay and Bering Strait. Sir John Franklin, an elderly man whose overland expeditions two decades earlier had charted much of the mainland coast of the North American Arctic, at a high cost in human lives, had been given command of what everyone believed would be the final expedition. Her Majesty's Ships *Erebus* and *Terror* set off down the Thames in May 1845 to a tumultuous and confident fanfare, but two months later, after their last contact with whaling ships in Baffin Bay, they entered Lancaster Sound and disappeared forever into the labyrinth of the arctic islands. Whalemen had a special interest in the progress of the Franklin expedition because they knew firsthand the dangers posed by pack ice, icebergs, and harsh weather, and because they were curious to see what might be discovered beyond the range of their own summer voyages in search of whales. Time passed and concern mounted. In 1847 William Penny made the first attempt to look for signs of Franklin's ships, during one of his whaling voyages, but was unable to penetrate Lancaster Sound. Two years later, by which time official searching expeditions were already in the Arctic, he and Captain Parker, commanding the *Advice* and *Truelove*, respectively, cached emergency supplies on the south shore of Lancaster Sound for any possible survivors of the missing expedition, which had not been seen for four years.

In his two cursory attempts to find traces of Franklin, Penny had been constrained by the need to pursue whales, which left him no time to pick up Franklin's trail, so he volunteered to lead a search expedition. With the support of Lady Franklin and her niece Sophia Cracroft, both of whom thought highly of Penny and campaigned vigorously on his behalf, he obtained overall command of an Admiralty expedition consisting of two vessels, with considerable latitude in the matter of outfitting and hiring crew. It was a unique distinction for a whaling master. The two vessels were named *Lady Franklin* and *Sophia*; Penny commanded the former and Alexander Stewart the latter. In the spring of 1850 they departed from Aberdeen, sailed to Baffin Bay, entered Lancaster Sound, and took up winter quarters off the south coast of Cornwallis Island. This turned out to be a popular place. Although the search for Franklin in the period 1847–59 extended over thousands of miles of arctic territory from Bering Strait to Baffin Bay, most of the maritime expeditions of 1850 converged on one small area. Penny's two ships, Captain's Austin's four naval ships, Sir John Ross's two ships, and Lieutenant De Haven's two American ships all converged at the junction of Lancaster Sound and Wellington Channel, like "a kind of explorers' club" (Corner 1972, 92). After De Haven's ships were carried back into Baffin Bay by drifting pack ice, the other eight vessels wintered within fifteen miles of one another.

The searching activities of 1850–51 have been described in many books and articles, so there is no need to outline here the discovery of Franklin's first winter camp on Beechey Island, the extensive explorations by man-hauled sledges in spring (which failed to find the missing men), or the acrimonious dispute between Penny and Austin, which led to an official inquiry. Penny returned from the expedition obsessed by the idea that Franklin's ships had sailed north through Wellington Channel and reached an ice-free polar sea, where they might still be found. Accordingly, he applied for leadership of another expedition, with steam-powered ships, to be dispatched immediately. It was too late in the season, the Admiralty said, with good reason. He then requested an expedition that would leave in the spring of 1852, but the Admiralty again turned him down. Although frustrated by their refusal, Penny may have drawn some satisfaction from the fact that he had become something of a public hero, an experienced whaling master whose bold enterprise had been reined in by less determined (perhaps even less capable) naval officers, and whose generous offer to help had been rejected by the jealous and closely knit naval establishment. The artist Stephen Pearce, who painted a famous composite picture of the "Arctic Council" of naval greats – men such as Back, Parry, and Richardson – had William Penny sit for him in 1852, at Lady Franklin's request (Woodward 1953, 809). Pearce included Penny's portrait among those he exhibited at Manchester in 1857, and he later reproduced it in his published memoirs (Pearce 1903).

With the door closed to further involvement in the Franklin search, Penny turned his attention back to whaling. His experience on the search expedition had helped him form ideas about how whaling could be improved. He saw that whalemen, like explorers, could winter safely on their ships and, like Eskimos, they could use dogsled transportation. He incorporated both these techniques in his next whaling voyage, with excellent results. His decision to winter in 1853 was also influenced by the news that a dozen men from the American whaler *McLellan* of New London, Connecticut, had successfully wintered ashore in Cumberland Sound in 1851–52. Penny saw this as an ominous sign of American territorial aspirations within a region tacitly understood to be British, and he spoke out firmly in favour of some British move to forestall the ambitions of the American interlopers.

Nationalism, concern for the future of whaling, and personal ambition were all reflected in the grandiose plan that Penny designed for arctic whaling. In 1853 he announced the formation of the Royal Arctic Company "for the purpose of carrying on whale and other fisheries, and for mining and colonising a certain tract of land in Davis' Straits, under a grant from the Crown" (*Aberdeen Journal* 1853). He proposed that, early in the season, large steam whalers (sailing ships with auxiliary steam power) would pursue seals and whales in the seas between Greenland and Novaya Zemlya. Then, in July, they would carry supplies westward for the settlement in Cumberland Sound. Finally, in November, they would return to Scotland with the produce of the colony. Although the company failed to obtain a royal charter (it was renamed the Aberdeen Arctic Company), did not receive a land grant or exclusive whaling rights, and had to postpone the acquisition of steam whalers, it did implement the settlement concept in a modest way.

In the spring of 1853, Penny headed for Cumberland Sound on a wintering voyage with two newly purchased vessels, the same *Lady Franklin* and *Sophia* with which he had searched for Franklin under Admiralty auspices. He commanded the former and Captain Brown the latter. The ships wintered at Nuvujen, and their phenomenal success in whaling exceeded all expectations. With the same vessels, Penny repeated the wintering experience in 1855–56 with Captain Martin in charge of the *Sophia*. Now, in 1857, he prepared to set off again with the same two vessels, this time with Captain Cheyne, a young man of twenty-six, commanding the *Sophia*. Summing up his experience,

Penny wrote, "I am perfectly acquainted with the arctic regions, my knowledge having been acquired by thirty-three voyages to these regions, and by spending three winters there. I have become intimately acquainted with the Esquimaux and their habits and manners" (William Penny 1856b).

MATTHÄUS WARMOW

The presence of Margaret Penny and her son William on the *Lady Franklin* made the voyage of 1857–58 unusual, to say the least, but there was another noteworthy passenger as well. Brother Matthäus Warmow had been sent along by the Moravian Church to assess the condition of the native people in Cumberland Sound and report on the feasibility of establishing a permanent mission there. No missionary had ever visited Baffin Island before.

The Moravians were experienced in arctic work, having operated missions on the west coast of Greenland for more than one hundred and twenty years and on the coast of Labrador for more than eighty years (Gad 1973, 254). But in 1857 the Eskimo population in the vast region that would soon become Canada was virtually untouched by Christianity. Two Moravians had briefly explored Ungava Bay in 1811. A Church of England clergyman had visited York Factory in Hudson Bay during the summers of 1820–23, reaching Churchill in the latter year. In the western Arctic, Johann Miertsching, a Moravian missionary serving as interpreter on HMS *Investigator* under Lieutenant M'Clure, had exchanged a few words and gifts with scattered groups of Eskimos as the ship skirted the mainland coast in 1850 on its way to three winters in the arctic ice and a miraculous last-minute rescue from an icebound harbour.

To establish northern missions took more than zealous men and ambitious policies. Accessibility was the key. The only feasible way to get men and supplies to remote outposts was by sea, but as ships were beyond the financial means of most missionary organizations, they had to depend on commercial vessels each summer for their needs. The sporadic missionary activity in southern Hudson Bay and among the Cree in James Bay before 1857 relied on the annual supply voyages of Hudson's Bay Company ships to its fur trade posts. Similarly, the Moravian missions in Greenland benefited from the commercial shipping links with Denmark.

The interior of Cumberland Sound lay roughly halfway between the two regions of Moravian missionary endeavour, approximately four hundred miles west of the Greenland coast and about the same distance north of Labrador. As whalers visited the region every summer, the idea of establishing a mission there was not unreasonable. The incentive that led to the dispatch of Brother Warmow to Cumberland Sound did not originate among the Moravians, however, but within the whaling fraternity. Two captains in particular, one English and one Scottish, had become alarmed at the impoverished condition of the Eskimos and felt that Christian teaching would be of great benefit.

At the end of the 1847 whaling season – a decade before Brother Warmow joined the *Lady Franklin* – Captain John Parker of the whaleship *Truelove* had taken a young Eskimo couple from Cumberland Sound back to Hull. The two young Eskimos were willing participants in his plan to enlist sympathy and support for the cause of Eskimo welfare on Baffin Island. With the *Truelove*'s owner Thomas Ward, Parker took them to the Moravian community at Fairfield, near Manchester, to discuss the possibility of introducing Christianity to the inhabitants of Cumberland Sound. The Moravians welcomed the idea and suggested that the couple should be given religious instruction at one of the Labrador missions before returning to their homeland. Memiadluk and Uckaluk, however, did not wish to go to Labrador, and Captain Parker decided to take them home on his next voyage to Davis Strait, but he agreed to stop at Lichtenfels, Greenland, to pick up Brother Samuel Kleinschmidt and take him to Cumberland Sound to assess the situation (*Periodical Accounts* 1849, 19:19–21).

Lichtenfels, where the Moravians had established a mission in 1758 (Gad 1973, xvi), was located about sixty-three degrees north latitude, approximately halfway between present-day Paamiut and Nuuk. It was not familiar territory to the whalers because when they made their counter-clockwise circuit of Davis Strait and Baffin Bay, they usually closed with the Greenland coast about four hundred miles farther north, in the vicinity of Disko Bay, and then worked their way to Melville Bay before crossing to the West Side. In agreeing to pick up Kleinschmidt at Lichtenfels, Parker was committing himself to an inconvenient detour that would take him away from the season's earliest whaling ground (called the Southwest Ice), between Greenland and Hudson Strait and would delay his advance northward to Baffin Bay. As it turned out, Parker did not succeed in reaching Lichtenfels; he pressed on farther north for the whaling. Sadly, the Eskimo woman died on board ship near Upernavik, but Memiadluk eventually reached home.

In 1849 Captain Parker again intended to reach the Greenland missions, where Brothers Kleinschmidt and Herbrich were making preparations to go with him to Cumberland Sound (*Periodical Accounts* 1849,

The Moravian mission at Lichtenfels, Greenland, where Brother Warmow
worked among the Eskimo people before joining the *Lady Franklin*
(Davis 1876, facing 50)

19:234); but efforts to follow up reports of Franklin's ships appear to
have taken priority, and the brethren waited in vain. Two successive
failures cooled everyone's missionary ardour for a while, but by 1852
the Moravians were again discussing "the plan of carrying the Gospel
to the heathen inhabiting the western shores of Davis Straits" (*Periodical Accounts* 1851, 20:342).

About this time, Captain Penny and a number of businessmen were
organizing the Aberdeen Arctic Company and thinking of establishing
a settlement in Cumberland Sound. Following the precedent of his
friend Captain Parker, Penny offered to take along a missionary on his
proposed wintering voyage of 1853–54, and the Moravians revived the
original plan whereby a whaleship would stop at Greenland to collect
a missionary. They advised Brother Matthäus Warmow to hold himself
in readiness, and they provided him with a letter of instruction outlining the purpose and duration of his work, the attitude he should
adopt towards whalemen and natives, and the duties he should per-

form on ship and ashore (see appendix 2). But Penny had no more
success than Parker. In early September contrary winds prevented him
from reaching Lichtenfels, and he was forced to cross to Cumberland
Sound without the missionary (*Periodical Accounts* 1853, 21:268–9).
After another failed attempt in 1855 on his way to a second wintering
in the sound, Penny proposed a new plan. "Would it not be possible
for you, with timely notice," he wrote to the Moravians, "to procure
me a missionary of your Church to accompany me from Aberdeen"
(*Periodical Accounts* 1858, 22:143). The Moravians agreed, and in October 1856 Brother Warmow travelled from Greenland to England
by way of Germany. The records of the the Moravian Church at Fulneck, Yorkshire, contain the following entry regarding Lovefeast celebrations on 26 April 1857, at which Brother Warmow delivered an
address: "Br Warmow – who has been spending some months here to
perfect himself in the English language and to be ready when summoned to sail with Captain Penny – expects soon to set off to the place
of his destination to preach the Gospel to the natives on the coast of
the Northumberland inlet – Our sincere and earnest prayers accompanied this dear brother – when he left us a few weeks later" (McOwat
1992).

After his crash course in English, Warmow travelled to Aberdeen in
June to join the *Lady Franklin*. The man who would be shipmate of
Captain and Mrs Penny for the next fourteen months was thirty-nine
years old. He had been born in Germany in 1818, educated in a village
school, and initiated into the brotherhood of the Moravians at Herrnhut in 1837. His training had been interrupted by two years of military
service, after which he had returned to Herrnhut in 1841. Five years
later he was sent to the mission at Lichtenau in Greenland, and
six years after that he was transferred to Lichtenfels, where in 1853,
1855, and finally 1857 he received orders to accompany Penny to Baffin Island (see appendix 2). His experience with Greenlanders and his
fluency in the Eskimo language had prepared him well for the task
ahead.

THE WHALING JOURNAL

Margaret and William kept their pen-and-ink record of the voyage of
1857–58 in three soft-covered "ciphering books," or school exercise
books, measuring about seven and a half by nine inches, whose thread-
bare front and back covers are now detached. Altogether, the journal
runs to about 18,000 words. The handwriting shows that William made
the daily entries for the first twenty-five days of the journal, during the

Atlantic crossing, and then Margaret took over. William later added a few words to her entry of 31 October, expanded her brief remarks on 28, 29, and 30 January 1858, and wrote all the entries for 31 January and 1 February. The journal contains four gaps. The first extends from the beginning of the voyage on 30 June to 5 July, while the ship was sailing around the tip of Scotland. The second runs from 25 to 29 August, inclusive, while the ship was in Kingnait Fiord. The third, at the winter harbour of Kekerten, runs from William's entry of 1 February until Margaret resumes writing on 13 May. The fourth gap, from the final entry on 7 July to 22 August, occurs during the voyage back to Scotland. Altogether, the gaps comprise more than one-third of the total number of days on the voyage. The shared authorship and the missing parts are not explained.

An inscription inside one of the detached covers, in William's writing, reads, "Journal kept by William Penny on board the Lady Franklin 1st November 1857." This indicates that the journal was begun as William's project (although the date is confusing because his regular entries had ceased in late July). Why did he make no entries until the ship was two weeks out from port? And why did he relinquish the journal to Margaret less than a month later? Perhaps at the beginning of the voyage he was too busy working the crew into their sea routine and navigating the vessel round the northern tip of Scotland to make any entries. After commencing the journal on 5 July, he may have handed it over to Margaret at the end of the month because he found it burdensome to keep a personal record as well as the official logbook of the ship. Margaret, after dutifully making entries for five months, may then have lost interest in the exercise, as many well-intentioned diary writers do. When her daily remarks became briefer in late January, William added his own comments. When her entries ceased altogether, he wrote at length on two days. But after that neither of them contributed to the journal for more than three months.

Perhaps Margaret was a victim of what psychologists dignify by the term "seasonal affective disorder," the overpowering lethargy that some experience during the light-starved days of midwinter, which in her case would have been intensified by the high latitude and by the lack of illumination, space, privacy, and comfort below decks. Her self-discipline and motivation may simply have faded away, not to be revived until the exuberant resurrection of the arctic spring. On the other hand, it is possible that she was distressed about something that was happening on board ship. Whatever the explanation, the blank pages during the long winter gap suggest that Margaret meant to return to summarize events later. Either she never got around to doing so or she considered it prudent to leave the pages empty.

One loose triangular fragment accompanies the journal. It appears to represent part of the bottom of a page, although no torn pages are now in the journal. One side, containing about thirty words, is in Margaret's handwriting. The closest thing to a complete sentence reads, "Mr. Warmow is a … companion so good & so cheery … Also an excellent young man." The other side bears about forty words in William's writing. It includes the name "Sophia" and the words "what a hard life they must … yet how happy a little bit of Tobacco … them." An English-Eskimo glossary of one page occurs at the front of the third scribbler (see appendix 5). This is in a different handwriting, probably that of Brother Warmow, who may have instructed Margaret in Inuktitut.

Writing a journal may be simply a personal ritual of record keeping for the satisfaction of the diarist at the time of writing, and perhaps for nostalgic reminiscences on subsequent occasions. Or it may be a form of delayed communication, a way of describing an experience later to family and friends, or even preserving it for future generations. The act of writing things down captures for the potential audience (whether oneself or others) the freshness and immediacy of the moment, without requiring retroactive recourse to memory after an intervening period of time. Although the unfilled gaps suggest that Margaret's record was intended merely for her own use, the document has outlived her, has given pleasure to subsequent generations of the family, and now reaches a wider audience through publication.

Margaret had plenty of opportunity to observe how sailing and whaling were carried out, and lots of time to establish friendly relations with Eskimo women at the winter harbour. Clearly, she was interested in the activities going on around her and was able to describe them with the keen enthusiasm engendered by a new experience. "It is so exciting to see all the operations going on that I can scarcely sleep any," she wrote on 11 May during the spring whaling from the floe edge. She exemplifies what Ronald Blythe, in a fascinating anthology of diary writings, calls "the diarist as eye-witness" (Blythe 1989, 7), and because she was a lone woman among a crew of men, her observations are of special interest.

EDITORIAL CONVENTIONS

My editorial changes to Margaret's journal are limited to the following: the addition of punctuation and capitalization to indicate sentences,

the expansion of a few potentially confusing abbreviations, the inser-
tion of words that are clearly intended but missing, and the explanation of words that are unfamiliar or badly misspelled. Illegible words
are indicated as such, and those about which I have doubts are followed by a question mark. I have left the original spelling unchanged.
When quoting other unpublished material, I have employed the same
editorial conventions.

In my text, sources of facts, opinions, and quotations are indicated in
parentheses by author's surname, year, and page; full details of publication are provided in the list of references at the rear of the book. However, no references are provided for the numerous quotations from the
logbooks of the *Alibi* (1856–57), *Lady Franklin* (1857–58), and *Sophia*
(1857–58), although they are included in the list of references. No references are given for specific documents relating to births, baptisms,
marriages, or deaths, because I have used photocopies, extracts, and
work sheets provided by several people whose help has already been
acknowledged and I have not myself examined the originals in Britain.

At the time of the voyage, Europeans usually referred to the original
inhabitants of Greenland and arctic North America as Esquimaux,
and they generally used the same spelling for singular, plural, and ad-
jectival forms. This is the word Margaret Penny used, though sometimes, like the whalemen, she shortened it to "Esque" or "Esqui"
(which probably evolved into the nickname Husky, which could still be
heard at Hudson's Bay Company posts in northern Canada in the mid-
twentieth century). Occasionally, whalemen called the native people
Inuit (and a Scottish whaling vessel bore the name *Innuit*), but usually
they called them Esquimaux. I have retained this historical term in my
text (in its accepted modern spelling, "Eskimo") to denote the original people of both Greenland and arctic Canada.

Eskimo words are spelled in almost every imaginable way in Margaret's journal, in the ships' logbooks, and in Warmow's letters. When
quoting the original documents I have left these unchanged, but for
standardization in my text I have used the accepted English renditions
of nouns if they exist (for example, "igloo," "kayak," "umiak"), and for
nouns that are not usually found in dictionaries I have used what I
consider to be a reasonable variant (for example, "angekok," "kamik,"
"maktak"). Eskimo personal names are also quoted as the Europeans
wrote them, but in my text I have arbitrarily adopted one phonetic ap-
proximation.

Place-names present a formidable problem for several reasons.
There were two different systems, one Eskimo and one Euro-American.

No written language existed for the Eskimo names, and when whale-men, explorers, and missionaries adopted them they spelled them in various ways. No central authority existed to approve place-names, so spelling variants and duplications often occurred. Although some of the names used by Eskimos and whalemen have made their way onto modern topographic maps or into the gazetteer of the Northwest Terri-tories, many others did not attain official status, and some are no longer used at all. In a few cases, the official government names of our era do not agree with nineteenth-century usage.

It is therefore difficult to design an appropriate policy for the rendi-tion of place-names in this book. My general policy has been to respect the nomenclature of the mid-nineteenth-century whalemen. All the names in Margaret's journal are reproduced as she wrote them, and when I have quoted from ships' logbooks I have left their rich variety of spellings unaltered. For standardization and clarity in my own writ-ing, however, I have adopted what I consider to be the most reasonable spelling for place-names used by the Europeans. But in cases where the early place-names are imprecise, confusing, or misleading, I have resorted to the modern official names (Canada 1980). For place-names on the coast of Greenland, there were three systems – Eskimo, Danish, and English – and in my text I use the English names that were familiar to the British whalemen.

A list of the various spellings of native place-names in Cumberland Sound that were mentioned in the primary sources, together with their official names (where such exist), appears in appendix 4. Read-ers who are interested in the confused but fascinating history of name giving in this region should consult the meticulous study by Philip Goldring (1985).

In the journal, in quotations from other primary documents, and in my text, air temperatures are in degrees Fahrenheit, distances in stat-ute miles, weights in tons or pounds, and lengths in feet and inches.

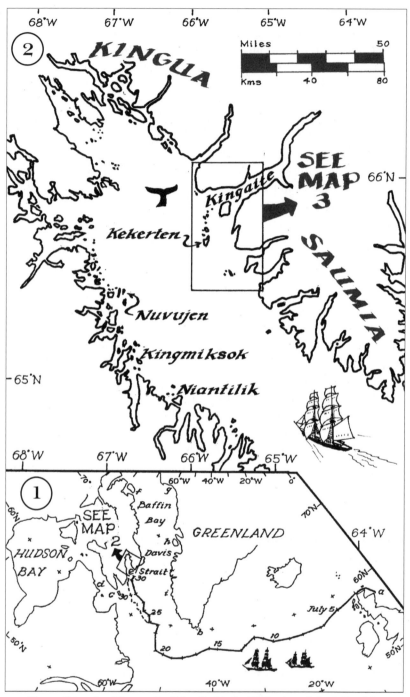

Map 1 (lower)   The track of the *Sophia* (solid line) and *Lady Franklin*
(dotted line) across the Atlantic to Cumberland Sound in July 1857
Map 2 (upper)   Cumberland Sound

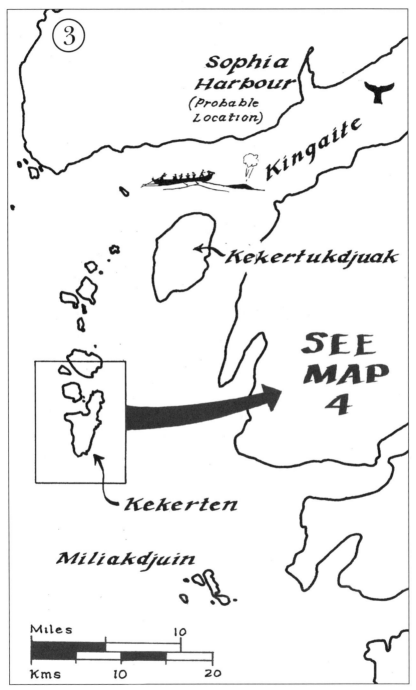

Map 3   Kingaite and Kekerten

Map 4   The island and harbour of Kekerten, showing foreshore flats
(dotted) and elevations (in feet)

This Distant and Unsurveyed Country

Icebergs and Bergy Bits

5–29 July 1857

Captain William Penny begins the journal. The two ships have already rounded the northern tip of the Scottish mainland and are starting across the Atlantic (see map 1).

‡ *July 5th* A.M. strong wind which made me very uncomfortable, the Lady Franklin rolling about with a strong E.S.E. wind which obliged the studding sails to be taken in and the light sails, but it soon moderated and all sail was again set. Latter part, slight showers. Trades people employed preparing for the fishery, seamen amongst the riggin. ‡

‡ *Monday, July 6th* Cloudy weather attended with a strong wind. Ship running to N.W., wind east, the Lady Franklin going through the water 8 or 9 knots and sometimes shipping a little water. Nevertheless all the trades people were employed on deck, blacksmith making conjurers [boat stoves], carpenters oars, cooper water casks, sailors fishing and flenching gear. From 6 to 6 past 138 miles. ‡

[*Tuesday July 7th*] ‡ Fine breeze and clear weather. Ship under a cloud of sail, royals, skysails, gaf topsails, the Sophia close in company. Wind S.S.W. At noon Rockall was seen. It looked like a distant sail. Numbers of sea fowls flying round the ship. Studding sails were set. ‡

‡ *July 8th* The weather was fine and every one actively employed, Lady Franklin a perfect work shop. Light and variable wind from S.W. to S.S.W., which ended in a calm and again in a strong S.S.W. breese. ‡

‡ *Thursday, July 9th*   Strong wind from S.S.W. and [word obscured] weather. Course, N.W. Squally at times. Taking in and setting sail. Work people employed preparing for the fishery. A visit was paid to the Sophia by the Captain to [see] how things were going on. ‡

‡ *July 10th*   Unsettled weather attend[ed] with showers. Seamen employed taking in and setting sail. Mr. Warmow employed smoking, chatting pretty good English, Dr. Grant teasing him and amusing him rather roughly. Sophia not far distant. Wind from W.S.W. to W.N.W. ‡

‡ *July 11th*   A gale with cross sea, all cabin passengers disposed to keep bed. Was under the double reefed topsails and jib handed for a few hours. By noon it was moderate and all sail was set again. Heavy N.W. seas. ‡

‡ *July 12th*   Moderate with all sail set, wind W. by N. [west ?]. At noon worship. Port tacks on board. Latter part light breese. ‡

‡ *July 13th*   Light and variable winds. Trades people employed at various works preparing for the fishery, the watch at various jobs about the riggin. Wind from N.E. to N.N.W. Lat[itude] obs[erve]d 57° 52['N]. ‡

‡ *July 14th*   Continued and variable changes round the compass, causing cross [seas] and making the voyagers very uncomfortable, besides making the sailors take in all the light sails and set them again several times. Blacksmith employed on our fishing plant, carpenter making oars, cooper fresh water [casks] for the boats. Lat. obsd. 57° 58. ‡

‡ *July 15th*   Light fair wind, Lady Franklin & Sophia a cloud of sail. Now a fine S.S.W. breeze hauling round with showers to the N.W. In studding sails, handed light sails. Trades people very busy. ‡

‡ *July 16th*   In the course of the 24 hours we had the wind from west to N.N.E., which obliged us to tack ship to the N.W., starboard tack on board. Handed top gallant sails. All the trades people very actively employed. Lat. 57° 45. ‡

‡ *July 17th*   Strong squalls from north & N.N.E. Middle and latter part more moderate, all sail set, also port studding sails. Watch and trades people actively employed. ‡

‡ *July 18th*   Again a strong wind from N.N.E., which caused the sails to be reduced to a double reef jib and trysail handed. Latter part more moderate. ‡

‡ *Sunday, July 19th*   More moderate. Out reefs. Soon again had all sail. At noon had service. Studding sail set, wind N.N.E. ‡

‡ *July 20th*   Continued to make the best progress with adverse winds and variable. One time calm, another all sail with studding sails going 6 knots. ‡

‡ *July 21st*   Ship close hauled on starboard tack wind from N.E. to N.W. Continued to ply north ward to the best advantage. Trades people employed amongst the fishing plant, seamen employed scraping masts. ‡

‡ *July 22nd*   Strong wind from N.N.W. Port tacks on board, making best proggress northward. Weather heavy, weather [two illegible words] L. 58° 24. ‡

‡ *July 23rd*   Blowing fresh breeze attended with foggie weather. At 8 A.M. a small stream of heavy ice was bearing N.E. Continued to ply to wind ward. Strong gale from north ward, under the double reefed topsails, jib, and trysail handed. Lat. obsvd. 59° 46 North. ‡

‡ [*24th*] *July*   Continued plying against a strong adverse wind under the double reefed sails. It moderated at midnight. Out reef and set jib and trysail. At daylight more moderate. Lat. 60° 1 N. ‡

‡ *Saturday, 25th*   Strong gale down the Straits. Continued to carrie a press of sail, tacking for streams of ice. Had the Lady Franklin from the double reefed topsails and reefed courses to the single reefed topsails & topgallant set. Got the ship cleaned up and all clear for a day of rest. ‡

‡ *Sunday, 26th*   Rather more moderate wind but strong from N.N.E. Plying to the best advantage, thick fog. ‡

‡ *Monday, 27th*   Still a continuance of unsettled wind and weather. Wind from N.N.W. to E.N.E., ship going from 7 miles an hour to 1 from studding sails set to light sails handed. Many washed pieces of

heavy ice. Trades people employed upon the boats & gear. Latter part handed the light sails. ‡

‡ *Tuesday, July 28th*   Strong wind in early part from N.N.E. Ship reaching to N.W. passing many ice bergs and bergie bits. At midnight handed the light sails and handed flying jib. Sent the crow's nest up. At noon lat obsd. 61° 26 North. Wind hauled from W.N.W. Made all sail, set topmast studding sail. ‡

‡ *Wednesday, 29th July*   Strong breeze. Continued to ply to the north ward under a press of sail. Wind from N.W. to N.N.W. Ice bergs and washed pieces of ice. At n[oon] Lat. observed 62° 44. Trades people employed amongst the fishing plant, seamen prepairing the fishing gear. Moderate and mild. ‡

The daily record kept by Captain Penny during the month of July resembles a ship's logbook more than a private journal. It contains nothing of a personal nature but simply presents details about the state of weather and sea, the progress of the ship, changes of sail, and the employment of the crew, during the Atlantic crossing from northern Scotland to Davis Strait. Curiously, the first entry is dated 5 July, by which time the *Lady Franklin* and *Sophia* had been under way for almost a week, so we are not given a glimpse of the scene at dockside in Aberdeen around the time of departure.

   The departure of an arctic whaler meant different things to different people. For most of the crew the occasion was the commencement of a grand adventure, a break from humdrum life ashore, a release from the constraining traditions of land-based society and the fetters of family life. As they took their leave of loved ones whom they would not see for months or years, they were already scanning the horizon of the arctic world, visualizing the rugged treeless landscapes, the precipitous mountain coasts, the immense and majestic icebergs. Undoubtedly, the thoughts of some of the men were turning to the pleasurable prospect of meeting Eskimos, especially those of the female sex, either at settlements along the Greenland coast or at the winter harbour in Cumberland Sound. Conversation was already undergoing a transition from the modes of expression acceptable in mixed company to the particular topics and distinctive vocabulary characteristic of male society on board ship.

As the Aberdeen Arctic Company's two whalers were making their final preparations, the eyes of the Aberdeen public were focused on Captain Francis Leopold M'Clintock, R.N., and the screw yacht *Fox*. In a last attempt to determine the fate of her husband, Lady Franklin, with support from many individuals, was sending out another search expedition, the fourth that she had sponsored. In the dozen years since HMS *Erebus* and *Terror* had been reported by a whaler in Baffin Bay, no European had seen the ships or their crews. Hope for their survival had diminished as expedition after expedition had searched the region stretching from Baffin Bay to Bering Strait and had failed to find the missing men. Then, in 1854, John Rae of the Hudson's Bay Company brought the first news of tragedy near King William Island in the central Arctic. Some Eskimos had told him about starving white men who had resorted to cannibalism a few years before, and they had provided him with articles that once belonged to Franklin and his men.

Many people in England were sceptical of these stories. The prestigious journal *Athenaeum* pompously declared that "all who know the Esquimaux know that they have no sense of truth. Like all savages they lie without scruple" (*Aberdeen Herald* 1854). Charles Dickens, who had never been to the Arctic, was nonetheless confident that Eskimos were "treacherous" (Berton 1988, 268). While the provenance of the relics could not be denied, many chose to believe that the Eskimos had plundered the abandoned ships and lied about the circumstances. Clinging desperately to the slender possibility that some of the men, including her husband, might still be alive, Lady Franklin had chosen M'Clintock to lead what a newspaper called "an ultimate expedition" (*Aberdeen Journal* 1857a) to the alleged scene of the tragedy.

M'Clintock was already a veteran of three expeditions in search of Franklin, and he was a strong proponent of arctic exploration from wintering ships by man-hauled sledges. It is strange to think that in a region where Eskimos had for centuries used dogs for traction, British explorers insisted on hauling the loads themselves – "the hardest work to which free men have been put in modern times" (Mackinnon 1985, 133). Nevertheless, it was an organized, planned system of travel over ice and snow, thanks in large part to M'Clintock's innovations and example, and during the Franklin search it resulted in the exploration of more than fifty thousand miles (M'Clintock 1875, 478). By 1857 M'Clintock himself had already covered four thousand miles by man-hauled sledging (*Aberdeen Journal* 1857b), and by that brutal method of travel he now intended to solve the Franklin mystery once and for all.

In April 1857 Lady Franklin purchased the privately owned steam-auxiliary yacht *Fox*, and more than a hundred men were put to work in the Aberdeen shipbuilding yard of Hall and Company to complete the modifications necessary for an arctic voyage (*Aberdeen Journal* 1857b). These included removing the "velvet hangings and splendid furniture"; reducing the size of skylights and companionways; sheathing the exterior of the hull against ice; encasing the stem in iron so that "it resembled a ponderous chisel set up edgewise"; fortifying the interior with beams; enlarging the boilers; and altering the rig (M'Clintock 1859, 5–6). Local newspapers took pride in the fact that another Franklin search expedition was setting out from Aberdeen, following those of Forsyth, Kennedy, and Penny in 1850 and 1851.

Lady Franklin had remembered a "small mahogany-built ice-boat" (a boat with runners on the hull to facilitate dragging it over the ice) which Sir John had ordered built years before. It had done good service on the expedition she had sponsored in 1852 on the *Isabel*, commanded by Edward Augustus Inglefield. But in the meantime the *Isabel* had been sold in Liverpool, with the boat mistakenly left on board, and no one knew of the steamer's whereabouts. Employing her famous resolve, and benefiting by her position and reputation, Lady Franklin secured the cooperation of Inspector Bates of the Liverpool police, who traced the ship to a small Welsh port with an unpronounceable name. The boat was found, shipped to Liverpool, and transported by rail to Aberdeen in time for M'Clintock's departure (*Aberdeen Journal* 1857c).

With her niece and constant companion Sophia Cracroft, Lady Franklin travelled to Aberdeen in late June. Although her purpose was to see M'Clintock off, she was anxious to see Captain Penny as well and to find out what he intended to do in the way of searching while on his whaling voyage. He was a great favourite with both women. Lady Franklin had once written to Margaret Penny, "Our silver Penny is worth his own weight in gold" (Franklin 1850). The feeling was mutual; Penny had great respect for Lady Franklin and her niece, and his ships had borne their names for seven years. While in Aberdeen, Lady Franklin met and talked with Brother Warmow, who wrote on the day before his departure with Penny, "Lady Franklin ... regrets that I cannot go in her ship. I have, at her request, given her a great deal of information regarding the Greenland language, and have furnished her with a number of phrases in writing" (*Periodical Accounts* 1858, 22:306). The *Fox* cast off and began moving out of the harbour on the evening of 30 June, but the pilot carelessly put the ship

Victoria Dock, Aberdeen, about 1870, looking towards the mouth of
the harbour (reproduced with permission from the George Washington
Wilson Collection, Aberdeen University Library, E-1644)

aground on a bar, and there she remained until high tide the following morning, when M'Clintock proceeded at last on his quest
(M'Clintock 1859, 15).

Penny's ships also left during the evening of 30 June. At 6 P.M. the
Lady Franklin and *Sophia* were lying in Victoria Dock behind a tide barrier while the tide in the River Dee rose towards its maximum. When
the water outside the barrier coincided with the level within the basin,
the gates were opened, the men cast off the mooring lines, and the
ships, with pilots on board, got under way. The emotional moment of
parting was on hand for forty-six individuals about to set off for more
than a year in the Arctic. They exchanged last farewells with "a great
concourse" of families and friends assembled on the dock (*Aberdeen
Journal* 1857d), and the steam tug *Victory* then towed the ships down
the river, past the breakwaters guarding its mouth, and into the North

Sea, where the men began to haul up the sails. A popular Scottish whaling ballad expressed some of the emotions they were probably experiencing:

We leave behind us on the shore
All them we love most dear
We leave our sweethearts and our wives
All weeping round the pier.

And our wee bairns hushed asleep
Their bosoms filled with pain
Dry up your tears for one half year
We'll soon return again. (Shuldham-Shaw and Lyle 1981, 17)

Like almost all of Britain's whaling ports, Aberdeen was on the east coast, facing the North Sea. The first part of any voyage to the Davis Strait whale fishery was therefore a loop around the tip of Scotland. Whaling ships often stopped at the Orkney or Shetland Islands to take on additional crew, but captains Penny and Cheyne had hired their full complement at Aberdeen, including fourteen Shetlanders, so a stop at the islands was not necessary. The ships proceeded northwards, took on pilots again at Noss Head, passed Duncansby Head, the northeastern tip of the Scottish mainland, and then turned the corner and navigated the dangerous tide races of Pentland Firth. After the pilots disembarked into a waiting boat in Thurso Bay, the *Lady Franklin* and *Sophia* continued westward, passed within ten miles of Cape Wrath, the northwestern point of the mainland, and headed out into the Atlantic.

The northern coast of the Scottish mainland is almost as far north as the southern tip of Greenland, beyond which lies Davis Strait. Penny's ships faced a voyage of about fifteen hundred miles westward along the fifty-ninth parallel to the longitude of Cape Farewell, then a northwesterly diagonal of eight hundred miles or so across the bottom of Davis Strait to Cumberland Sound. But sailing ships are rarely able to follow a straight path towards a destination, owing to the impossibility of advancing directly into a headwind. Winds in the North Atlantic between Scotland and Baffin Island, although variable in direction, generally blew from the westerly sector, in opposition to the course of westbound ships. Whaling captains making their way from Europe to Davis Strait therefore expected a relatively slow voyage, with some uncomfortable days beating upwind. Keeping near the fifty-ninth parallel enabled them to avoid battling the full force of the Gulf Stream, the broad flow of surface waters between the southeastern United States and Europe.

The *Lady Franklin* and *Sophia* off northwest Greenland in 1850 during the search for Sir John Franklin, with the ships commanded by Austin, John Ross, and Forsyth

(Illustrated Arctic News 1850, 13)

The *Lady Franklin* and *Sophia* were not large vessels. With tonnages of 201 and 113, respectively, they were smaller than all the other sail whalers leaving Britain for Davis Strait in 1857, whose average was about 335 tons. The upper deck of the *Lady Franklin* was approximately 100 feet long, while that of the *Sophia* was 80 feet. Carrying stores for more than a year, fresh water, and everything necessary for whaling and for the transportation of blubber or oil, the ships could not have had much space for living quarters. But at least they were comparatively new, having been built only seven years before. They were rigged as brigs, carrying yards and square sails on both masts and a spanker (fore and aft sail) on the mainmast. No illustration clearly showing the ships has come to light, but Peter Cormack Sutherland (1852, 1:13), who sailed as surgeon with Penny on two whaling voyages and one Franklin search, described the *Lady Franklin* as she appeared under sail from the *Sophia* in 1850: "In her hull, in the symmetry of her rigging, and ropes, in the exact proportion of her masts and their rake, and in the beauty of her white widely-spread but neatly-cut and well-set sails, the Lady Franklin was certainly an object of great beauty and attraction." Sutherland noted that the *Lady Franklin* was the faster of the two, especially in heavy weather. This is borne out by notations in Penny's logbook in 1857. On 10 July he wrote, "Hauled up fore sail to enable the 'Sophia' to come up"; and four days later: "Lost sight of the 'Sophia' for 6 hours but hauled up and picked him up again."

Despite their different speeds, the impediments of darkness and fog, the vagaries of weather, and the various sail and course alterations necessary to suit the fluctuating moods of North Atlantic weather, the *Lady Franklin* and *Sophia* managed to maintain contact during the next four weeks, losing sight of one another only a few times over a distance of more than two thousand miles. Keeping two ships in company sounds deceptively simple today, accustomed as we are to propelling ships with engines, navigating with satellites and computers, communicating with radio, probing depths with sonar, and seeing through darkness and fog with radar, but it was vastly more difficult a century and a half ago, before the inconstant power of wind could be replaced with something more reliable and before the normal boundaries of hearing and sight could be so cleverly extended. Sailing in company required constant attention and care, especially at night or in fog, but it enabled captains to compare chronometers and check their estimated positions from time to time, and it brought a measure of security in case of trouble. They would, of course, give each other a safe amount of sea room until they had to close in to exchange information by speaking-trumpet.

Except for a passenger ship, which dropped gradually out of sight west of Cape Wrath, diverging on a more southerly path towards the port of Quebec, the two whalers sailed alone on the surface of a sombre sea, the only vertical elements of relief within the vast and featureless circle bounded by the horizon – two small wooden hulls driven by sails of cloth and men of steel. In fine weather the trades people and seamen tightened rigging, scraped masts, made water casks and oars for the whaleboats, sharpened harpoons, lances and flensing tools, overhauled whale lines, and stored whaling gear in the boats. But when the winds exceeded gale force and the decks were awash, all outside work was suspended.

Captain Penny's journal entries tell far more about the employment of the crew than the activities of the three passengers – his wife Margaret, his son William, and the missionary Matthäus Warmow. But he made one small observation on 10 July: "Mr. Warmow employed smoking, chatting pretty good English, Dr. Grant teasing him and amusing him rather roughly." It seems that Brother Warmow, despite his course in English language in Yorkshire (or perhaps because of it), was the target of the gibes of a feisty and inconsiderate young Scot. In the ship's logbook Penny recorded another incident. Early in the voyage, he released two carrier pigeons, which he named Margaret Penny and Mate (either a nickname or an abbreviation of Matthäus) Warmow. Whether this was a serious attempt to send news home, as Sir John Ross had done during the Franklin search, or simply a frivolous gesture to amuse his guests is unclear, but we are told that the pigeon Penny returned immediately to the ship while the pigeon Warmow flew away out of sight. The behaviour of the birds reflects the personalities of the two individuals after whom they were named. Margaret was practical, realistic, and down to earth; Warmow was headstrong, dedicated to his cause, and willing to place himself in the hands of the Lord.

As a source of information about life on board ship during the first month of the voyage, Warmow is even more disappointing than Captain Penny. In a report sent back to the Moravians in August, he wasted no words describing the Atlantic crossing. "On the whole," he wrote, "but little of interest occurred" (*Periodical Accounts* 1858, 22:452). Can anyone sail across an ocean and honestly claim that little of interest occurred? Does the remark really indicate that Brother Warmow was unmoved by the profound solitude of the boundless sea, insensitive to the ocean's inconstant moods, uninterested in natural phenomena? Or did he think that indifference to the natural world was the correct posture to adopt for the Moravians to whom he was writing?

The transatlantic voyage of the *Lady Franklin* and *Sophia* was very different from the peregrinations of whalers in the Pacific, where there were so many whaling grounds and so many ships that encounters with other vessels were commonplace, and where "gams" (visits to other ships for the exchange of news, mail, and good cheer) provided social occasions to offset the loneliness and boredom of the long sea voyages. Because many American captains were accompanied by their wives, and sometimes their children as well, their ships bore a passing resemblance to households and families, if only at the command level.

Several months before Margaret Penny left for the Arctic, an American whaling wife, Mary Chipman Lawrence, sailed on the *Addison*, commanded by her husband Samuel (Garner 1966). They took along their daughter Minnie, who was five years old when the ship left New Bedford, Massachusetts, in the fall of 1856. During the three-and-a-half-year voyage down the Atlantic, round Cape Horn into the Pacific and up to the Hawaiian Islands, north to the Bering and Chukchi seas, south to New Zealand, and home again by the Horn, the ship spoke other whalers on more than 180 occasions. Almost 160 of these meetings were accompanied by gams, sometimes on board the *Addison* and sometimes on other vessels; and on two dozen of the gams – one out of every seven – Mary Lawrence met other captains' wives. The most fulfilling occasions were those on which both wives and children were present. "This meeting with families at sea is very pleasant for all concerned," wrote Mary, "particularly so for the children" (Garner 1966, 212). But sometimes, when rough seas or high winds intervened, she could do no more than wave a handkerchief at the lonely figure of a woman on the upper deck of a passing ship.

If time was available, whaling prospects poor, and the weather gentle, a gam might last all day and include tea and dinner. The captains' conversation habitually centred on the whaling success of various ships, accidents and disasters in the whaling fleet, and the latest prices of oil and bone, while that of the women focused on more personal matters – children, clothes, and religion, and social events at such ports as Lahaina and Honolulu. For whaling captains and their wives, gams were the closest thing possible to going out to dinner at a friend's house ashore, and they sometimes took along a bottle or two of wine, some comparatively fresh vegetables, and a few small presents for the children. Margaret Penny enjoyed no pleasures of this sort in her voyage from Scotland to Davis Strait. The ships were in direct transit to the whaling grounds; there was no time to waste; the weather was less suitable for intership visits by boat; and in any case they saw no other whalers at all.

Margaret's impressions of life on board ship are not recorded. Certainly she would have found space at a premium, for the *Lady Franklin* was relatively small, had much of the interior reserved for fresh water, stores, oil and bone, and carried a crew larger than an ordinary merchantmen of equal size in order to man several whaleboats. As was usual on ships, there was a basic rule for accommodation – the higher the rank, the farther aft. The seamen slept and ate in the forecastle, while those of higher rank lived in the rear section of the vessel. Usually the captain's day room, with a dining table for his officers, extended across the stern, and his sleeping cabin and water closet were next to it. Running forward from the captain's quarters along both sides of the ship were tiny shared cabins for the doctor, mates, cooper, carpenter, cook, and steward. To fit three passengers into the limited space allotted for officers and crew must have demanded considerable ingenuity from Captain Penny and a deal of tolerance from all concerned. Margaret probably slept in her husband's cabin, sharing an enlarged berth. If the arrangement was similar to that experienced by Henrietta Deblois on the American whaler *Merlin* in 1856, the sleeping cabin – sometimes ostentatiously termed a "stateroom" – measured a mere six by ten feet (Druett 1991, 35). But as the *Lady Franklin* was considerably smaller than the *Merlin*, the captain's cabin may have been even more cramped. During the day, Margaret undoubtedly used the day cabin, where she could knit, read, write, sew, wash and iron clothes, and perhaps take young William through some lessons.

Whalemen expected to encounter floating ice south and west of Cape Farewell, where the floes and bergs carried southward by the East Greenland Current are swept around into Davis Strait. They therefore gave the land a wide berth. The *Lady Franklin* and *Sophia* were two hundred miles southwest of Greenland when, on 23 July, they first met drifting pack ice, elongated by the wind into a series of "ice streams." Each day's sail carried them deeper into the polar world. During the remainder of the voyage, several forms of floating ice were an integral part of the seascape through which they travelled: landfast ice, also called land ice or fast ice (a fringe of salt-water ice attached to coasts); pack ice (floes of salt-water ice of varying sizes, moving in response to winds and currents); icebergs (large masses of fresh-water ice calved into the sea from glaciers and drifting with the currents); and bergy bits (small fragments of icebergs). Because whales were often found near the edge of the pack-ice zone and because bergs, and sometimes ice floes, lingered throughout the summer, it was inevitable that whalers would meet up with ice of one form or another during a voyage. Sailing among rock-hard pieces of ice was one of the the most hazardous parts of any arctic whaling voyage. In navigating through relatively open pack ice – what the whalemen referred to as sailing ice – the captain usually climbed to the crow's nest and conned the ship from there, shouting commands to the helmsman below. It required a cool nerve and superb judgment, and if visibility was obscured by fog, snow, or darkness, it could be a terrifying experience with a very high risk of disaster.

One of the advantages of wintering voyages, strangely enough, was that ships were exposed to ice hazards for a shorter time than those making one-season voyages. They arrived on the whaling grounds much later. Captains Penny and Cheyne were approaching Cumberland Sound in late July, by which time the margin of the pack-ice zone had already retreated a hundred miles from its maximum position, greatly reducing the total area of ice-covered water. Within the pack-ice zone, open leads and pools had expanded, providing more space in which to advance. And the ice itself, responding to warmer air and water temperatures, had become softer, weaker, and less capable of holing a hull. By contrast, ships on one-season voyages, arriving at the edge of the pack-ice zone around the beginning of April, had to contend with extremely severe conditions of weather, ice, and sea. Almost four months before the *Lady Franklin* and *Sophia* passed Cape Farewell, several whalers had arrived in the Davis Strait region to start whaling. On 1 April the Hull whaler *Anne* had experienced a gale that continued for eight miserable days before showing any signs of moderation. As her surgeon later described it, "The ship was a mass of ice; her sides, bows, and bulwarks, inside and out, deck and lower rigging, were all covered thickly, so much so that in some places it was more than a foot thick. Every sea that came on the vessel left a fresh coating of ice – the spray froze on the rigging – and the oilskins of the sailors hung with icicles" (*Hull Advertiser* 1857b).

Not only did the one-season ships arrive much earlier, in winter weather, but they remained close to the dangerous pack ice for three or four months as they advanced slowly northward to Melville Bay and then tried to cross to Lancaster Sound. On wintering voyages, however, whaling captains delayed their arrival until relatively late in the season, sailed directly to Cumberland Sound, and made sure they tucked their ships away in a sheltered harbour in time to avoid being caught in an exposed situation by fall freeze-up. After the disruption incurred by autumn gales, the sea ice changed from foe to friend. Although the ships spent the next ten months icebound, the winter ice cover was usually stable and held the ships safe. They enjoyed the protection of harbour ice until the middle of the next summer, by which time the seas were again comparatively unencumbered by pack ice, permitting navigation.

On 23 July the observed latitudes of the *Lady Franklin* and *Sophia*, as recorded in their logbooks, differed by about four minutes – only a few miles – and both logs recorded course changes to avoid "Cape Ice." Evidently they were still sailing in company. But soon after this they become separated, probably during thick fog on the twenty-sixth. By the twenty-eight they were at least seventy miles apart, and two days later the distance had increased to one hundred and fifty miles or more, with Captain Cheyne forging ahead on a more northerly course towards the mouth of Cumberland Sound while Captain Penny, unaware of his consort's position, continued towards the southeastern tip of Baffin Island. Penny's last entries in the journal (which was about to be taken over by his wife Margaret) refer to heavy pack ice and a number of "ice bergs and bergy bits." The men had sent up the crow's nest and were putting the final touches to the whaling gear.

The Kind-Hearted Esquimaux

30 July – 14 August

Margaret Penny now takes over the journal as the ship makes a landfall and continues to Cumberland Sound (map 2).

[*July 30th*]   Weather fine, sky cloudless. In the morning there was a considerable swell on the sea. About 12 A.M. it subsided and a gentle breeze blew which carried us on well. A number of icebergs of immense size were seen, some assuming the appearance of fortifications, & others that of ruined castles. In the evening we saw something like land to windward & felt all very cheerful & happy at the prospect.

July 31st   I was awoke at 4 A.M. this morning by the joyful news that it had been land we had seen last night, for it was now seen close on the weather bow. It turned out to be Resolution Island. The weather was delightful, & I remained on deck the whole day amusing myself by looking through the telescope at the rugged coast. The sea was so calm we could see a great distance. The land is very high & mountainous. I was much surprised to see so little snow, but those who have been here many voyages tell me they never saw [so] little. The coast is studded with ice but not a bit of floating ice to be seen. The Dr. has managed to reach the crows nest today.

August 1st   Weather still delightful, sky without a cloud. Thermometer 63 degrees in the shade. A party went in a boat to pick up some peices of ice which had broken off from an iceberg lying close by, when it broke. It was like the noise of thunder & it was beautiful to hear the echo dying in the distant hills. The ice when melted is the most pleasant water I ever tasted. The men are now all actively employed prepairing their fishing gear.

August 2d   After plying through islands of mountainous height, where one not accustomed could never imagine a ship could enter, we arrived at Naujartalik harbour about 4 P.M. Not being possessed of language in which I could describe the scenery here I must sum up by saying it is "terrifick grand." We saw the figure of a human being on the top of one of the mountains & when our eyes got a little accustomed we could distinguish an Esquimaux hut near the waters edge, where they generally place them just beyond tide mark. Mr. Penny, Mr. Warmow, & the Dr. set off with a boat party to land & we saw from the vessel three Esquemaux sitting on a ridge of the hill tossing up their arms & crying out "Chimo" "Chimo," an expression of their joy at seeing the party land. They took them into the boat & brought them on board when we learned that they were females, one with a sucking child in her hood. Their condition is past all description. They had nothing to eat except some small fish left by the tides in the crevesis of the rocks, Captain Souter, a man belonging to Peterhead, having taken away their husbands or sons (on whose hunting they depended for support) to assist him with his whale fishing & left these poor creatures in this miserable state. Mr. Penny gave them something to eat immediately, which they did with great relish. They gave us very bad intelligence of the Alibi. She had wintered here instead of going where she had been directed by Mr. Penny, where the whales were in hundreds. It has cast a gloom over all on board our vessel to hear that 5 of the Alibi's men had died & that the poor Dr. had been very ill used by the men & that he had fallen over board & been drowned. We had service in the cabin in the afternoon as usual, after which Mr. Penny said a few words to the men with regard to their melancholy intelligence. They seem to have confidence in his experience & are sanguine of success, so we must trust in an over-ruling Providence to protect us, taking every precaution ourselves to prevent ill health. The men went in the evening to an island where the Alibi's people had buried their comrades. They brought back with them a blind man, his wife & child. He is very intelligent & is called the blind Priest. His wife is very ill & the child is covered with boils. The Dr. opened the [boil] under its arm & Mr. Penny washed it & put some healing ointment on it, which seemed to give it some relief for it slept immediately. Mr. Warmow commenced his labour of love the moment he came in contact with these poor people. He went on shore with them & was left in their hut with them for 2 hours & they seemed to understand very well.

August 3rd   I went on shore today with Mr. P., Mr. Warmow, & the Dr. We paid a visit to the Esquimaux hut & were received by her in a very graceful & kind mannner for her condition. She presented me with a small seal skin. Upon the whole, her tent was not so uncomfortable, being covered with seal skin. She seemed well provided with deer skins for sleeping amongst. We had a delightful climb up the mountain. In little spots between the rocks there was all sorts of wild flowers, fine grass with a sweet smell like English hay, an immense quantity of crow-berries, blue berries, & cran berries, but they are not quite ripe yet. We brought away a great many specimens of the flowers which we intend to preserve. I enjoyed this day very much. It has been warm & pleasant. The men have been busy coiling the whale lines into the boats today & as they finished with each boat they gave three hearty cheers.

August 4th   Got under way for N[uvujen]. The weather is still beautiful & we have been plying through islands all day. The men have been drawing lots for their boats & placing the [harpoon] guns in them. In the evening a party went on shore to an island; they reported it very pleasant & fertile for this climate. They saw some birds nests & found some copper ore, also an Esquimaux lamp.

August 5th   [Entry written, then crossed out] The wood for the house was rafted ashore to-day, and I have been there amuseing myself.

August 5th   We arrived at N[uvujen] about 3 P.M. after plying through a great many islands & sunk rocks. We came so near some of the rocks that we could have jumped upon them from the vessel. Natives were seen on shore. A boat was immediately dispatched for them & they came on board, had tea, & remained until evening. They are really a most interesting people, particularly the females.

August 6th   I went on shore early this day to see the site for the house. It is situated in a pleasant valley well sheltered by surrounding hills & a fine beach for fishing. The men have been most active in rafting the wood ashore. I really do not think that any class of men can go through so much work as sailors. I paid a visit to some Esquamaux huts & have been much amused wandering about amongst the rocks gathering flowers in which I have been assisted by two native females. We managed to understand each other very well. Mr. Warmow, the Dr., & William went to an opposite island this evening on a shooting excursion but were unsuccessful. I have made an appointment with my female friends to go tomorrow. The weather here is delightful.

August 7th   I went on shore this morning & found the people all very busy putting up the house. It will be walled in tonight. Mr. Warmow has been in the Esquimaux huts all forenoon & told them this day of their Saviour. They seemed all much impressed & one woman said without doubt I shall never forget what I have been told. In the afternoon we went to the opposite side of the bay. I had much difficulty in climbing up the steep rocks but after ascending about 200 feet we had a fine view & descended on the other side to some lakes where we gathered a number of beautiful flowers. We likewise saw a few eider ducks. I was quite pleased to see the kind-hearted Esquimaux, how anxious they were to assist me up & down the rocks, one always going before to look for the easiest way, another keeping close & sometimes placing her foot firmly against a rock to make a step for me when I found it difficult.

August 8th   Found myself very tired on getting up this morning. Did not go on shore today, it being rather damp. The house is all finished tonight & the men came on board all very tired. However they seemed soon rested for on going on deck about 8 o clock I found them dancing reels with the greatest spirit.

August 9th   We all went on shore today & Mr. Warmow, assisted by the Dr., read service in the house. The assistant carpenter leads the choir. He sings very well, indeed as also several others of the crew, which added very much to the solemnity of the scene. Mr. Warmow read the beautiful litany of the Church of the United Brethren. The Dr. afterwards read the 21st chapter of Matthew & the remarks upon it from the light of the dwelling. The 103 psalm & the 64 paraphrase were sung.

August 10th   Weather beautiful. Provisions, casks, coals &c. &c. going on shore to the house. Had a walk on shore.

August 11th   I have been on shore all day wandering about amongst these solitary wilds. I am much pleased with the poor natives, particularly Mackitow, the wife of an old man. She is very kind & attentive to him. It was quite amuseing to see them examining my dress.

August 12th   Mr. Warmow & the Dr. have been away all day in search of game but have been unsuccessful. Today we have had the pleasure of a visit from Mackitow dressed in a jacket & petticoat neatly made after the English fashion.

August 13th   The men have been engaged all day in carrying coals & provisions to the house. They are all very tired & complain much of pains in their joints, but I think it is from being overheated in carrying such burdens over the rocks & then the cold air in the evening. The weather continues very fine. I have been on shore to the house to take a farewell of my Esquimaux friends for a time.

August 14th   The weather has been rather cloudy to-day. Mr. Warmow & the Dr. have been away dredging & have found a curious looking animaul. They have preserved some to bring home. At 4 P.M. the ship was got under way for Kingite, two men being left in charge of the house to set up casks & catch whales if they can. The Esq. seemed very sorry to part with us.

At the end of July the journal begun by William Penny, arctic whaling master, ceases to be a nautical record of weather and sea, ship's course, sail changes, and jobs carried out by the crew. Fading away like jetsam in the vessel's wake are the references to setting studding sails, handing top gallants, double-reefing topsails, shaking out reefs, and other procedures of vital concern to a sea captain. From then on, Margaret describes scenes and events from the unique vantage point of a woman who is the wife of the ship's commander.

The tenor of Margaret's journal entries leads us to suspect that she was not a total stranger to ships and the sea. They contain none of the remarks we might expect from a true landlubber about the novel and often disturbing aspects of life on the ocean wave, such as gyrating decks, flying spray, crowded quarters, lack of privacy, and the incessant cacophony of shipboard noises: creaking timbers, clattering blocks, rattling galley pots and pans, the dull thud of the bow against head seas, the thunder of men's feet when all hands are called at night to shorten sail, the muffled bark of commands carried away on the wind, the pistol-shot of sails flapping as the vessel comes about onto a different tack. Nor does Margaret say anything about seasickness, though Captain Penny himself had admitted feeling "very uncomfortable" a few days out from Aberdeen.

It would not be surprising to learn that Margaret had had some previous experience at sea. The railway had not yet reached northeastern Scotland, and overland travel was limited to foot, horseback, or horse-drawn carriage on rough roads. As most of Scotland's towns and cities were on the coast, they depended largely on the highway of the sea. Ships carried most of the freight and many of the travellers who left or entered ports such as Aberdeen. If Margaret Penny had ever had occasion to visit Peterhead, Dundee, or Edinburgh, she had probably made the journey by sailing vessel or steam packet. On the other hand, the paucity of remarks in Margaret's journal about the novelty of shipboard life could simply be the result of a steady osmosis of maritime lore from her seafaring husband during seventeen years of married life.

For the next fourteen months Margaret Penny would be alone in a male community, one woman among twenty-six men and two boys. Her husband, at forty-nine years of age, was the oldest person on the ship, slightly older than his mate, James Birnie. Only one other man was of more than forty years. Seven were in their thirties, twelve in their twenties, and three in their teens. The youngest on the crew list (appendix 1) was George Gibson, a seventeen-year-old apprentice, but there was also an unlisted cabin boy, undoubtedly younger.

With an average age of only twenty-eight, the crew could be described as young, but not uncommonly so for an arctic whaler of this period. The crew of the *Sophia* averaged only twenty-six years of age, and other whaling crews were similar. This was partly a reflection of the demographic characteristics of the period. The average life expectancy for males in Scotland in the middle of the nineteenth century was far lower than it is today; moreover, there were fewer older men in proportion to total population than there are now. In addition, whaling was an occupation that depended heavily on hard physical labour, and in the arctic environment every task was more more arduous and dangerous than usual; so when hiring a crew, a whaling captain looked not only for experience but also for robust health, strength, endurance, and resistance to cold – qualities more likely to be found in young men.

A man's character had to be considered as well. On a small, crowded ship, interpersonal contact was constant and unavoidable. Men who were intolerant of others or were habitual complainers or militant "sea lawyers" could easily undermine the morale and effectiveness of a crew and jeopardize the success of the voyage. On a wintering voyage to arctic regions, all the usual sources of friction and tension among a crew were multiplied many times over by the increased length of the voyage, the idleness, confinement, and discomfort experienced during the winter months, and the heightened level of danger in sailing a wooden ship and rowing open whaleboats through cold seas encumbered by floating ice.

Captain Penny had been able to hire twelve men who had sailed with him on his previous wintering voyage to Cumberland Sound in 1855–56. Thus, almost half the crew were well known to him, had already experienced the rigours of an arctic winter, and had elected to repeat the performance. At least nine others had previously served on whalers, and three had served on merchant ships. Only two appear to have been true "landsmen," or "green hands" – the surgeon and the apprentice.

Although whaling crews were less formally structured than those of naval ships, they were nonetheless organized in a hierarchy of ranks and functions. Authority flowed down fom the master, or "captain," through the chief or first mate and (on large ships) the second mate. Other individuals were responsible for specific operations: the spectioneer directed flensing; the skeeman took charge of making off the blubber below decks; and the boatswain supervised the maintenance of the vessel and its equipment. At the bottom of the hierarchy the seamen, or "foremast men," carried out the bulk of the manual labour related to the operation of the ship and the catching and processing of whales. On the *Lady Franklin* the "ordinary seamen" and the slightly more experienced "able-bodied seamen" amounted to nine men, roughly one-third of the ship's complement.

Depending on the size of the ship, the nature of the voyage, and the experience of the crew, some individuals might "wear two hats." Mates and spectioneers usually served also as harpooners. On the *Lady Franklin* one man was designated in the crew list as "harpooner & skeeman" and another was identified as "b'swain and harpooner." Another was listed as "ice master" but served also as harpooner. In addition to the officers and men who sailed the ship, manned the whaleboats, and flensed the whales, there were always some experienced artisans, or "trades people," who made, maintained, and repaired articles of wood and metal. On the *Lady Franklin* these included two coopers, a carpenter, a second carpenter, and a blacksmith. In addition, there was a cook to prepare the food and a steward to serve it. Another person with specialized training and function, though not a professional sailor, was the surgeon. British whalers were required by law to carry a licensed doctor or medical student.

Each whaleboat operated like a small replica of the whaling ship, with its own chain of command and division of labour. A harpooner was in overall charge and was responsible for the most critical operations; after pulling the bow oar during the approach, he would stand up to harpoon the whale and later to lance it. A boatsteerer manned the steering oar and helped keep the line clear; a line manager pulled the after (or stroke) oar and coiled the line. Usually, three or four seamen pulled the remaining oars. It was not unusual for a ship captain to command one of the boats. Both Penny and Cheyne intended to take their place at the bow oar, operate the harpoon gun, and wield the lance.

On board ship, life followed the familiar progression of hours, days, and weeks, but with the additional rhythm of sea watches. The crews of sailing ships did not simply retire to bed in the evening and rise leisurely in the morning to sip coffee and peruse the sports section of the paper. At all hours when the ship was under way, a "watch" – which usually consisted of a third or half of the ship's company without the trades people – had to be on duty under the authority of a mate or other experienced officer to operate the ship, watch out for danger, and carry out a variety of maintenance jobs, such as checking rigging, pumping bilges, and washing decks. Each watch lasted four hours, except for the two-hour "dog watches" between 4 and 8 P.M.

Margaret, her son William (or Billie), her fellow passenger Brother Warmow, and the ship's doctor Erskine Grant were outside the watchkeeping system and were more or less free to follow their own inclinations. How they spent their time during the Atlantic crossing is not a matter of record, but we can visualize them accustoming their landlubberly legs to the incessant roll and pitch of the ship, strolling on deck in fair weather, enjoying the vigorous sea air, marvelling at the unfamiliar limitlessness of ocean space, and observing how the bewildering forest of yards, sails, sheets, braces, and halyards was managed by the nimble sailors. We can imagine them at other times sitting below in their cabins, reading, chatting, or writing up journals. Meals provided the best opportunity for social interaction, and if they dined with the ship's officers, the presence of a woman, a missionary, and a boy must have taken some of the sting out of the salty language of the whalemen and brought about fundamental changes in the subject matter of table conversation. The sabbath was rigorously respected. All work stopped at midnight every Saturday and was not resumed for twenty-four hours. On Sunday morning, Warmow and the doctor joined forces to conduct a service of divine worship, a practice that continued through the winter.

Young William, who was aged twelve at the beginning of the voyage and a teenager by 7 July, must have eagerly eyed the shrouds that rose enticingly towards the mastheads – a boy climber's delight! His father probably encouraged him to ascend and may even have ordered him to do so, no doubt despite the trepidation of an anxious mother. An American boy, Reginald Hegarty, who went to sea on his father's whaling ship when only seven years old, later recalled the thrill of his first climb up the ratlines to the masthead, using the futtock shrouds to snake round the overhanging edges of the platforms of the main top and the topmast crosstrees, while each additional foot of height above the distant deck imparted a wilder gyration from the ship's motion. Then, following the example of experienced men when they were in a hurry to descend, the seven-year-old boy gripped the backstay with his bare hands and slid all the way down to the deck. With more practice, he learned to "run the rigging," which entailed travelling the entire length of the vessel from the overhanging after end of the spanker to the forward-thrusting tip of the bowsprit without ever touching the deck. His most daring stunt was to slide down the curve of a trysail when it had a bellyful of wind, but this foolhardy amusement ceased after his father casually asked him what would happen if the wind suddenly ceased as he started his descent (Hegarty 1965, 15–7, 72–4).

For the twenty-one-year old doctor, Erskine Grant, the boyhood appeal of climbing may have been mitigated slightly by advancing years, and the rashness of youth tempered by the maturity of adulthood and the dignity of his profession. Was it simple curiosity, then, or a lingering boyish sense of adventure – or perhaps peer pressure – that induced him to conquer height on board ship? On the last day of July, Margaret reported in her journal, "The Dr. has managed to reach the crows nest today." Brother Warmow, on the other hand, apparently felt quite close enough to God down on the deck.

A day after Margaret made her first journal entry, remarking on "a number of icebergs of immense size … some assuming the appearance of fortifications, & others that of ruined castles," Captain Penny made his landfall at Resolution Island, a barren rock mass, triangular in shape and roughly twenty-five miles on each side, rising slightly more than 1,500 feet from the sea. A prominent sentinel at the entrance to Hudson Strait, the island was a landmark well known to masters in the employ of the Hudson's Bay Company, for its vessels had been sailing through the strait and across Hudson Bay for almost two centuries, carrying supplies and trade goods a thousand miles into the interior of the continent to fur posts at Churchill, York Factory, and Moose Factory. But the *Lady Franklin* was destined for Cumberland Sound and therefore altered course and proceeded northward along the coast. There was no sign of the *Sophia.*

Between Hudson Strait and Davis Strait, the southeastern part of Baffin Island points towards the Atlantic Ocean with three parallel fingers. From the south, in sequence, these are the Meta Incognita Peninsula, the Hall Peninsula, and the Cumberland Peninsula. All are mountainous, with elevations approaching 3,000 feet in the first and exceeding 3,000 and 7,000 feet, respectively, in the last two. Nestled between them lie the long troughs of Frobisher Bay and Cumberland Sound. The latter indentation, where Penny intended to carry out whaling, is approximately the size of Lake Ontario; if placed in a north-south alignment in Britain, it would extend from Edinburgh to Liverpool, or from Hull to London.

Despite its severe climate and very restrictive navigation season, the southeastern part of Baffin Island had become known to Europeans surprisingly early. Three decades before the French and English established settlements at Port Royal (Nova Scotia), Jamestown (Virginia), and Quebec, Martin Frobisher had already made three expeditions to the bay that now bears his name. Although mining rather than colonization was his intent, the scale of his ventures was impressive. His third expedition in 1578, to extract what was falsely believed to be gold, contained fifteen ships and four hundred men, with a prefabricated house for a wintering party, which in the end did not stay over. It has been called "the largest arctic expedition that has ever been fielded" (Kenyon 1975, 10). Several years later, Frobisher's fellow Elizabethan, John Davis, also made three expeditions to southeast Baffin Island, mapping most of the coastline between Hudson and Davis straits and becoming the first European navigator to sail into Cumberland Sound. For the next two and a half centuries, however, the large gulf that he found and named was not visited.

As the *Lady Franklin* cruised northward past the opening of Frobisher Bay, along the stern rocky coast of the Hall Peninsula and into Cumberland Sound (see map 2), the awesome grandeur of the scenery

The coast of Baffin Island south of Cumberland Sound,
where Margaret was struck by the grandeur of the scenery
(photo by the author, July 1973)

was not lost on Margaret Penny. She passed an entire day on deck, admiring the rugged treeless land by telescope, and confessed that she lacked adequate words to describe it. After "plying through islands of mountainous height," where she could scarcely imagine that they could safely pass, the ship dropped anchor in the harbour of Niantilik, and the pièce de résistance was served at what had already been for Margaret a sumptuous banquet of new sights and experiences. She set foot ashore for the first time in a month, climbed the hills, enjoyed the fragrant smell of the coarse grass ("a sweet smell like English hay"), collected flowers, and made her first acquaintance with the local inhabitants.

In addition to hearing a lot about the Eskimos from her husband, who had passed two winters among them, Margaret had met a few of them in Britain. "I had a visit from Tackritow," she would write on 18 August, "my old acquaintance whom I had seen in England," and she must have also known Eenoolooapik, the man who had accompanied Penny to Aberdeen in the fall of 1839, lived there during the winter, and departed for Baffin Island with him in the spring of 1840, a few months after Margaret's marriage to the whaling captain. Margaret must have been eager to see the native people in their own environment, and at last the opportunity had arrived. At Niantilik and a few days later at Nuvujen she visited women in their tents, admired their fur sleeping blankets, examined their clothing (not less eagerly than they examined hers), and walked with them on the hills, delighted when they thoughtfully helped her clamber over the rocks. She found the females "kind-hearted" and "most interesting." As the first white woman among them, she was herself an object of intense curiosity, but the relationship that developed steadily between Margaret and the native women was much more than mutual curiosity. It involved shared activities, companionship, and friendship. It included understanding, sympathy, and compassion.

In both their culture and hers there were traditional gender-related roles in society and the family. As a married Scottish woman, Margaret was familiar with the domestic responsibilities of managing a household: shopping, cooking, cleaning, making and mending clothes, raising children, cultivating a garden, putting up preserves, and performing other such chores, mainly during the hours or months when her husband was away "earning" a living – that is to say, doing work that brought in cash to purchase many of the goods and services required by the family. Despite numerous contrasts between Scotland's commercial economic system, based on money and specialized occupational roles, and the subsistence economy of the Eskimos, in which money played no part and virtually every man was a hunter, there were some fundamental similarities in female roles. Margaret found much in common with the Eskimo women who, like her, were responsible within the family for collecting edible plants, preparing food, making and mending clothing, and nurturing young children. Because of this, she may have felt much closer to the Eskimo women ashore than to the Scottish men on board the ships. And circumstances favoured contact between the women. Margaret was excluded from the men's work of sailing the ship, pursuing and flensing whales, erecting buildings, and hauling ice for winter water supply, just as the Eskimo women were normally excluded from the hunting and whaling activities of their husbands and sons. When the men were involved in their activities, there was often time for the women to meet and socialize.

During seventeen years of operating in Cumberland Sound, British and American whalemen had exerted a strong influence on Eskimo life and culture. The relocation of Eskimos from their customary places of residence to localities where whales occurred was one of the unfortunate aspects of whaling contact. Once the value of Eskimos as whalemen had been demonstrated and the tradition of hiring them for the season had become established, it was inevitable that some interruption of their usual cycle of nomadic hunting would occur whenever they elected to work for whaling captains. If they were hired for the summer, they missed some of the hunting for birds, fish, and sea mammals. If their employment extended into the fall, they sometimes missed the most important caribou hunt of the year, when skins were in prime condition. If they continued to work for a wintering vessel, they had less opportunity to hunt ringed seals and other winter-resident animals. The more time they spent helping the whalers, the less time they had to secure what they needed for themselves: meat and fish for food; animal skins for clothes, blankets, tents, boats, dog harnesses and traces; wood, ivory, and stone for weapons and tools; soapstone for pots and lamps; animal oil for lighting, heating, and cooking; and sinew for thread.

To their credit, most whaling captains assumed some responsiblity for the dependants of the Eskimo men they hired. They made up for some of the shortfall in products of the hunt by distributing ships' provisions, and they provided substitutes for some of the traditional articles and materials that the native men and women no longer had the time to make or collect, by paying for their labour with goods such as whaleboats, knives, needles, clothes, metal, wood, and cloth. When a captain had occasion to shift his hired men to another locality, he generally had the sense to ship entire families rather than the men only, in order to avoid leaving the women and children to fend for themselves. But as Margaret saw at Niantilik on 2 August, not all captains were so considerate. Captain Sutter (probably commanding either the *Clara* or the *Innuit* from Peterhead) had shipped all the able-bodied men of the small community, leaving behind four women (one of them too ill to walk), two babies (one covered with boils), and a blind man, all of whom were desperately in need of food. Margaret did not hesitate to attribute the "miserable state" of the "poor creatures" to the whaling captain who had removed the husbands and sons on whose hunting the women, old man, and children "depended for support."

There was more bad news at Niantilik. The Aberdeen Arctic Company's third whaler, *Alibi*, commanded by Alexander Stewart, had wintered there instead of at Kekerten, contrary to Penny's instructions. The ship had subsequently departed, but the Eskimos supplied the "melancholy intelligence" that, during the winter, six of her men had died, five of them (as they later learned) from scurvy, and one – the doctor – in strange circumstances. It is easy to believe that this shocking information and the macabre sight of half a dozen fresh graves on a desolate island in the harbour "cast a gloom over the ship's company," as the logbook stated. It was not the sort of news to inspire con-

The harbour of Niantilik, where the whaler *Alibi* lost five men to scurvy during the winter of 1856–57 (photo by the author, August 1976)

fidence among the men and woman of the *Lady Franklin*, who were themselves about to spend an arctic winter on board ship.

After dismantling a hut which the men of the *Alibi* had erected on shore, and leaving a message in case the *Sophia* turned up, Penny took the *Lady Franklin* about fifty miles up the coast to Nuvujen Island. He could have laid a course through the middle of Cumberland Sound, but instead he chose to pilot the vessel through an intricate maze of uncharted islands and reefs along the coast. A century later the official navigational guide for arctic waters, describing the "wide bays, filled with numerous islands and rocky patches" of this section of coast, noted that "the channels between the islands and the western shore afford a nearly continuous inside passage for boats with local knowledge" (Canada 1959, 2:180). Penny either had obtained enough local knowledge on his previous voyages to take the inside route rather than a safer passage in the middle of the sound, or he was taking this route for the first time in order to obtain that knowledge.

To thread narrow gaps among islands in a square-rigged sailing vessel without the advantage of charts, engines, echo sounders, radar, or satellite navigation may seem like a ship master's nightmare. The technique was to proceed cautiously under shortened sail, with men at the bow sounding with lead and line, the anchor hanging ready to let go,

The whalemen's graveyard at Niantilik, where the crew of the
Lady Franklin saw the graves of men from the *Alibi*
(photo by the author, August 1976)

deck-hands standing by for sudden manoeuvres, and the captain in the crow's nest looking for submerged rocks and shouting orders to the helmsman. We can almost feel the tension when Margaret remarks that at times they could have jumped from the ship onto the rocks, and even the terse nautical language of the ship's logbook imparts some of the excitement of entering harbour: "At noon abreast of Neuvowen Island. At 2 entered harbour by the north entrance but the tide being too strong was obliged to drop out again, ply south, and enter through several rocky islets, haul up short, make a tack, and drop anchor in 17 fathoms with all sail set."

Kingmiksok (now Imigen Island) in the middle ground, the birthplace
of Eenoolooapik and site of the first intentional wintering,
by men from the American whaler *McLellan* in 1851–52
(photo by the author, September 1976)

Penny was an enterprising whaling master and a bold navigator.
When he followed a beaten path, his eyes were continually sweeping
the terrain to right and left, looking for new routes that might lead
him more swiftly to his destination – or that might perhaps lead to
an entirely different, more profitable objective which others had not
considered. He had pioneered the whaling advance into Cumberland
Sound and had initiated the practice of wintering on board ship. Now
we see another of his ideas about to be implemented for the first time.
"This island," as the ship's log stated, "is to form one of the summer
fishing stations." Penny intended to put the *Lady Franklin* and *Sophia*
into a harbour at Kekerten, near the northeastern coast of Cumberland Sound, and to send the whaleboats out cruising for whales from
there, but as the daily range of the small open boats would not be
great enough to intercept whales migrating along the opposite shore,
approximately forty miles away, a subsidiary base at Nuvujen would
cover that area and thereby increase the chances of securing whales.

The plan required that a house be provided at Nuvujen to accommodate the boat crews and the equipment necessary for whaling, and
the *Lady Franklin* carried the lumber for this purpose. Evidently, the
structure was partly prefabricated, for the logbook mentions taking
"the lower frame of the house" ashore. At Aberdeen, before departure,

Brother Warmow had seen one of the houses destined for the whaling stations (perhaps it had been assembled to make sure everything was in order). He had not been impressed, remarking that it appeared to be more suitable for Surinam than the Arctic, but adding that Penny intended to insulate the walls with animal skins inside and snow outside, and then provide heat with iron coal-burning stoves (*Missionsblatt* 1857, 131).

Now it was time to erect the building at Nuvujen. Rising at five each morning and working well into the evenings under the direction of the carpenter, the sailors erected the lower part of the frame on 6 August, laid the floor, and put in the walls and ceiling the next day, and completed the doors, windows, and roof on the following. Divine service was held inside the house on the ninth, and the next four days were spent transporting and storing sixty tons of wooden shakes and iron hoops, seven tons of coal (all carried in bags on the men's shoulders), and a quantity of provisions and gear. It was gruelling work, made especially difficult by a twenty-two-foot rise and fall of the tide and by the awkward rocky topography of the place. Although Margaret described the site as "a pleasant valley sheltered by surrounding hills, and a fine beach for fishing," Brother Warmow declared, "So rugged was the ground that it seemed hardly suitable," and he wrote of "the difficult task of landing the building materials and dragging them over the rocks" (*Periodical Accounts* 1858, 22:452). The work took its toll; both Margaret's journal and the ship's logbook mention the aches and pains prevalent among the crew.

Captain Penny sent ashore two whaleboats, along with lines and gear, and he selected his spectioneer Andrew Lindsay and his cooper John Falconer to take care of the station. As Margaret noted on 14 August, the two men were to "set up casks & catch whales if they can," but she did not explain how two men were going to accomplish this. By themselves they could not operate a whaleboat, let alone two, and the only people on the island were three women, a lame old man, and a child. Warmow's account provides a clue. He stated that on 5 August, as he helped choose a site for the house and then visited the Eskimo tents, "we were surrounded by a pack of dogs, so numerous, as to remind me of a flock of sheep. Of course, I did not count them, but should think there were not less than 200" (*Periodical Accounts* 1858, 22:453). It was common practice for Eskimos to leave their sledge dogs on an island during the summer to subsist on lemmings, birds, eggs, and anything else they could scavenge, and it was usually an island at or near which the Eskimos planned to spend the winter. The presence of many dogs and several people suggests that the rest of the band intended to return to Nuvujen. Presumably, the two whalemen expected their arrival and were counting on them to provide at least ten men to complete the whaleboat crews.

On 14 August Margaret Penny took leave of her latest "Esquimaux friends," and the *Lady Franklin* set sail across Cumberland Sound for "Kingite" (now called Kingnait Fiord).

Tackritow, My Old Acquaintance

15 August – 2 September

The Lady Franklin *is crossing Cumberland Sound to Kingaite.*

August 15th   We expected to have been at Kingite this morning, but the weather is so foggy & calm that we have made no progress. In the afternoon the Traveller & her steam tug was seen to leeward, apparently bound for the same harbour as ourselves.

August 16th   Still unable to make any progress. Weather warm & beautiful. Divine service in the afternoon as usual. It is very pleasing to see with what respect & attention the sailors listen to the word of God.

August 17th   Boats seen some distance up the harbour. Two came rowing to us. They belonged to the Alibi. The mate & men came on board to breakfast & confirmed the accounts given us by the natives at Naujaktalik. The poor Dr. had been labouring under mental derangement all winter. He had several times attempted to commit suicide & although carefully watched at last succeeded in throwing himself overboard. A boat had been immediatelly lowered to save him but the swell was too heavy at the time to permit of their doing so. Mr. Skelton, who is now mate, can not be too highly thought of for his kindness to the sick. He is a fine specimen of a true-hearted Englishman. About 12 A.M. Capn. Stewart & Capn. Cheyne came on board. The Sophia was directed to proceed to Kakertine islands & erect his house, at least land the materials for it. The Alibi has seven whales & she was ordered to proceed to a harbour a little farther up. There [are] too many vessels in the harbour with her. We passed the Traveller, the Jackal, the Gem & the Arctic, & proceeded farther up the inlet. About 4 P.M. we saw a steamer coming up after us. It turned out to be the Isabella [*Isabel*] of Hull commanded by Capn. Couldrey, with Capn. Parker of the Emma on board. They belong to the same company & had come up from the Kakertine Is. in search of whales & a good harbour. They offered us a tow as it was calm & a strong tide setting down the inlet against us. Capt. Parker gave us the news of the vessels who had been up the country and we were sorry to learn that the Undaunted & Gipsy belonging to Peterhead had been wrecked & that only six whales had been captured among the whole fleet. Our second mate was sent on in a boat to sound for fear of sunk rocks, the Isabella towing us at the rate of a knot & a half in the hour. Our mate was sent on board to watch for rocks, he having often passed up & down this inlet before, as also had the second mate, who was [pioneer?] in the boat. Capt. Couldry came on board to tea & we had scarcely finished when Capt. Penny was called on deck to see the steamer grounded. She had slipped on the rocks so quietly that they never knew until the Lady Franklin came alongside, & we did not feel the least motion in her. I was rather afraid when she began to lay over, first to the one side & then to the other, but thank God we got off all safe & the Traveller a few minutes after us & were both safely anchored about 2 A.M.

August 18th   I had a visit from Tackritow, my old acquaintance whom I had seen in England. She has made a great improvement amongst the natives & is herself quite civilized. The men have been very busy today repairing the jib boom.

August 19th   I was surprised at 4 A.M. by a visit from a party of Esquimaux who had been away hunting. They had been very successful & gave us some haunches. They had been absent 10 days & had shot 9 deer & two salmon. They had seen a great many [salmon] but unfortunately had nothing to catch them with. We had some of the deer fryed for breakfast & it proved very tender & fine. Amongst the party of natives is Tessiwin & his wife. He is one of those who have been on board the Alibi all winter & he has got for her 4 whales & lost three. He is a most intelligent man in his own way & is very anxious to get to England. He has been promised by Capn. Stewart to get [there] this winter but when told by Capn. Penny that he must stay & superentend one of the houses he is quite pleased to do so. The natives on this side are far advanced in civilization & I feel very happy to think that my husband has been one means of bringing them to what they are. In the

Captain John Parker, commander of the Hull whaler *Emma*, whom Margaret
met in Cumberland Sound (Town Docks Museum, Hull [TDM])

afternoon they all came on board again with Capn. S, dressed in their
best clothes & very clean. Some clothes were sent by some of the Directors & I am sure they would have been highly pleased if they had seen
the happiness they had conferred upon these people.

August 20th   The weather is beginning to get a little colder. We are
getting casks &c. from the Alibi. A boat party has gone on shore to

hunt & botanize. A number of flowers have been found but no success by the hunters, although several deer were seen. They also saw a whale feeding but it was too dark to send away the boats.

August 21st   I got up this morning at 6 A.M. to see the boats start in pursuit of the whale seen last night. It is a lovely morning & the water as smooth as a sheet of glass. The Alibi is lying close to us. They are busy painting. Captn. Stewart has been on board here several times today. We got under weigh for Kikertine at 1 P.M. but were obliged to let go anchor again after drawing into the middle of the harbour. We have had Tackritow & Mary on board to tea. They really conduct themselves with great propriety & are anxious to learn. The one is to go to Kickertyne to keep the house clean there & the other to Newbeanen for the same purpose, as also to collect the Esquimaux who are scattered about hunting. An Esq. boy brought me two deer's tongues in a [present?] to-day. They are going off soon to catch salmon, which are in great abundance & very fine.

August 21st [*sic*]   We weighed anchor this morning for Kickertine. While at breakfast J. Donaldson announced that a whale had attempted to rise alongside, but made off when she saw the ship. There was an immediate rush on deck by the cabin party, who were disappointed in not having the pleasure of seeing [it]. At 11 A.M. Mr. Penny saw one from the crows nest. Two boats were sent off in pursuit of her, but no success. In the mean time another rose in an oposite direction. After watching for 5 hours she also made off. In the evening the ship was anchored in Sophia harbour, the wind being too strong to proceed farther. A number of Esquimaux came on board in the evening, amongst them many old acquaintances. They remained all night.

August 22nd   Still unable to get away. An Esquimaux came with some bone [i.e., baleen] & told of a small whale being ashore at a short distance. Divine service as usual. The greater part of the crew on shore gathering blue berries. They have brought some on board for me. I have enjoyed them very much.

August 23rd   Esquimaux on board all day. I have been much pleased with one of them, Oshallee, an old man who benevolently maintains by his labour five orphaned children along with his own family. You can teach them anything. They are so biddable & willing to please. The hills here are about 2000 feet high & much more fertile than on the other side. I had a pail full of delicious blue berries gathered from the hills. They are covered with them.

August 24th   We started this morning for Kickertyne. It has been rough all day & the wind against us. The navigation here is very difficult, sunk rocks in every direction. Mr. Penny at the mast head & a man kept constantly sounding. Wind increasing & very cold all day. In consequence of eating too many berries Mr. Warmow shot a turkey [a ptarmigan?]. We had it cooked.

August 30th. Sunday   Divine service early to-day to allow the men to get a walk on shore & get berries, which are here in great abundance.

August 31st   It has rained the whole day. The boats have been unable to go away as intended to look for whales. We are lying in a fine harbour, completely land-locked but it is blowing a gale out side.

September 1st   Three boats started at 10 A.M. to look for whales. They returned at 2 P.M., having seen none. The weather fine again.

Sept. 2nd   Weather fine. Four boats started this morning at 4 A.M. in pursuit of whales. They returned at 3 P.M. having seen none.

During the first two weeks in Cumberland Sound (map 2), the *Lady Franklin* had not encountered any other ships. The *Sophia*, her constant companion on the Atlantic crossing, had wandered off somewhere between Greenland and Baffin Island and had not turned up at either Niantilik or Nuvujen. The *Alibi* and an American whaler *George Henry*, both of which had spent the winter at Niantilik, had left by the time Penny arrived. A Scottish vessel had hired native men at the harbour and sailed away. Everyone on the *Lady Franklin* must have been eager to meet up with other ships and hear their news. Why had six men died on the *Alibi*? What were the real circumstances behind the doctor's death? Had the whaling fleet been successful in Davis Strait and Baffin Bay? Had any whales appeared in Cumberland Sound yet?

   The answers were waiting on the opposite coast in Kingaite (Kingnait Fiord), a narrow trough winding more than fifty miles into the lofty glacier-capped mountains of the Cumberland Peninsula. Several whalers had congregated in a place which the whalemen called Sophia Harbour but which Warmow called by its native name, Tornait. Although its location is not described in Margaret's journal, in Warmow's letters, or even in the logbooks of the *Lady Franklin* and *Sophia*, it appears to be the bay that penetrates two miles into the northern wall of the fiord several miles east of its mouth and is now called Kingnait Harbour. There, the *Lady Franklin* encountered the two other ships of the Aberdeen Arctic Company (*Sophia* and *Alibi*), four ships from Peterhead (*Arctic*, *Gem*, *Jackal*, and *Traveller*), and one from Hull (*Isabel*). On board the latter was another Hull captain, John Parker. He was the man who, a decade earlier, had introduced Memiadluk and Uckaluk to Britain, had petitioned Queen Victoria for Eskimo assistance, and had attempted to introduce Moravian missionaries to Cumberland Sound. Parker had left his own ship *Emma* anchored on the north side of another bay, called Kingitlook in Captain Penny's logbook (probably Kangertlukdjuak, about twelve miles east, on the opposite coast of Kingnait Fiord). Margaret's entries in mid-August reveal that some of the ships in this small fleet possessed steam propulsion. She took no special notice of this fact, but it is of considerable interest.

The potential advantages of steam power in ice-laden seas had been recognized early, but the first attempts to use it in the Arctic had not been crowned with success. In 1829, a year after writing a book on steam navigation, John Ross had gone in search of the Northwest Passage in the steam-auxiliary vessel *Victory*, which had previously been a paddle-wheel packet in the Irish Sea. This bold but premature experiment, during which the unreliable engine was jettisoned in frustration and the ice-trapped *Victory* abandoned, ended four years later with Ross and his men rowing out through Lancaster Sound, where they had the extraordinary luck to be saved by a passing sail whaler. In 1845, when Sir John Franklin set off through Baffin Bay to reach the Pacific, HMS *Erebus* and *Terror* possessed steam locomotive engines and propellers as well as sails. They had not returned. Searching for Franklin in 1850–51, Captain Horatio Austin employed the steam-auxiliary vessels *Intrepid* and *Pioneer* in conjunction with two sailing vessels. The results were not spectacular. William Penny, who at the time was commanding another Admiralty search expedition on the *Lady Franklin* and *Sophia*, felt that Austin was not using steam to full advantage. He urged him to take the steamers up through Wellington Channel, where he firmly believed Franklin had gone. Austin's refusal led to a bitter disagreement between the two men and ultimately to an official inquiry. The same four ships used by Austin were sent out again under Captain Sir Edward Belcher in 1852, but if Austin had been cautious, Belcher was excessively so. In 1854, fearing that ice would not release the vessels in time to get home, he abandoned all four ships in the Arctic and retreated on board a transport and two ships of another expedition. A court martial followed.

Despite the unimpressive achievements of auxiliary steamers on naval expeditions, there was a growing belief that steam ought to be used in the whaling fleet, a view expressed often in the newspapers of Hull, Peterhead, Dundee, Aberdeen, and other ports during the 1850s. Whaling men may have drawn a few conclusions from what they could observe in their home ports, where steam tugs were in use. If steam tugs could tow a whaleship from dockside through a crowded anchorage and out through a narrow harbour mouth, both in calms and against adverse winds, and contrary to flood tides, then why could a ship with power not tow a whaler among the ice floes, narrow channels, and adverse currents of the whaling grounds? Along the northwest coast of Greenland in 1852 and 1854, as whalemen trudged along the edge of the landfast ice, leaning into their harnesses like beasts of burden to tow their bulky ships foot by foot up the narrow shore lead, they had seen the Royal Navy's steam-auxiliary ships *Intrepid* and *Pioneer* cruising easily past them in calms, each with a sailing ship in tow. An experience like this could certainly convince a man that steam power had some advantages. Why could whaling ships not also be provided with auxiliary steam engines and screw propellers?

In 1857, the year of Margaret's voyage to Cumberland Sound, steam power was applied to British whalers for the first time. Three approaches were adopted almost simultaneously. The first was to convert an existing ship to a steam-auxiliary whaler by installing an engine, a shaft and propeller, and allocating space for coal. Shipowners in Hull, Peterhead, and Dundee adopted this method, turning the *Diana*, *Innuit*, and *Tay* into steam-powered whalers in time for the 1857 season. The second approach was to build new ships incorporating both steam and sail propulsion, as Dundee did in time for the 1859 season. The third approach, considered "an intermediate stage between the old sailing whaler and the auxiliary screw vessel which was shortly to succeed her" (Lubbock 1955, 360), was to send out a small steamer in company with a sail whaler, to tow her in calm weather and in constricted waterways, and to carry some of her provisions, blubber, and baleen if necessary. The pairing of a powered vessel with one entirely dependent on sails – the technique adopted by the Franklin search expeditions of Austin and Belcher several years earlier – was in essence a tug philosophy extended into the arctic regions. In 1857 the Hull whaler *Emma* was operating in Cumberland Sound with her steam tender *Isabel*, and the Peterhead whaler *Traveller* was sailing in company with her steam tender *Jackal*. Both tenders, of course, were equipped with sails as well as engines, as were all of the so-called steam whalers that were used in arctic whaling until its demise around 1910.

After criticizing Austin for not using steam power more decisively in the Franklin search, William Penny had gone on to promote the application of steam power to whaling ships. Among the objectives of the Aberdeen Arctic Company, which he had helped organize, was the "application of the power of the auxiliary screw to whaling vessels" (*Literary Gazette* 1853). But when whaling interests in other ports began the transition from sail to steam, his own Aberdeen company hesitated. Now Penny had the humiliating experience of seeing steam-powered tenders from Peterhead and Hull operating in his domain of Cumberland Sound, while he remained in command of a sail whaler. Although he had been one of the most persistent proponents of steam and one of the greatest innovators in the history of the whaling industry, he had to stand on the deck of an engineless ship while a generous captain from a rival port gave him a tow.

The news from the other ships was discouraging. Captain Parker had brought the *Emma* from Melville Bay, where he had witnessed the destruction of two nearby ships by pack ice. Whereas Penny's two ships had sailed directly to Cumberland Sound late in the summer with the intention of wintering, most of the Scottish whalers had proceeded along the coast of Greenland three months earlier, hoping to get round the top of Baffin Bay, pursue whales off Pond Inlet and in Lancaster Sound, and then sail south along the Baffin Island coast on their way home at the end of the summer. This had been the usual routine for one-third of a century, and it depended on the fact that as the ice cover of Davis Strait and Baffin Bay diminished after April, a shore lead gradually opened up between the stable landfast ice attached to the Greenland coast and the drifting floes of the Middle Ice offshore. This lead, which widened and extended northward as the season progressed, provided a pathway up the coast and around Melville Bay towards the open area of the North Water, which in turn gave access to Lancaster Sound.

The pathway, however, was exceedingly dangerous. The restless floes of the Middle Ice, several feet thick and rock hard, responded to the subtle thrusts of currents, the pulsating rhythm of tides, and the

S.S. "Diana" off Cape Farewell." 29th April 63.   Evening "

A steam-auxiliary whaler, the *Diana* of Hull, several years
after Margaret's voyage (TDM)

unpredictable whims of winds. When strong westerly winds drove large
floes against the rigid margin of the landfast ice, they became battering rams of extraordinary force, and any ships "nipped" between the
attacking legion of advancing floes and the unyielding fortress of the
land ice were in severe jeopardy. "A ship thus circumstanced, although
exceedingly strong, is as easily crushed as an eggshell in the hand,"
observed one whaleman (*Hull Advertiser* 1858a).

The loss of the Peterhead whalers *Gipsy* and *Undaunted*, "two of
the finest, strongest, and swiftest clipper vessels ever sent to the fishery" (*Hull Advertiser* 1857a), vividly illustrates the risks that attended
the passage around Melville Bay. In mid-June, off the prominent landmark of Devil's Thumb, more than seventy-four degrees north, the two
ships, in company with the *Emma*, were several miles ahead of the
rest of the fleet when a series of strong southwesterly gales closed the
shore lead and trapped them against the edge of the landfast ice. The
crews worked feverishly with fourteen-foot ice saws to cut rectangular

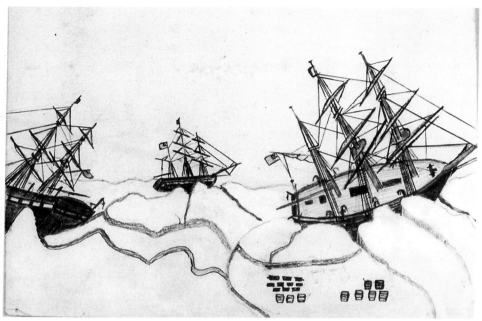

The whalers *Gipsy, Undaunted,* and *Emma* beset in Melville Bay in 1857.
Only the *Emma* escaped destruction, later reaching Cumberland Sound, where
she encountered Captain Penny's ships (sketch by William Barron, TDM)

"docks" into the land ice to give the ships some temporary protection.
The men of the *Emma* are said to have cut no fewer than eighteen
docks in a period of six weeks (Lubbock 1955, 367).

On 29 June gale-driven pack ice stove in the staunch timbers of the
Gipsy, forcing the crew to hurriedly grab some clothes and provisions
and set up camp on the land ice. After setting fire to the wreck – a
common practice in the whaling fleet – they made their way over the
ice to the *Undaunted,* which was still under assault by the numberless
floes, whose appetite for destruction was yet unsatisfied. During one
siege, the ship was lifted five feet out of the water and pushed onto her
side, though a slackening of pressure then released the bruised and
strained hull back into the water. The pressure continued for a fortnight. On 11 July ice at last penetrated the hull, and the ship began
to break up. As the wooden timbers, beams, planks, masts, and yards
yielded noisily to the grinding ice, the men saved what they could,
fired the wreck, and managed to haul some of their whaleboats over
the ice to the *Emma,* which by good fortune had escaped the severe
nip. Later, when the ice opened slightly, some of the men were able

to head south in whaleboats. As the pressure diminished, Captain Parker managed to extricated the *Emma* from the imprisoning ice and reach the rest of the fleet several miles away. He distributed the shipwrecked men among the other ships, sailed south, crossed Davis Strait to Cumberland Sound, and was in Kingaite when Penny arrived in mid-August.

Margaret's remark on 2 August that the *Alibi*, commanded by Captain Stewart, had wintered at Niantilik "instead of going where she had been directed by Mr. Penny" shows that her husband's authority was not limited to his own ship but covered all three ships of the Aberdeen Arctic Company. Penny was the senior captain and general superintendent. He drew up the strategy for each season, issued instructions to the other captains, and took overall command of activities on the whaling grounds. In the spring of 1854, after his ships had wintered at Nuvujen, Penny had discovered what he called in his logbook a "splendid haven" at Kekerten. He had intended to winter there on his next voyage in 1855–56 but for some reason had ended up in another harbour. In August 1856, before starting for home with the *Lady Franklin* and *Sophia*, he had pointed out the harbour to Captain Stewart, who had just arrived from Scotland with the *Alibi*, and had instructed him to winter there. In choosing Niantilik rather than Kekerten, Stewart had disobeyed orders.

Margaret must have met Captain Stewart in Kingaite on 19 August, when he came on board accompanied by his hired Eskimos, "dressed in their best clothes & very clean." She recorded no other details about his visit. The matter of the winter harbour was certainly discussed on that occasion but probably by the three captains in private. In the ship's logbook, Penny reported that Stewart could not give any good reason for placing his ship at Niantilik, adding that "the man who has not the wisdom to take advantage of the experience of others how to pass arctic winters with safety to the lives of those under his command … is unfit to command." In Penny's mind, events had proved that Stewart's action had been not only insubordinate but irresponsible, because six men had died during the winter. Five deaths from scurvy were shocking enough, but the suicide of Dr Robertson was particularly disquieting. According to Margaret's understanding of the matter, the *Alibi*'s doctor "had been labouring under mental derangement all winter." This is borne out by the logbook of the *Alibi*, which contains several references to the doctor's irrational behaviour, beginning eight months before his death:

28 November 1856 The surgeon of the ship, after having for days past shown symptoms of being in a deranged state of mind, gone on shore and attempted to deprive himself of life by cutting and wounding his own throat with a penknife but prevented by the natives.

27 December At 3 A.M. The Surgeon awoke the Master to inform him that he had taken a quantity of laudanum in mistake for tincture of rhubarb. The master instantly forced him to take one or more doses of tartar emetic and by constantly drinking warm water he soon vomited it all [out] of his stomach without leaving any bad effects after it.

By 3 January 1857 the doctor was "very troublesome at times and appears to be quite in an insane state of mind." On the following day, although restrained in his berth and watched by a sailor, the doctor "in a fit of insanity" somehow leaped out of bed and ran forward to the crew's quarters to plead for their protection against people who intended to kill him. "Got him pacified as soon as possible," the log stated. From this time onwards, the doctor was irrational, paranoic, and sometimes delirious. He had to be "continually watched like a child and confined in his bed every night." No entries appear in the *Alibi*'s logbook after 22 February, but a short newspaper account several months later outlined the circumstances of Dr Robertson's death: "The doctor had been out of his mind most of the winter, it was about the middle of July, in a gale of wind, when the ship was making for a harbour [apparently Sophia Harbour], that he leaped overboard and was drowned, though every effort was made to save him" (*Peterhead Sentinel* 1857b).

Captain Penny had first learned of the doctor's death from Eskimos at Niantilik who had spent the winter in the vicinity of the ship and seen the doctor's strange behaviour. They had also observed the attitude of the ship's crew towards the doctor, something that was not mentioned in the *Alibi*'s logbook. Penny wrote in the *Lady Franklin's* logbook, "I sincerely trust the account they [the Eskimos] give of the cruel treatment the Surgeon had received at the hands of the crew is not true." Later, after meeting up with Captain Stewart in Kingaite, Penny stated in his log that he would not comment on the surgeon's death but would leave the matter to "the laws of his country." It was an extraordinary remark to make in an official logbook, a thinly veiled accusation that Stewart was ultimately responsible for Robertson's death. Evidently, Penny believed that the sailors' teasing of the doctor had contributed to – or even caused – his mental deterioration and eventual suicide, and that Captain Stewart should have curbed the men's insensitive harassment. If Stewart and his men had remained healthy and had secured many whales, Penny might have treated his disobedience lightly. But things had not worked out at Niantilik. Six men had died, and Penny was in a position to say "I told you so."

Part of Penny's vision of the Aberdeen Arctic Company was that its vessels would operate under the umbrella of one strategic plan. On three successive voyages (1853–54, 1855–56, and 1857–58) the *Lady Franklin* and *Sophia* had sailed together, passing every second winter in Cumberland Sound. Sailing alone, the *Alibi* had wintered there for the first time in 1856–57 after the other two ships had returned to Scotland, and it was intended that she would return to winter there in 1858–59. By alternating the winterings of its three ships, the company was exerting a continuous presence in Cumberland Sound. The overlap of departing and arriving ships each summer facilitated the exchange of news, supplies, and personnel.

Margaret's remark on 18 August that she had received a visit from "Tackritow, my old acquaintance whom I had seen in England" reminds us that the contact between Europeans and Eskimos did not occur solely within the arctic domain of the native people. Margaret may have met several individuals from Baffin Island in Britain during the two decades leading up to her whaling voyage.

Along the east coast of Baffin Island, and especially in Cumberland Sound, where ships had begun wintering in 1853, the Eskimo people had many opportunities to admire the material possessions of British and American whalemen. Through trade and employment they were able to acquire for themselves a varied assortment of imported weapons, tools, implements, and materials. Those hired as "ships' natives" met and interacted with whalemen on a daily basis, learning more about their language and customs. But they were exposed to a biased sample of Euro-American culture and society, composed entirely of men and only of those whose occupation was whaling. They must have wondered about the land from which the whalemen came – what animals and plants it had, what type of dwelling the people lived in, what they ate, and how they amused themselves. Judging from the immense sailing ships in which the whalemen travelled, the sophisticated equipment they carried, and the effectiveness of their techniques for working with metal, wood, and cloth and for hunting the big whales, they must surely represent a civilization of high attainments. What other things, possibly even more astounding, existed in their own land? Curiosity and a sense of adventure doubtless created in the minds of a few individuals the desire to visit the land over the sea.

At Durban Island on the north shore of Cumberland Peninsula during the 1830s, a teenage Eskimo boy named Eenoolooapik (and called Eenoo, Robbie Durban, or simply Robbie by the whalemen) begged various captains to take him home with them. In the fall of 1839, after the protestations of his mother were overcome, he joined Captain Penny on the *Neptune* and set off for Aberdeen, where he passed the winter. On 1 April 1840 he left for Baffin Island with Penny on the whaler *Bon Accord* and helped pilot the ship into Cumberland Sound, the first European vessel known to reach that region in two and a half centuries. There can be no doubt that Margaret met Eenoolooapik during his sojourn in Aberdeen, the period during which her courtship and marriage took place.

Several years later, Margaret may have had another opportunity to meet a resident of Baffin Island. In 1846 Captain Kinnear of the whaler *Caledonia* returned to Kirkcaldy with a fourteen-year-old boy, Aukutook (or Aquatook) Zininnuck, sometimes called Kookie Ekie by the Scots. Evidently, his precise origins were not of great concern to local newspaper reporters, who simply called him the "son of one of the chieftains of those wandering tribes who roam about Greenland and Davis' Straits" (*Fifeshire Advertiser* 1846a). They described him as "tolerably well-grown," "handsomely dressed in blue clothes, sailor fashion," "polite," "very kind and docile in his disposition, and very apt." He lived with Captain and Mrs Kinnear during the winter, and with the help of a public subscription was given some "useful education as well as religious instruction." The intention was that "he might become an instrument, in God's hands, to go to his benighted countrymen (who are in the deepest paganism) when he returns" (*Fifeshire Advertiser* 1846b). The presence of an Eskimo boy in Scotland would have been common knowledge within the whaling community, but the port of Kirkcaldy is approximately eighty miles south of Aberdeen, and whether Margaret and Aukutook ever met is unknown.

The following year Captain John Parker brought the whaler *Truelove* into Hull with two Eskimos on board. They were Memiadluk (aged seventeen) and and his wife Uckaluk (aged fifteen) from Niantilik in

Cumberland Sound. Today, life masks of Captain Parker and the two Eskimos are on display at the Town Docks Museum in Hull. Looking at the silent plaster replicas, one wonders what ties or obligations linked the native couple from Baffin Island with the whaling master from Hull in such an adventure. One marvels at their sense of trust in committing themselves to the custody of a man they knew only from occasional summer visits and upon whom they would have to rely in order to cope with the intricacies of daily life in a distant country populated by tens of thousands of unfamiliar people speaking a different language.

In his whaling voyages into Cumberland Sound, Parker had been struck by the impoverished condition of the inhabitants. At Niantilik, twenty out of a population of about one hundred and seventy had died from starvation during the summer of 1847; the survivors had fallen ravenously on the greasy whale flukes and flippers brought up from his ship's hold. By bringing Memiadluk and Uckaluk to England, Parker hoped to publicize the plight of their people, raise money for the purchase of material goods, enlist government support for relief, and (as described in the introduction) persuade the Moravians to send a missionary to the region. There was an even wider vision. In February 1848 Parker addressed a memorial to Queen Victoria, by way of his local member of Parliament, outlining a scheme that would alleviate the misery and destitution of the Eskimo settlements. It read in part as follows:

Your Majesty's Memorialist has been deeply impressed, from personal observations, with their miserable lot; and with great humility ventures to suggest that the most effectual method of securing their permanent benefit will be to colonize the western side of Davis' Straits, – making Hogarth Sound [Cumberland Sound] the principal station, – in the manner which has for many years been adopted by the Danish Government on the eastern side, where the natives are comparatively happy and where there is no risk of their being subjected to the horrible calamities which those on the western coast have continually to endure. (Parker 1848)

If the Government could not see its way clear to establishing settlements on the coast of Baffin Island, Parker added, then perhaps the Moravian Brethren who operated missions in Labrador could be persuaded to expand their activities northward to the region. He explained, however, that he had already approached the Moravians about establishing a mission, and a shortage of funds appeared to be a real obstacle to their participation.

Parker's memorial made the rounds of Colonial Office advisers, who condemned the colonization proposal as unfeasible. In a classic expression of the imperialist viewpoint, one of them expressed satisfaction that Parker had not blamed the miserable state of the Eskimos on "causes connected with European interference" when clearly their condition seemed "only the too common fate of the inhabitants of extreme climates." Another, responding to Parker's plea for additional guns to help the people procure food, remarked, "The Ordnance used to have a quantity of old guns which were discarded in the Army; & perhaps a few might be obtained as a gift." Finally, a reply was drafted, which said, "Sincerely as Lord Grey [the colonial secretary] laments the sufferings and distress of these tribes, it has not been in his power to advise Her Majesty to sanction the formation of any settlement in their neighborhood, or adopt the other measures suggested in the memorial for their relief" (Parker 1848).

During the winter, Parker exhibited the young couple in several English towns and cities, including Hull, Manchester, Beverley, Driffield, and York. To be displayed as curiosities to paying audiences around the north of England must have been degrading and humiliating, but it was a means by which public support could be secured. The exhibits were said to have an educational value as well. A lecture at the Mechanics' Institute in Manchester was described as follows: "The male gets into his canoe, holds the paddle, and poises the spear. A description ... is given by Mr. Gedney, surgeon of the Truelove; and afterwards Captain Parker explains the condition of the people on both sides of Baffin's Bay, and draws that contrast between the Danish and the British rule which is so little to the credit of our country" (Times 1848a). Donations and proceeds from the exhibits enabled Parker to purchase guns, ammunition, and other useful articles to the value of one hundred pounds for the people of Cumberland Sound, and at a ceremony in Hull a few days before departure, the wardens and elders of Trinity House presented the couple with more firearms. After two appearances in the Public Rooms of Hull, where many of the townsfolk came to bid them farewell, Memiadluk and Uckaluk sailed for home on the Truelove on 22 March (Times 1848b; Eastern Counties Herald 1848a).

An interesting sidelight to the story of these two Eskimo visitors is that they were vaccinated on arrival in Hull, probably by G. William Gedney, who had served as surgeon on the Truelove and who played a prominent role in exhibiting them and caring for them during their stay. Gedney was about fifty-two years of age at the time. He is known to have been a druggist or medical dispenser but may have been a qualified doctor as well. Memiadluk and Uckaluk may have been the first

Eskimos to be protected in this manner against smallpox, but there was a tragic irony. On the way to Davis Strait, when the *Truelove* stopped at Stromness, the twenty-six Orkneymen who were hired to complete the crew came on board with measles among them. What happened next was reported half a year later in Hull newspapers when the ship returned to port:

Almost immediately after leaving the Orkneys the measles broke out amongst the Orkneymen, five or six of whom were attacked, and each receiving the assistance of Mr. Gedney, the surgeon, recovered. Memealuk was the next subject of the complaint, and he also speedily regained his health. Ukaluk appears to have received the infection from her husband. Although she recovered from the measles, they left a cough and spitting, with which she was afflicted when the vessel reached the ice on the 25th or 26th of April. This, notwithstanding the best attention and comfort that the ship could afford, turned into consumption, under which she rapidly wasted away, and expired on the 23rd June, on board the Truelove, at Frow Islands, on the east-side of of Davis' Straits. Her remains were interred, with Christian burial, the service being read by the surgeon. (*Hull Advertiser* 1848b)

Like another Eskimo, Kudlago, who became mortally sick on the whaler *George Henry* while returning in 1860 from a winter in the United States – and who asked in his final moments, "Do you see ice?" (Hall [1864] 1970, 23) – the unfortunate Uckaluk survived a long journey only to die on the eve of arriving home.

Uckaluk's husband Memiadluk continued on the ship to Baffin Island and landed near Cape Searle on the north coast of the Cumberland Peninsula, where friends and relatives received the collection of knives, guns, and other articles with "extravagant delight" (*Hull Advertiser* 1848b). As bearer of this magnificent cargo, and with heightened prestige derived from his travels to the far-off land of the whalers, Memiadluk had no difficulty in finding another wife. But his new affluence brought about a change in lifestyle. A decade afterwards, another Hull whaleman, William Barron, met him somewhere on the West Side and reported that "he was too idle to hunt and fish any more so long as the presents lasted which he had received in England" (Barron 1895, 80).

Tackritow, to whom Margaret referred on 18 and 21 August, was unquestionably the most famous Eskimo woman traveller. She was a younger sister of Eenoolooapik and may have been inspired to quit her native shores by stories of his experiences in Scotland a dozen

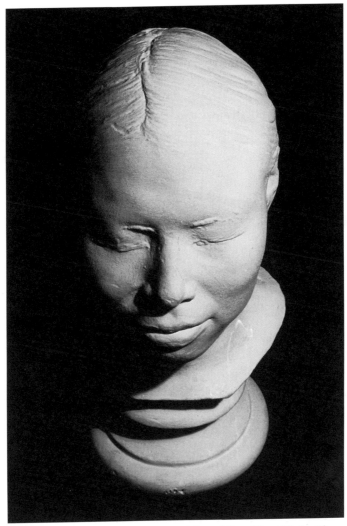

Life mask of Uckaluk, who sailed from Niantilik to Hull with
Captain Parker in 1847 and died on her return voyage (TDM)

years earlier. With her husband and a young boy, she was taken to England in 1853 by a Hull entrepreneur, John Bowlby, on a small schooner named the *Bee*. They remained in Britain for almost two years.
Sometime during this period Margaret met Tackritow, either in Hull
or some other British city where the Eskimo group was exhibited,
or in Aberdeen, where Tacritow boarded Captain Penny's ship *Lady
Franklin* in late June 1855 to return to her homeland (William Penny
1856a).

Bowlby was a merchant and shipowner who in 1848 had sent the *Bee* and a converted revenue cutter the *Seaflower* to Davis Strait to fish for cod and halibut (*Hull Advertiser* 1848a). His new plan, in 1853, was to set up "a sort of fishing colony" in Cumberland Sound (*Eastern Counties Herald* 1853a). Newspaper accounts mentioned harpooners, so it seems that whales as well as fish were to be sought. Three ships, the *Seaflower, Bee,* and *Wellington,* left Hull on 23 June, carrying building materials for a large house and everything they would need for a three-year stay, including some goats (*Eastern Counties Herald* 1853c) – surely the first of their race to visit Baffin Island. The first two vessels reached their destination safely, but the *Wellington,* a cockleshell of only twenty-nine tons manned by five men and a boy, failed to arrive. Bowlby and his men erected their house on the island of Nuvujen but had no success in whaling or fishing. After two months, they abandoned the scheme and returned to Hull. The crew of the *Wellington,* rescued from starvation and shipwreck by a whaler, later reached home safely. In the sketchy reports of this badly conceived and poorly executed settlement scheme, there is no explanation of Bowlby's purpose in taking three natives back to Hull. Possibly the idea was not Bowlby's at all but that of the surgeon, the same G. William Gedney who had been on board the *Truelove* in 1847 when Captain Parker returned with Memiadluk and Uckaluk, and who had lectured about Eskimo life wherever they were exhibited.

Within a few days of the ships' arrival in early October, newspapers reported that Bowlby intended to introduce the three Eskimos to Queen Victoria (*Eastern Counties Herald* 1853b). Were he and Surgeon Gedney callous promoters, or were they sincere campaigners for social justice and native welfare? In the absence of evidence to the contrary, one must assume that, like Captain John Parker in 1847, they were using a few Eskimos in order to bring to the attention of the British public and government the harsh conditions of life on Baffin Island, to draw attention to the impressive achievements of the Danish colonial administration in Greenland, and to enlist support for a scheme of settlement in Cumberland Sound that would permit the introduction of education, religion, and material welfare. "One part of Mr. Bowlby's design," one newspaper reported, "was to raise the conditions of the western natives to a condition of comfort, intelligence, and moral standing, equal, at least, to that of the tribes on the opposite coast" (*Hull Packet* 1853).

Tackritow, who was then sixteen, her husband Hackboch, aged eighteen, and seven-year-old Hackaluckjoe, who was from another family,

comprised the small Eskimo group. On 3 February, wearing traditional arctic skin clothing and accompanied by John Bowlby, his agent
Mr Bowser, a "talented lecturer" Mr Buckingham, and (as interpreter)
Mr Gedney, they arrived at Windsor Castle to appear before Queen
Victoria, Prince Albert, the Duchess of Kent, the Duchess of Sutherland, and others of the royal entourage. Before their presentation
they were shown around the castle and grounds by the steward of the
household. Tackritow had made a pair of slippers, which she presented to the queen (*Eastern Counties Herald* 1854a). Later that day,
Queen Victoria wrote in her journal:

Had seen before luncheon 3 Esquimaux, a married couple, & a little boy,
natives of Keimensoka & Newganemyatt, on the West coast of the Cumberland
Straits, Davis Straits. They are the 1st to have ever come over. They belong to a
very poor tribe of about 500 or 1000 & have been brought over, in the hopes
of raising funds to assist them. They are my subjects, very curious, & quite different to any of the southern or African tribes, having very flat round faces,
with a Mongolian shape of eyes, a fair skin, & jet black hair. They are entirely
clothed in skins. The boy is a pretty little, red-cheeked, black-haired thing,
7 years of age, the man 18, and the woman 16. (Victoria 1854)

The occasion made a profound impression on Tackritow, and she described her appearance before royalty on many subsequent occasions.
As far as she was concerned, Queen Victoria was "very kind, very much
lady" (Nourse 1879, 443).

Within the month Mr Bowser, the agent, received a cheque from
Buckingham Palace for twenty-five pounds (*Eastern Counties Herald*
1854b). In the meantime, the Eskimo group had been on show at the
Lowther Arcade Rooms in London, "surrounded by their huts, canoes
and hunting implements, many of which display in their construction
a vast amount of rude ingenuity." The exhibition, which included an
illustrated lecture by Mr Leicester Buckingham on "the principal characteristics and leading productions of the Arctic Regions and the
manners and customs of the natives," was judged "well worthy of public patronage" (*Illustrated London News* 1854). In late March they appeared in the Music Hall in Hull, "surrounded by the native scenery,
and their hunting and war implements," along with "several good
specimens of stuffed seals, birds and other animals, inhabiting the
North Pole regions" (*Eastern Counties Herald* 1854c). One wonders
what "war implements" they chose to brandish. Similar exhibitions
were held in many other places, including the Corn Exchange at

ESQUIMAUX RECENTLY ARRIVED IN LONDON.

"The Esquimaux Family" in London after their appearance before
Queen Victoria at Windsor Castle. Tackritow (Tookoolitoo) is at right
(*Illustrated London News* 1854).

Driffield in early April, the De Gray Rooms in York on 17–20 April
(admission one shilling during the afternoon, sixpence during the
evening, half-price for children), the Mechanics' Institute at Pockling-
ton on 21 April, and the Zoological Gardens of Hull during the first
week of June. On this latter occasion they demonstrated the use of the
kayak on a small lake, in front of students from several local schools
(*Yorkshire Gazette* 1854; *Eastern Counties Herald* 1854d).

In England, Tackritow's husband was referred to as Hackboch, Harboch, or Harkbah. But the American explorer Charles Francis Hall (who met the couple near Frobisher Bay in 1860, employed them on his expeditions of 1864–69 and 1871–72, and took them to the United States) called him Ebierbing and used the nickname Joe (Hall [1864] 1970, 132). The editor of Hall's second book (Nourse 1879, 441) sometimes combined these names as Joe Ebierbing, and the man has also been called Eskimo Joe. Hall was told "that this couple had been taken to England in 1853, and presented to Her Majesty Queen Victoria" (Hall [1864] 1970, 132), so there can be no doubt that all these names refer to the same person. Yet there is no similarity between the names Ebierbing and Hackboch! Perhaps a misunderstanding by surgeon Gedney, or even by Hall, underlies the confusion.

In England, the Eskimo woman whom Margaret called Tackritow was referred to as Tackilictoo, Tickalictoo, Tickaluck-too, and Tarchuctoo. Hall spelled it Tookoolito, and she signed a published portrait of herself slightly differently, as Tookoolitoo. All of these were attempts to render into written English the sound of her native name. But according to the Hull whaleman William Barron, who with her help learned some Eskimo vocabulary while in Cumberland Sound in 1852, she was usually called Hannah by the Americans "on account of her native name being too long" (Barron 1890, 45). This nickname was made popular by Hall, but in England it was sometimes undestood as Anne (*Hull Advertiser* 1858b). As part of the veneer of English manners and appearance that she affected long after returning to Baffin Island, or simply as a convenience for tongue-tied whalemen and explorers, she sometimes introduced herself as Hannah or Anne. (Within the past few decades a heightened sensitivity for the accurate rendition of Inuktitut names on Canadian historic plaques has replaced Hall's famous friends Ebierbing and Tookoolito – alias Joe and Hannah – by two apparent strangers, Ipirvik and Taqulittuq.)

When Captain Penny returned to Aberdeen in late August 1854 after his first wintering whaling voyage, he brought "an Esquimaux youth of about 14, a pleasing lad, who rejoices in the name of Neu Terrallie" (*Aberdeen Journal* 1854). Penny's motive in bringing another young man to Scotland is unknown. The absence of press attention during the winter suggests that, unlike Parker and Bowlby, he did not arrange for Neu Terrallie to be exhibited and did not campaign widely for public donations. The objective may have been to obtain geographical information or to train him as an interpreter. By this time, William and Margaret Penny had been married for fourteen years and had four children between the ages of seven and thirteen living at home.

There may not have been room there for Neu Terrallie, but even if the boy was consigned to another family or put up in a boarding house, Margaret could hardly have avoided meeting him, and it would have been normal for her to help him adjust to life in the strange city. He may have accompanied the *Lady Franklin* and *Sophia* when the ships sailed again for Cumberland Sound on 23 June 1855.

Peterhead played host to an Eskimo visitor in 1856–57, the winter before Margaret and William Penny set off for Cumberland Sound. The man who arrived with Captain Sutter on the whaleship *Clara* on 14 November was described as "an Esquimaux of low stature, but an athletic looking person, and … a most expert harpooner" (*Aberdeen Journal* 1856). Sutter was involved in a dispute with Captain Stewart of the *Alibi* over the ownership of a whale taken near Niantilik in mid-October, and he had brought the native harpooner who had first struck the whale to Scotland "as evidence" (*Peterhead Sentinel* 1856). Although unnamed in the brief newspaper reports, subsequent references to the dispute indicate that the man must have been Newbullygar (a rendition of his native name), or Bullygar (as the whalemen usually called him). As the *Alibi* (with all the witnesses for the defence) was spending the winter in Cumberland Sound, the case could not proceed, and Newbullygar must have returned to Cumberland Sound on board a whaling ship in the summer of 1857, because Margaret's journal reveals that he was working for Penny's two wintering ships in May 1858. As Aberdeen and Peterhead are only about thirty miles apart, it would not be surprising if Margaret had met Newbullygar during his sojourn in Scotland.

On the various occasions after 1838 when English and Scottish whaling masters returned from Davis Strait with Eskimo visitors, the initiative, persistence, and vision of the whaling masters John Parker and William Penny stand out. Both realized that whalemen could benefit from native geographical knowledge and skills, and that teaching some individuals to speak English would improve communication on the whaling grounds and perhaps lead to greater success. But in addition to recognizing the potential value of Eskimos to whaling operations, they recognized that whalemen had an obligation to treat the Eskimos decently. Furthermore, they believed that the British government should bear some responsibility for the material and moral welfare of the native population. The government, however, did not concur with this opinion.

On linking up again with the *Sophia* in Kingaite in mid-August, Penny had ordered Captain Cheyne to take his ship down to Kekerten, the place he had previously selected as a winter harbour for the ships and a site for his second permanent whaling station. On 24 August Penny sailed the *Lady Franklin* down to join her. He found that Cheyne and his crew had already surveyed the harbour entrance, discharged building materials and coals, built a foundation for the prefabricated house, and erected the framework of the building. In his logbook Penny reported that he went ashore and "found the house all formed in the very best position that have been selected around the harbour." As his son William went off hunting with Brother Warmow (unsuccessfully), the crew of the *Lady Franklin* joined with the men of the *Sophia* in landing stores and finishing the house.

Penny felt a sense of urgency because the whaling season was drawing to a close. "Continued our labour," he wrote, "being anxious to get clear for our fishing." He added, "The fourteen days lost by the 'Sophia' has been a great disappointment." Evidently, he was not pleased that on the incoming voyage the *Sophia* had sailed directly to Kingaite and had not been available to help erect the houses at Nuvujen and Kekerten. Although Captain Cheyne's boat crews had cruised for whales from Sophia Harbour on nine days before Penny arrived with the *Lady Franklin*, they had failed to capture any whales. Now, when the whaling prospects were likely to improve, the crews of both ships had to expend valuable time getting things ready for winter at Kekerten. On the last day of August, Penny wrote, "Pretty far through with the house. Very anxious to get of to our fishing." On the next day, as Margaret records, three of the *Lady Franklin*'s boats went whaling for four hours. The *Sophia*'s crews had set off at five in the morning and did not return until four in the afternoon. Meanwhile, the tradespeople worked feverishly to finish the house.

All Belonged to One Company

3–27 September

The two ships are anchored in the harbour at Kekerten (maps 3, 4).

Sept. 3rd   Four boats again started at 4 A.M. They returned at 4 P.M., saw two whales but did not get near enough to fire at them. Captn. Cheyne, the mate & harpooners were assembled in the cabin of the Lady Franklin this evening to receive instructions from Captn. Penny, which were nearly as follows. Each harpooner was to take a half-turn of his line round the billet-head, as whales in this clear water run so fast that the lines are very apt to be cut by the rocks when the boat is not well up to them. Each boat was to keep at a proper distance from each other, so that a fish coming up between two of them they would see which way she headed & allow the boat which had his tail turned next to them to fire first. Also to be careful & not make the slight[est] noise with their feet in the boat & to show themselves as little as possible & never use their oars but in a breeze of wind. Likewise to remember that they all belonged to one company & must assist each other in everything, their interests being one.

Sept. 4th   At 5 A.M. Capt. Cheyne hailed the Lady Franklin to say he saw a barque in the offing & thought it was the Alibi. Capt. Penny ordered a boat to be lowered immediately & started in pursuit, but found her too far ahead so returned & got the Sophia under weigh & followed her. What could be Capt. Stewart's motives for such proceedings I cannot conceive, as it was arranged that he was to remain in

Sophia Harbour until the Sophia came for the spare provisions, boats, &c. &c., which were to be left with the Company's ships about to winter. Capt. Cheyne came on board the L.F. to take charge & get her up again to Sophia Harbour. We started about 2 P.M., leaveing the cooper of Sophia & cooper & mate of the Lady Franklin in charge of the house & to set up the casks before the frost sets in. The weather is very calm.

Sept. 5th   We had through the night alternate calms & gales & reached Sophia Harbour about 6 A.M., when the anchor was let go in safety. The crew had then 4 hours rest when two boats started to look for whales. They saw one. There was a great swell in the water so that they could [not] remain long out. We have now Sophia Harbour to ourselves all the other vessels having removed to some other situation. Mr. Warmow & the Dr. accompanied Capt. Penny. I am longing very much for the return of the Sophia & feel strange to be left alone in this wild country, although everyone on board is kind to me. The sailors have music & dancing every night. Some of the airs they sing are very pretty.

Sept. 6th. Sunday   All quiet, wind & rain the whole day. Capt. Cheyne & Billie on shore. They walked as far as red river about a mile inland.

Sept. 7th   Boats started this morning at 5 A.M. Saw a great number of whales in droves of from 5 to 14, but caught none.

Sept. 8th   The boats again started this morning, went up the feiord, saw 4 whales but it came on a gale of wind & they were obliged to return. The second anchor was let go as soon as they came on board. Billie went on shore with a gun & shot a snow bird.

Sept. 9th   Weather rather cold. Boats set out about 12, saw some fish. Capt. Cheyne shot, fired at one & missed her. He was much disappointed.

Sept. 10th   Boats again set out at 6 A.M. Capt. Cheyne got fast but the harpoon came out & lost her. At 4 P.M. the mate saw the Sophia coming up the inlet. I was glad to hear the news. At 6 she was anchored in the harbour beside us. Capt. Penny had been very busy in his excursion, having picked up a number of Esquimaux of whose assistance we stood much in need. Capt. Stewart had behaved in a most disgraceful manner to the Arctic Co., particularly in pretending to have orders contrary to those delivered to Capt. P. & in trying to deprive the Coy. of the natives who have been maintained at their expense, also throwing out dark hints about Capt. Martin with regard to his conduct last year to me while beside us. He also hinted that some dark deed had been done by him, but I trust God will protect us.

Sept. 11th   Never was a more beautiful morning seen than when the 6 boats left at 6 A.M. The day has continued fine throughout. At 2 P.M. we saw Mr. Penny's boats returning & as they drew near I saw that they had met with something to disapoint them. They had seen a great many whales & one was singled out & watched by three of the boats & they had almost got within shot of her when Mr. Cheyne dashed in with his boat before them & frightened her away.

Sept. 12th   Boats again set off this morning but saw only one whale at a great distance. There is one of the Esquimaux women here named Maria, a very interesting person. She had a fine boy named Eenoolooapick after his uncle. Everything seems to remind her of all his little ways & her tears flow fast whenever she sees any one who had been kind to him. We have tried to explain to her the resurrection of the dead & she seems more reconciled. Mr. Warmow is to take her with him [on] a short excursion & explain to her more fully about our Saviour. We have had a very disagreeable scene with Mr. Cheyne but he seems now brought to his senses & I trust all will go on amicably together.

Sept. 13th. Sunday   The men are all on shore to get a walk. Mr. Penny had a very narrow escape with his life, he having walked on a good way beyond the others, came to a place where he thought he could get down, but when about half-way down the face of the cliff he came to a perpendicular rock a little slippery with frost. There was no place for his feet & he could not ascend again from the small ledge where he stood [but] fortunately had a knife & cut his neckloth into strips which he tied to the roots of a small willow & let himself down so far that he again got hold with his feet & thank God he was enabled to reach the ground in safety. In the afternoon we had our service as usual.

Sept. 14th   Three boats have gone up the fewin [i.e., fiord] & three to Kicertye to look for whales. If any are seen they are not to return to-night but three crews to sleep in a tent up the f[iord] & the other three to go to the house at Kickertyne. However, they saw few whales & all returned about 6 P.M. Mr. Penny shot 2 ducks [with] Towlow. Mr. Warmow has been on land all day & two Esq. with him looking for game. They returned about the same hour. They had shot nothing all day but just as the boat landed to bring them on board the boy Dick saw a seal on the rock & Mr. W up with his gun & shot it, bringing it on board with them. As the boats were all nearing the ship George Ross, one of the harpooners, was guilty of a breach of etiquette. The mate was very angry with him & Mr. Penny reproved him also, but he said it was a mistake of his boatsteerer's, who had come too near before he could turn & got between the mate & the ship, this being the offence, but I consider whatever the mans offence was with regard to etiquette the mate was guilty of a greater when he told his master that he had no right to interfere in his affair as [he] was quite able to settle his own quarrels. I must confess I felt very queer when I heard him say so as I expected other things of Mr. Birnie.

Sept. 15th   The boats set off this morning in their usual manner, three up & three down the inlet. They were not long gone when a fish made her appearance. George Ross fired at her & would have got her had not his gun hung fire. He tried another & lost her also. Mr. Cheyne likewise lost one. They all returned about 5 P.M., much disappointed & in rather bad humour. Mr. P. called George Ross into the cabin to make inquiry how he had blundered the fish. He explained & was very sorry for his mistake. After tea the subject was referred to & some ill feeling displayed by the mates. Mr. Warmow also behaved in a most unbecoming & un-Christian manner. My attention was drawn to him by seeing him laughing so I asked him what was the cause of his merriment & he said he was laughing at the self-confidence of St. Peter in thinking he could walk upon the sea. I have always felt sorry whenever I heard anyone speak without solemnity of anything sacred & I expressed myself so to Mr. Warmow.

Sept. 16th   Wind strong from the eastward. Boats unable to leave until 8 A.M. Mr. Penny crossed the inlet twice. Several fish were seen but they were unable to come near them. They all returned except one boat. A whale was seen in the mouth of the harbour. Mr. Penny & the mate started in pursuit. Just as they were doing so someone called from the hill that the absent boat was fast in a fish. The parties on board were all delighted & were guessing how large she would be & great was our disappointment when it turned out a false report.

Sept. 17th   A strong wind & heavy sea running. Notwithstanding, the boats left at 7 A.M., but could not get near the fish they are so restless. I feel sorry for the men. They come back so disappointed.

Sept. 18th   The people all employed today bringing water from the land, the wind being too strong for fishing. Towlow & his boats crew left today for deer hunting. Oshilee, an Esque, one of Mr. Penny's faithful followers, brought on board a fine haunch of venison & said he had shot five deer & would bring more when he got it home. His wife is a most active woman & very fond of her husband. I was much amused at her dressing his hair & trying to make him look well.

Sept. 19th   Weather more moderate. Boats all started at 6 A.M. We were looking out for their return about the usual time but could see nothing of them. We came to the conclusion that they had either got a fish or then gone down to the house at Kickertyne. At sun down a boat came in sight, which turned out to be Towlow from his hunting excursion. They had shot two deer, a hare, & snow bird. We have now plenty of venison & very fine it is.

Sept. 20. "Sunday"   Weather beautiful & dry. The boats had gone to Kickertye. They had slept at the house & started at 6 A.M. for the ships, a distance of 25 miles. The two coopers left to set up the casks had been very diligent & were very happy to see their friends again, having now been a fortnight alone.

Sept. 21st   Boats left at 5 A.M. They have crossed & recrossed the feiord several times. We have seen a number of fish from the vessel but the boats were not so fortunate. A fresh arrival of Esquemaux from Sumea.

Sept. 22   Mr. Penny, the second [mate], & Towlow, with their boats, went up the inlet, Mr. Cheyne & the mate going down. We observed from the vessel a number of whales on the opposite side of the inlet. They remained there about four hours. I persuaded the blacksmith to man a boat & cross to see if he could catch one. He got very near them, but Mr. C. saw him & crossed also. The whales had heard the noise & we saw one throw up her tail to a great height & they all made off immediately.

Sept. 23rd   Mr. Penny arrived last night about 12 P.M. They had seen no whales, but met in with a party of Esquimaux & got a dozen of fine large salmon from them. The second mate was left to proceed to the head of the inlet, which is about 35 m[iles] long. Two whales seen from the vessel. Mr. P. went in pursuit, but they made off. The boat arrived from the head of the inlet. They had seen no whales, but report abundance of game & brought with them 150 lb. of rein-deer which the natives sent to Mr. P.

Sept. 24th   Boats all employed today taking in water. As it has been very frosty for the last few days we are afraid of the brooks being dried up soon. In the forenoon two whales seen. Mr. P. & Lucas crossed to try & secure them but did not get nearer than half a mile. This has been a clear, beautiful frosty day.

Sept. 25th   Towlow returned this morning. He had shot a rein-deer & a hare, which he brought to the vessel. He again started along with Lucas & two boats crews for Kingua, to see if the whales are congregated there. Mr. Warmow accompanied them. This is the first day we have had snow.

Sept. 26th   Whales seen, but no boats sent away, it being deemed prudent by Mr. Penny to show to the harpooners that they [i.e., the whales] did not come in at night & go out in the morning as supposed by them, but would play there for days if not frightened off by their noise.

Sept. 27th. Sunday   Divine service read by the Dr. in Mr. Warmows absence. Men all on shore in the afternoon. Saw several whales & now see the neccessity of Mr. P['s] instructions

It was now September. The brief arctic summer had run its course and winter was in the air. The days, sunlit for almost twenty-four hours around the time of summer solstice in June, now contained nearly equal segments of darkness and light. The waning power of the sun, depriving water, earth, and air of energy, was initiating the hibernation of plants and insects and triggering the southward migration of many sea mammals and birds. After a summer's feeding, winter-resident land animals were clothed in thicker fat, fur, and feathers for the cold months ahead. Night-time temperatures frequently dropped below freezing, producing thin skins of delicately veined ice on tundra ponds. Mountain summits were already capped in white from premonitory flurries. The landscape, once briefly bright with floral glory, was becoming muted and sombre. Scattered residual pinpoints of autumnal reds and yellows on the tiny leaves of ground-hugging plants were losing their brilliance, and technicolour extravagance was fading towards the stark winter black and white of rock, snow, and ice.

It was a time when most arctic whaling ships would be starting for home at the end of their voyage around Baffin Bay. Some were already on their way across the North Atlantic, and others were in various harbours along the coast of Baffin Island, the crews making their last half-hearted sorties in the whaleboats and securing things on board ship for sea. After half a year away from familes, friends, and fresh food, several hundred men on two dozen ships would be releasing the fetters on thoughts and desires, and eagerly anticipating the comforts and pleasures of life ashore at home.

For the forty-three men, two boys, and one woman on the *Lady Franklin* and *Sophia*, however, the whaling voyage was still in its early stages, and the challenging prospect of an arctic winter loomed ahead. Neither ship had secured a whale, but there was still time. In Cumberland Sound, whales tended to be abundant in the fall as they migrated southward from Baffin Bay through Davis Strait towards their wintering territory. Perhaps they took advantage of a last opportunity to feed on zooplankton in the sound before their winter fast.

The broad gulf took a long time to freeze over, and beyond the slowly congealing waters along its coasts there was still plenty of room for whales. But it would be foolhardy for a captain to pursue these whales through September and October, and then attempt to traverse Davis Strait through November's massing floes, shrieking gales, bone-chilling temperatures, driving snow, and deepening darkness, to reach the stormy North Atlantic. The only reasonable way to prosecute the fall whaling was to take up winter quarters in a protected harbour, send the whaleboats out cruising for as long as weather permitted, and then settle in to wait out the winter months. The small open whaleboats could operate well past the time when it was prudent to cease ship navigation. A lost whaleboat would be a troublesome inconvenience, but a lost ship would be a major disaster. The wooden world of a whaleship was domicile, workshop, warehouse, and transport, the key to survival and link to home port.

Not only would a wintering crew be able to prosecute the "fall fishing," but several months later, when the whales began to reappear in May on their way north, the men would be in position to resume whale-

Whalers and boats off Cape Searle, Baffin Island
(sketch by William Barron, TDM)

boat operations long before it was possible for any incoming ships to penetrate the blockade of pack ice outside the mouth of Cumberland Sound. Whales could thread their way among the innumerable floes and dive beneath ice barriers, but the larger, more cumbersome sailing ships would have to wait until late June or July before attempting a passage into the sound. Wintering thus enabled a ship to have access to the whales in two additional seasons, fall and spring.

With a whaling base established at Nuvujen on the southwestern coast of the sound, Penny was now ready to initiate whaling from his two ships on the opposite coast. He sent boats cruising for six hours on 1 September, ten hours on the next day, and twelve hours on the following. Then, in the manner of a coach giving a pep talk before a crucial match, he assembled his harpooners and boatsteerers in the ship's cabin on 3 September and issued instructions. Margaret, not the sort to ignore interesting events on board ship, attended the gathering and recorded some of her husband's remarks.

"Each harpooner was to take a half-turn of his line round the billet-head," Margaret wrote. The billet-head, or loggerhead, was a strong upright post in the bow of British whaleboats, a simple but indispensable feature of the boat's architecture. It played an essential part in the whale hunt. An adult whale could weigh more than fifty tons. Its tail flukes, some twenty feet from tip to tip, exerted enough power to push the animal through the water at a cruising speed of three or four miles per hour and a sprint three times as fast, and could propel the immense body vertically out of the water in prodigious leaps during times

Eskimo whaleboats in Cumberland Sound
(Anglican Church of Canada, General Synod Archives)

of play or when in flight from attacking killer whales. A manned and equipped whaleboat, on the other hand, weighed only a ton and a half, and its five or six pairs of human arms could not drive it as fast as a fleeing whale.

The whale had an enormous advantage in weight and power, and to offset this, European and American whalemen had long used the ingenious system of harpoon, line, and drag. From their small boats, they struck the whale with a hand-thrown harpoon whose barbed or toggling head was designed to penetrate the skin and remain fixed. A rope line attached to the harpoon ran to the whaleboat, passed through chocks at the bow, looped around the vertical billet-head, and ended in line tubs, carefully coiled to prevent snagging. Once the harpoon was firmly embedded, the boat was connected to the whale, exerting drag. In order to avoid being pulled underwater, the crew had to let the line run out whenever the whale dived, then haul it in again and coil it down carefully in the tubs each time the whale surfaced or slowed. Like a deep-sea sportfisherman playing a marlin five times his own weight, or a fly fisherman playing a vigorous salmon with a light line, the whaleboat crew had to maintain just enough tension to tire the prey and gradually bring it closer for the kill, but without letting the whale pull the boat underwater or break the line. The loggerhead was the key to this operation. By exerting friction on the encircling line, it acted as a brake and enabled the crew to absorb the enormous strain of the fleeing whale.

Taking a turn of the line around the loggerhead was therefore normal whaling practice, which Margaret may not have realized. The real point of Captain Penny's remark was that with boats operating from shore rather than from a ship at sea, the harpooners should keep the line between boat and whale as short as possible in order to avoid bights of line becoming snagged and cut on reefs or shoreline rocks. A broken line could mean a lost whale.

Penny also emphasized the importance of ascertaining a whale's direction of movement so that it could be harpooned from one of its rear flanks. As very little of a whale's body was visible above the surface, it was often difficult to distinguish head from tail when it was resting or moving slowly, especially if a sea was running. But it was very important to make the distinction. For a harpooner to approach head-on would be like a cowboy on horseback attempting to rope a charging steer from the front, rather than overtaking it from the quarter. It was essential to keep out of the whale's line of sight, to avoid its forward momentum, and to steer to one side or the other of its dangerous flukes.

Penny also advised that if more than one boat was near a whale, the boat approaching from the rear should "fire" first, which tells us that the whaleboats of the *Lady Franklin* were equipped with harpoon guns. They were favoured by British whalemen because their greater range brought more whales within reach and enabled the harpooners to strike from a safer distance. These weapons, however, were not comparable to the guns used on modern whale catchers, which are far larger and more powerful and which fire a huge harpoon bearing an explosive head to kill the animal. The harpoon guns of Penny's day had the same function as the traditional hand-thrown harpoon – to attach a line to the whale by puncturing its skin. They did not kill the whale.

When one thinks of a whaleman using the traditional hand harpoon, the image of a javelin thrower at a track-and-field meet may spring to mind, but the analogy is not a good one. The modern javelin is a superbly crafted, free-flying, aerodynamic projectile weighing less than two pounds. It is grasped slightly behind its point of balance and launched, after a short run, into a trajectory that will attain the greatest possible distance, which for a world-class athlete could approach three hundred feet. By contrast, the whaling harpoon was a relatively cumbersome weapon weighing four to five times as much. It consisted of an iron shank and head mounted on the end of a stout hardwood shaft about six feet long and more than two inches thick, fastened to a

Harpooning a Whale

Whaling with hand harpoon (sketch by Timothy Packard of the whaler *Andrews*, 1867. By permission of the Houghton Library, Harvard University)

line of about two and a half inches in circumference. The harpoon shaft was cupped by the hand behind its rear end and was hurled with an overarm motion by a man standing in the bow of a moving boat. Its effective range was only thirty feet or less (Scoresby 1820, 2:242) because the farther the harpoon travelled through the air, the more line it drew after it, thereby increasing the drag weight and reducing its velocity.

Harpooners had often been frustrated because they could not get close enough to a whale before it sounded or dived beneath ice floes. The idea of a gun to propel harpoons farther had challenged men's imagination as early as 1731, but a century passed before an effective and reliable swivel gun for mounting on a whaleboat's bow was produced by the famous gunsmith William Greener of Birmingham, England, in 1837. William Penny was not the sort of man to ignore an invention that might treble the effective harpoon range. According to a testimonial published in an American whaling newspaper in 1852, he had used Greener's guns when he commanded the Dundee whaler *Advice* (Lytle 1984, 83), which must have been in 1849.

Whaling with gun harpoon (sketch by William Barron, TDM)

Lancing a harpooned whale (sketch by William Barron, TDM)

In his instructions to the harpooners on 3 September, Captain Penny also reminded the men of the need for stealth when approaching a whale, especially during calms, when the silent sea would fail to mask the sounds of shuffling feet or dipping oars and when sudden movements could be detected by the animal's acute eyesight.

Whales began to appear in Kingaite in early September, and sightings became almost a daily occurrence. Margaret's entries refer to "many," "a great number," "a great many," and "droves." One whale surfaced tauntingly in the mouth of the harbour and lived to tell the tale. Despite Penny's admonishments to his harpooners, the first month of extensive whaleboat cruising brought a plague of missed opportunities. Captain Cheyne fired and missed once, struck and had the harpoons draw out twice, and managed to frighten away a whale that Penny was preparing to strike. Harpooner George Ross missed once, struck and drew once, and had a misfire another time. On the seventeenth, Penny's own boat somehow alarmed a whale during the approach and lost the chance to strike, an event which Margaret discreetly refrained from mentioning in her journal.

The run of spoiled chances would continue into October. On the seventh, two boat crews, using oars in their approach instead of the sails which Penny recommended in relatively smooth water, alarmed their quarry and missed their moment. Even when success seemed inevitable, circumstances seemed to conspire against them. The incident that Margaret was to describe on 6 October must have been exasperating in the extreme. In the ship's logbook Penny recorded that a whale rose "close ahead of us. Up sail. Run right upon her, had the gun ready to fire when the cry 'Donaldson over board.' Down sail, swept the boat round. I could not see him for the sail. When it was taken down he was 200 yards astern. He was about to lost spirit when [he] cheered up [and] struck out again. Had the gun ready to fire over him. However, picked him up but lost the whale. Set sail and run to the harbour."

Penny had been about to use the harpoon gun in a way that Margaret described as "the manner of Manby's apparatus." George William Manby was the inventor of a method of shooting a line to a disabled ship so that people could be rescued from the shore; he had once made an arctic voyage on the whaler *Baffin* under command of William Scoresby, Jr, in order to find out why whalemen were reluctant to adopt whaling guns and to experiment with one that he himself had developed. Manby would have been delighted to learn that Penny, who had intended to fire a harpoon over the head of the man in the water so that the line would fall within his reach and enable him to be hauled to the boat, had come close to combining the two devices in one instrument.

Sometimes the condition of the weather or sea stood in the way of whaling success. On 14 September the logbook of the *Lady Franklin* recorded, "Several near chances of whales but none secured it being too calm and the water like a mirror." Conditions went from one extreme to another. Two days later, in the wake of gale winds blowing down Kingaite, the open boats were shipping water in rough seas as they tried unsuccessfully to overtake the whales.

During September, with the *Lady Franklin* riding at anchor in Sophia Harbour, Margaret was confined to the ship with little to do while most of the men were away in the boats. From each day's early hours until mid- or late afternoon, she had as company only Dr Grant, Brother Warmow, her son Billie, and a few shipkeepers. When the boat crews returned in time for tea or dinner, the talk undoubtedly centred on whaling. Margaret's journal entries reflect the way she was attuned to their departures and arrivals, their adventures in the boats, and their disappointment and frustration at near misses and bad breaks. It is the experience of the whalemen rather than Margaret's own activities and feelings that her diary records. We long to hear about the cabin she occupied with her husband, the washing and sanitary arrangements, what clothes she had with her, where she took her meals, whom she dined with, what food they ate, what they talked about, how she occupied her time between meals, and countless other mundane details of her shipboard life. But in this we are disappointed.

The *Lady Franklin*, *Sophia*, and *Alibi* – the entire fleet of the Aberdeen Arctic Company – were all present in Cumberland Sound. It was, of course, not unusual for two or more vessels to keep company during the whaling season. The high risk of ship damage or loss in the ice-bound regions and the unforgiving severity of the climate made it advisable to keep close to other ships. Generally speaking, ships sailing together remained independent of one another in whale catching, but if they wintered together their captains sometimes decided to share the hunting effort and the catch. At a winter harbour in Hudson Bay during the winter of 1864–65, for example, five captains "made agreements to join company in floe whaling" and drew up a contract (W.G. Ross 1975, 53).

The cooperation between the *Lady Franklin* and *Sophia* – and in theory the *Alibi* as well – was more than a spontaneous arrangement to suit shared circumstances at a particular time and place. It was a deliberate strategy arranged in advance, involving the ships of one company under the overall direction of one captain, and it covered many aspects of the voyage. The underlying principle, which had originated with Penny, was that three ships cooperating in the entire whaling operation would be more effective than three ships working independently. Essential ingredients of this synergistic approach were loyalty to the company, obedience to the senior captain, and mutual cooperation. When Penny addressed the harpooners of the *Lady Franklin* and *Sophia* on 3 September, he reminded them, as Margaret noted, "that they all belonged to one company & must assist each other in everything, their interests being one."

Reading Margaret's journal and the ships' logbooks, one wonders whether Penny's vision of a unified command over three vessels was too idealistic. Captain Cheyne appears to have accepted Penny's authority, and except for a few incidents – the "disagreeable scenes" mentioned by Margaret on 12 September and 19 October – they appear to have got along well. On the other hand, Captain Stewart, who had already wintered and was to sail for home in early October, clearly ignored Penny's overall authority during the two months in which they overlapped on the whaling grounds. After learning that Captain Stewart had wintered at Niantilik contrary to orders and had lost six men, Penny now discovered that Stewart had promised to take the native harpooner Tessuin back to Scotland, even though Penny intended to employ him during the winter. In addition, Stewart was supposed to transfer whaling gear and surplus food to the *Sophia* for the use of the two ships that intended to remain out over the winter, but on 4 September he attempted to sail away without doing so, and Penny had to take command of the *Sophia* and go in pursuit. Margaret remained on board the *Lady Franklin*, so she was not an eyewitness at the subsequent confrontation between her husband and the renegade captain of the *Alibi*. She could only refer to the incident retrospectively, on 10 September, from what she had been told. The logbook of the *Sophia*, written by Penny for six days, records the events and includes the doctor's declaration as witness: "From the 4th Septr. up to 10th Septr. the events above stated fell under my observation, [signed] Erskine B. Grant."

The *Sophia* overtook the *Alibi*, anchored somewhere near Niantilik, and Penny, Grant, and Warmow all went on board. When Penny asked Stewart why he had not landed the provisions as instructed, Stewart "grew most abusive." He refused to let Grant examine half a dozen men who were reported to have scurvy. "The man would hear no reason," wrote Penny, who sent the doctor back to the ship to fetch a letter from the managing directors of the Aberdeen Arctic Company, which authorized Penny "to take full command of all their vessels in Cumberland Sound." But Stewart was not impressed:

Capt. S refused to read it or hear it read. Capt. P. ordered the Surgeon to read it wh. he did, upon which Capt. S. said he did not care for those instructions as he himself had written orders which he would obey: on being asked by Capt. P. to read him these instructions, he refused. The natives who had worked all the year round with him and who have served Capt. P. ever since he came amongst them he also refused to hand over. He also refused to leave provisions, lines &c. on wh. Capt. P. in a great measure depended; but in hopes that he may change his mind Capt. P. sent him a dispatch ordering him to land all spare provisions, lines, lances, and the natives at the house at Nubuivan when he had done with them himself.

Penny stated that Stewart had been "engaged with the full knowledge he was to serve under me." It seems unlikely that there was any ambiguity about the command hierarchy, yet Stewart would not adhere to it. He said he intended to hand over his ship's natives (most of them trained by Penny) to the *Arctic*, a Peterhead whaler. Stewart seems to have developed a degree of cooperation and friendship with her master, Captain Reid, that far exceeded his allegiance to his own employers. Next morning, the *Sophia* encountered difficulty getting under way and began to drift dangerously towards a lee shore; but on the nearby *Alibi*, Captain Stewart made no move to help. Penny considered this "an action most unworthy of a seaman."

There seems no doubt that Stewart's actions were in defiance of his instructions and contrary to the interests of the company. To deprive Penny and Cheyne of the required provisions, equipment, and native whalemen shortly before they committed their vessels to winter quarters and to fail to assist a ship in distress constitute a degree of irresponsibility that is rare in the history of arctic whaling. Was Stewart simply an irrational and malevolent character, or did he harbour some deep-seated grudge against Penny? Seven years earlier, when Penny and Stewart had sailed in seach of Franklin, Penny had been in overall command of the two ships; but with his propensity for generating publicity, the venture had become known in the public mind as the "Penny expedition." And although it was a party under Stewart that had discovered the graves of three of Franklin's men on Beechey

Island, providing the first evidence that the missing expedition had passed its first winter safely at that place, newspapers tended to credit Penny with the achievement. Had Stewart grown to resent his subordinate position in an enterprise that had earned abundant praise for Penny yet pitifully little for himself? If so, why had he agreed to sail again under Penny's authority?*

---

* As there were two or three Scottish whaling captains named Alexander Stewart in this period, it is conceivable that the cantankerous master of the *Alibi* in 1857 was not the man who had commanded the *Sophia* on Penny's Franklin search expedition of 1850–51. Until contrary evidence comes to light, however, I shall assume that they were the same person.

What a Size of an Animal!

28 September – 28 October

Both ships are anchored again in Sophia Harbour.

Sept. 28th   Mr. Penny & Mr. Cheyne set off with their boats this morning, leaving the mate & Ross at a little distance to watch their motion.
About 10 A.M. the blacksmith, who was watching in the crow's nest,
called out one of the boats had got fast in a fish. He immediately set off
with a boats crew to assist in killing her. It took him an hour to cross &
they were just taking her in tow when he joined them. Mr. Penny had
shot her & the other boats had joined him to help. I was very happy
that they had been enabled to make a beginning. Mr. Penny was so
anxiously wishing for it so that he might have food for the Esquimaux
& their dogs & just as I saw the boats in sight towing the whale, a tribe
of Esqi of between 50 & 60 in number, landed at the vessel from the
other side. Great was their astonishment when they found no body on
board but myself & two little boys. They are a fine looking set of men &
women. One man, Noodlook, in particular, is as handsome as any I
ever saw in Britain, with black curly hair (this is one of those men who
Mr. Penny thinks must be descendants of some of the early voyagers,
who we know lost their vessels in this quarter[]); their joy was great
when I explained to them that Mr. Penny was bringing across a whale
to the vessel & they were anxious to be off to assist him. However, when
I looked again I saw Mr. P. coming along with the Dr., who had likewise
gone off in a boat with some Esq. females to get a look of the whale. It
was now 3 P.M. & at 7, just before dark, the[y] brought her along side.

What a size of an animal! You would scarcely think that such a monstrous creature could be killed. She is 56 feet long. Her whale bone is 12 feet.

Sept. 29th   All hands are employed flinching to-day with 12 Esq. assisting. I have been watching the process the whole day & I have managed to overcome prejudice & eat a bit of the skin, which is a preventative for scurvey.

Sept. 30th   All hands have again commenced flinching this morning. The whale is so heavy that they can scarcely get her turned round. A number of thrashers are congregated about the whale, they being very fond of the blubber. I have seen the men kill two of them.

Oct. 1st   All hands employed cutting up the bone & stowing it. The boat returned this afternoon from Kinguwa, having seen no whales. They encountered stormy weather & found a good deal of ice in the inlet. We have had snow all day.

Oct. 2d   Six boats set off this morning. Some whales were seen, but they took the alarm. The boats returned about 4 P.M., bringing with them some natives from the oposite side.

Oct. 3d   Snowing at intervals all day, wind strong. No whales seen to day. All hands busy cleaning the vessels. All the Esquimaux came on board in the evening to get a dance with the sailors, this being the night of drinking the health of sweethearts & wives.

Oct. 4th. "Sunday"   A heavy gale through the night. The Sophia was dropped astern of the Lady F. at 2 P.M. & both anchors of both vessels let go. It continued blowing until 12 noon. After that it became more moderate. Divine service immediately after dinner. A boat on shore saw 3 whales. A number of Esquimaux on board in the evening. Mr. Penny & Mr. Warmow tried to instruct them a little with regard to God. They seemed most attentive & interested. On asking them if they knew who made the earth one of them said it must have come out of the sea for he had seen whales bones on the tops of the hills.

Oct. 5th   Eight boats this morning set out for the fishing. A great swell in the sea, few whales seen. The boats returned at 5 P.M.

Oct. 6th   Boats all set out again this morning at [7?]. A good many whales seen. Mr. Penny was just about [to] fire at one & had a fine chance of her when the cry of a man overboard was heard. Of course he immediately gave up the whale to save the man, who was about a lines length from the boat. Mr. Penny called out to him to swim on & he caught him with the harpoon as he was about to sink. They were all sadly grieved at the loss of this fish, but it was fortunate the man was saved. I heard Mr. Penny telling them that in any case of immergency where a man could not swim or [could] get exhausted they should fire the harpoon gun with the line in the manner of Manby's apparatus. Strong wind. Second anchor let go at 2 P.M.

Oct. 7th   A great many fish seen today, but they were all frightened. One of the Esquimaux had a fine chance but the second mate came up with his oars & frightened her.

Oct. 8th   Eight boats all left at 6 A.M., Mr. Penny & the Esquimaux taking the upper part of the inlet. One of the Esq. boats nearly got fast. Had they not taken down their sail they would have been right upon her.

Oct. 9th   All hands again started at 6 A.M. The snow has been falling thick all day. Some whales seen, but snow too thick to calculate distance. Boats returned about 3 P.M.

Oct. 10th   Sophia came alongside to put her coals on board Lady F. so that her tancks may be ready for a fish. Obliged to be swung off again at 8 P.M., a gale of wind blowing. All the anchors let go.

Oct. 11th. Sunday   A fine clear day. People on shore. Six or 7 whales seen. Divine service at 2 P.M. The Esquimaux seem to understand very well that they are to respect this day, for they go about very quietly & forego their usual occupations.

Oct. 12th   Boats all away today but too great a swell & obliged to return.

Oct. 13th   The Dr. went in Mr. Penny's boat this morning. They were both sanguine of getting a whale. They saw several & were near one but could not capture her. They all returned about 12 noon, it being impossible to sit in the boats. Many days when they return I see the ice hanging on their beards three or four inches long.

Oct. 14th   Mr. Penny intended to remove to Kickertyne to-day, but the wind has changed & a snow storm has come on. The natives are all to go with us. They have brought all their things on board & seem highly pleased at the prospect of change. No boats away today, only Mr. Penny on shore to look if he can see any whales. Returned in about 2 hours. Saw some, but sea rough.

Oct. 15th   Sea very rough to day, weather cold & snowy. Both anchors hove up.

Oct. 16th   Thick snow. Boats went off to look for whales. John Lucas nearly fast. A gale of wind & obliged to return. All quiet in the afternoon.

Oct. 17th   Started this morning at 11 A.M. for Kickertyne, a fine fair wind. A native oumite [i.e., umiak] & kyack came alongside with some of Mr. Penny's oldest acquaintances. One of them, Pacak, is the native who brought down the news of Franklin's people from Ongoomuite [i.e., people of Pond Inlet and vicinity]. We see very distinctly that he is conversant with the facts, but it is very difficult to get them from him. He says, however, that they lost their ships far to the north & came in five boats. He also says that one man with a large head & red hair set off to go to the east side by crossing Lancaster Sound. He speaks too about someone who did everything with his left hand. In a little time perhaps he will let out more. He gives out that they went back again in their boats. He likewise says that he got a gun from them & that he gave them [a] large salmon.

Oct. 18th. Sunday   Arrived at Kikertyne this morning about 8 A.M. & anchored in a fine safe harbour. Fine clear weather. Divine service at 2 P.M.

Oct. 19th   Wind very strong. Mr. Penny went in his boat to look for whales, mate left on board. Another disagreeable scene with Mr. Cheyne about his not stating correctly in his Official Log Book the facts with regard to the harbour in which the house is built. They are there that Mr. Warmow & Mr. Penny landed on Kikertye & saw

from a height a fine harbour which Mr. P. thought would be very
suitable for the house to be placed & named it Warmow Haven, the
house at Neubeonean having been named New-Haddo.

Oct. 20th   A fine clear day. Some whales seen at a distance. Mr.
Warmow & the Dr. went down to Kikertyne with the mate of the Sophia
& a party of Esquimaux females. They had a fine sail down & enjoyed
themselves very much, but in returning at night one of the coopers
came in his boat along with them to take down some things he wanted.
When it began to get dark they lost sight of each other & Mr. Warmow
waited so long, being afraid the cooper would not find the harbour
where the ships were, he not having been there before. However, he
[i.e., the cooper] got one of the Esquimaux, who was out in his kyack,
to pilot him & was much better off than the other boats crew, for they
almost lost their way & had their boat half full of water, which made
them very uncomfortable & out of humour.

Oct. 21st   Very squally to day. Mr. Penny on shore looking for whales,
none seen. The cooper set off again for Warmow Haven & they saw
from the land that he had a very narrow escape from being lost in a
squall, but he was very active & got his boat kept upright & he was seen
in safety before they left the land. No boats away in the afternoon.

Oct. 22nd   No whales in sight today. Mr. Penny has gone with his
boat & taken down 7 Esquimaux to Warmow Haven to make them
commence building [snow?] houses for themselves for the winter. This
has been the coldest day we have had. Mr. Penny returned at a quarter
to 7 P.M. & had a very cold sail. The other boat did not arrive until
an hour & a half after & we were beginning to be anxious about them.
Mr. P. made those on board fire one of the harpoon guns & hoist a
light at the gaff end for their direction. They had found it very difficult
to row, but soon forgot their hardship in a glass of grog.

Oct. 23rd   Strong wind & snow. No boats away to day. Ice beginning to
make.

Oct. 24th   Very cold to-day, ice forming very fast. No whales seen.
Two Esquimaux left to go down to Kikertyne with a boat, the one there
having been driven ashore & so much damaged that she is unfit for use
until repaired.

Oct. 25th. Sunday   Very cold & strong frost. Ice getting thicker every hour. Divine service at 2 P.M. Men always very attentive.

Oct. 26th   Ice so strong to day that Mr. Penny thought it advisable to move down to Warmow Haven & got up the anchors for that purpose. The Lady Franklin was to hang by the Sophia & Mr. Cheyne was told not [to] heave up his chain for the purpose, but he thought he would be too long after us of getting under weigh & hove up too soon. The consequence was both ships drove & would have been ashore had it not been that the bay ice kept us off until a kedge was got on shore. The anchors were obliged to be let go again & give up all thoughts of moveing for a night. We have 70 Esquimaux on board the two ships. They are also going down to Warmow Haven. Some of them sing very sweetly. The whole of them are fond of music & think it a great treat to get down to the cabin to hear the accordion played by the second mate, who has a fine ear for music & both sings & plays well. The Dr. also sings well & Mr. Warmow occasionally gives us an Esqui. hymn.

Oct. 27th   We got under weigh this morning at 9 A.M. & arrived at Warmow Haven at half to 1. Immediately after dinner the natives & their luggage was got on shore & we are safely moored in our old quarters.

Oct. 28th   We are removed to day to the inner harbour, which is to be our winter quarters. A whale was seen in the mouth of the harbour & Mr. Penny & the other boats set off after her, but she was too quick for them.

With the first whale killed on 28 September, the men had at last made "a beginning," as Margaret noted in her journal. The ships had been away from home port for three months. Their whaleboat crews had been cruising for a month and a half whenever weather and other circumstances permitted, spending long hours criss-crossing Kingaite, sighting dozens of whales and striking at least three of them, only to have their harpoons draw out and the prey escape. But now, with the capture of a huge whale (harpooned by Captain Penny), their streak of bad luck seemed at an end. The dismal prospect of returning home without a single cask of blubber after months of effort, as one out of every nine Davis Strait whalers had done during the 1840s, was happily ended.

The whale was taken in conditions that were less than optimum – a calm sea only occasionally rippled by light breezes. After sighting several whales frolicking on the opposite side of the fiord at about four in the morning, the boat crews had set off from the ship "cautiously," as the log recorded, using paddles instead of oars for stealth and later hoisting sails. At approximately ten o'clock Penny struck with a gun harpoon. The whale fled, drawing out three and a half lines – about half a mile of rope – as it towed the boat behind it. The men, hauling the rope in with bare hands as the wounded animal tired, drew the boat foot by foot towards the prey until, after a few hours of exhausting effort, they were close enough to kill it with the hand lance. The next task, challenging in its own way, was to get the immense carcass to the ships for flensing.

When whaling was carried out on the high seas, the ship could sometimes be sailed up close to a floating whale carcass. But in what was generally called bay whaling, in which the boats operated from a ship at anchor, there were seldom enough officers and men left on board to hoist anchor and set sail, and in any case the nearby hazards of uncharted coasts would have made such a course of action risky. So the whaleboat crews had to perform the extraordinarily arduous work of towing the whale to the ship. In this back-breaking enterprise all available boats worked together, fastened in line ahead, using either oars or sails, and sometimes both together. The tow could take many hours, depending on the distance to the ship, the direction and force of the wind, and the state of the sea. The men had to endure whatever harsh turns the weather took, bailing out by hand the frigid water which the waves threw into the open boats and relying largely on muscular exertion at the oars to keep warm in temperatures that were often below freezing. Occasionally, boat crews had to interrupt their tortoiselike journey towards the ship in order to wait out bad weather in a bight of landfast ice or in the lee of an island. Only in the most extreme circumstances did they abandon their whale.

About fifteen hours after setting off in the morning and six hours after subduing the whale, the weary boat crews of the *Lady Franklin* and *Sophia* at last pulled slowly into harbour, secured the immense carcass alongside Penny's ship, and boarded their vessels for some hot food and a night's sleep.

At fifty-six feet (more than half the length of the *Lady Franklin*), Penny's whale made a strong impression on Margaret, who wondered

Towing a whale back to the ship (sketch by Timothy Packard, by permission
of the Houghton Library, Harvard University)

that an animal so large could be conquered. It was always difficult to
obtain a correct measure of a whale's length, since most of the carcass
was submerged and the flukes were canted where they were secured to
the ship abaft the bow. There was neither need nor time for accurate
measurement, and if the log keepers recorded the length of a whale,
they rarely bothered to explain how the measurements were taken,
whether along the curve of the body or along a straight line from end
to end. Probably, the position of the nose and tail were roughly noted
and the distance between them measured along the deck with a sounding line or simply paced off. A few masters who were scientifically
inclined and whaling surgeons who were interested in natural history
approached the matter with more care, recording girth, breadth of
flukes, and so many other body measurements that a tailor could have
made a well-cut suit of cetacean clothes.

Sixty-five feet, or possibly seventy, was regarded as the probable maximum length of Greenland whales by the great arctic authority and
whaling master William Scoresby, Jr (1820, 1:454) – though in more
than three hundred kills, he had never encountered one longer than
sixty feet (Jardine 1837, 77). Dr Robert Goodsir, who sailed as surgeon
with Captain Penny on the whaler *Advice* in 1849, recorded the length

of a female whale "from the fork of the tail, along the abdomen, to tip of lower jaw" as sixty-five feet (Goodsir 1850, 96). His words "along the lower abdomen" suggest that the measurement was taken along the curvature of the body, which would exaggerate the length (like measuring human height with a tape measure by running the tape over an undulating topography of beer belly, slumping chest, fleshy neck, multiple chins, and protuberant nose).

Whaling logbooks seldom recorded the length of captured whales. The usual indicator of whale size was the longest blade of whalebone, or bone (baleen), in the whale's mouth. Because baleen was relatively short and had to be cut out and hoisted on deck, it was far easier to measure than the entire body of a partly submerged whale. Baleen length was roughly proportional to overall body length and, more importantly, to the quantity of oil in the blubber. According to Scoresby (1820, 1:457), whalebone never exceeded fifteen feet, and bone of thirteen feet was "seldom met with." Penny's whale, as Margaret tells us, yielded twelve-foot bone (the ship's log called it eleven feet eleven inches), which is certainly indicative of a very large whale – "a splendid whale" as the ship's logbook noted.

When whales were killed, they were processed as quickly as possible in order to minimize losses to scavenging killer whales ("thrashers," as Margaret called them), to get the blubber safely stowed below deck before a gale could intervene, and to free the men for further whale catching. On both ships, the next three days were devoted to the tasks of flensing, or "flinching" (peeling strips of blubber off the carcass and cutting out the baleen), and "making off" (cutting the blubber into small pieces and storing them in tanks below). The men were called at four o'clock on the morning of 29 September, and after breakfast they began the work. The two ships were moored together alongside the whale so that they could cooperate in the process. As the flensing was carried out by the crew of the *Lady Franklin*, the blubber was conveyed to the deck of the *Sophia* for making off. The men, assisted by a dozen Eskimos, worked at the job for seven hours on the first day and ten hours on the second. On the third, they seem to have spent about ten hours completing the making off, gumming and stowing the whalebone, and cleaning up the greasy decks. It thus took approximately fifty-four men more than twenty-seven hours to reduce the carcass to blubber and baleen, a total of about fifteen hundred man-hours of work. The effort yielded one and a quarter tons of whalebone and enough blubber to make about twenty-two tons of oil.

Captain Parker's ship *Emma* flensing a whale (sketch by William Barron, TDM)

Normally, British whalers carried the blubber back to their home port at the end of the voyage, where it was rendered into oil in boiling yards ashore. American ships, on the other hand, melted the oil out of the blubber on board ship during the voyage (doing so in try-pots erected on the upper deck) and arrived home with casks of oil rather than casks of blubber. Penny had designed a compromise system to suit his wintering mode of arctic whaling. This was to complete the flensing and making-off on board ship, as usual, and later to render the oil during the winter. In this way he was able to sail home with a cargo of oil, as the American whalers did, but without taking the time to try it out during the whaling season and without encumbering the decks of his small vessels with bulky try-works. In addition, the task of rendering oil out of blubber provided a healthy diversion for the men during the winter months, and the residue could be used to feed Eskimo dogs and, if necessary, people.

Before the brutally effective weaponry and equipment of twentieth-century whaling, the industry was notoriously wasteful, using only the blubber and baleen (sometimes solely the latter), and leaving the remainder of the carcass to drift away, decompose, and sink. This was a particularily unfortunate loss in arctic regions, where the Eskimo population depended on animal meat, fat, skin, sinew, baleen, and bone for almost all the necessities of life. On wintering whaling voyages, however, it was usually possible to make some of the discarded parts of flensed whales available to the natives. When the last of the blubber had been stripped off Penny's whale, the ship's logbook reported, "Towed the carcase on shore for the Esquimaux and dogs for food and all the skin."

In August, September, and October, Margaret recorded the arrival, departure, and activities of a number of Eskimos. Some, like Tessuin, were either working for another vessel or travelling from one region to another, but most seem to have been working for Penny. Mary and Tackritow were to be employed as cleaning women at Kekerten and Nuvujen. Towlow, who commanded his own whaleboat crew, supplied some meat to the ships. Oshilee brought meat as well. A group of fifty or sixty, including Noodlook, came on board, helped to tow the dead whale, and supplied a dozen men for flensing. Others arrived in time for a Saturday-night dance with the sailors. When the ships left to take up winter quarters at Kekerten, they took the Eskimos on board, and they picked up another group, including Pakak, along the way.

Margaret's frequent references to Eskimos underscore the extent to which the natives of Cumberland Sound had become integrated into the labour system of commercial whaling. The whaling ships were self-sufficient in the sense that they carried enough men to trim the sails, man the boats, pursue the whales, and flense the carcasses; but although their complements were well suited for one-season voyages, the practice of wintering on board ship introduced challenging new requirements which the whalemen by themselves could not satisfy. First among these was the necessity of procuring fresh meat during the winter to supplement the preserved food and prevent scurvy. Second was the need to implement a transportation system in spring to move blubber and bone from the edge of the landfast ice to the frozen-in ships for processing. The whalemen's equipment, experience, and expertise were inadequate for these vital tasks, and they had to turn to the native people for assistance.

On his first wintering whaling voyage in 1853, Captain Penny had hired Eskimo men to hunt during the winter, to drive dogsleds during the spring, and to man whaleboats during the summer. This set a precedent for all subsequent wintering voyages. Because the native men could perform useful tasks in all seasons, it became normal for the

ships' captains to employ them for the entire duration of their sojourn
in Cumberland Sound. Consequently, Eskimos had to move with their
families to the winter harbour selected by a captain and to reside there
for the better part of a year. To compensate the Eskimos for the reduction of the time available for their own subsistence hunting, a whaling
master had to assume some responsibility for feeding the men and
their families while they were working for his vessel. And, of course, he
had to pay them for their services by providing them with goods such
as used whaleboats and whaling gear, guns and ammunition, tools and
implements, metal and wood, clothes and cloth.

Enterprising natives who obtained a used whaleboat and gear as
wages in kind were in a position to offer any ship their services as a
distinct whale-catching unit. Whaling masters departing from Cumberland Sound, anxious to promote continuity in their native labour
force, sometimes arranged to purchase on their return a year later
any whalebone that had been obtained by the Eskimos during their
absence. Penny's strategy appears to have been to have a ship of the
Aberdeen Arctic Company wintering in Cumberland Sound every year,
passing on its ship's natives to the incoming vessel. But as the events of
September show, the infidelity of an ornery master could threaten the
success of such a plan. For reasons that are not obvious, Captain Stewart had determined to hand over the *Alibi*'s natives, including the expert harpooner Tessuin, to a non-company ship. Penny's anger about
this development is perfectly understandable.

Margaret found the man named Pakak, who came on board on 17 October, of particular interest because he told a story – somewhat inco-
herent yet tantalizing – about white men arriving at Pond Inlet in five
boats following the loss of their ships farther north. It was only natural
to think of Franklin's two ships, last seen twelve years earlier when
beginning their search for the Northwest Passage. Brother Warmow
wrote a detailed description of the encounter with Pakak. He reported
that while the ships were sailing from Tornait to Kekerten, they met
two leaky skin boats from Saumia (the southeast coast of the Cumberland Peninsula) containing eighteen people who had been travelling
for two weeks with little food and "were consequently in a wretched
state." Seven of them boarded the *Lady Franklin* and eleven the *Sophia*.
Warmow's account continued:

But in spite of their distress, one of the men was very conceited. When I asked his name, he replied, laying his hand on his breast, "Me Captain Pakak!" I thought this was indeed a wonderful captain, with nothing to command, and indeed possessed of nothing but his miserable life. Still he appeared by no means stupid. But I have never had so bad an impression of any Esquimaux as this man. In this opinion, our captain quite agreed with me, although this man was treated with much attention on board, probably because he was skilful in the whale-fishery. He told me, that he once lived at Pond's Bay, formerly a very populous place, called by the Esquimaux, Aggamiut, – the windward side. He also gave a circumstantial account of the destruction by his fellow-countrymen, – probably in 1851 – of a provision-house, which had been erected on Leopold Island for the use of Sir John Franklin. He declared that was a fine time, for, although the contents of many of the barrels were spoiled and useless, the Esquimaux still obtained abundance of meat, brandy, tobacco, and wearing apparel. He made also some other statements, which were exceedingly interesting to me, on account of the sad fate of Sir John Franklin. They were to the effect, that a party of people, who had suffered shipwreck, had been in the neighbourhood referred to, several years ago; – that he himself, however, had not seen them, as this was before his arrival there, – that is, probably previous to 1850; – that these people had lost their ships in the ice, further up in the north, where the sun does not shine for several months altogether, and had then travelled in two divisions in boats; and that the one which came to Aggamiut had five boats, and remained there with the Esquimaux fifteen days, while the other division with only one boat had proceeded westwards. May not this have been Sir John Franklin's party? (*Periodical Accounts* 1858, 23:89–90)

The man's announcement, "Me Captain Pakak," which caused Warmow to wonder about a captain "with nothing to command," may have been his imitation of the customary introduction used by Captain Parker among the Eskimos. In any case, the words stuck and he became "Pakak" to the Europeans. Warmow probably felt a special interest in the man's story and its possible bearing on the Franklin mystery because he had lived for many years in Greenland, on the threshold of the Northwest Passage, and in Aberdeen he had met Lady Franklin and had refused her invitation to join the searching expedition on the *Fox* under M'Clintock. Penny also had good cause to be interested in Pakak's account, for he too knew Lady Franklin and had participated in the Franklin search several years earlier. Indeed, it is likely that everyone on the ships was fascinated by what Pakak had to say about possible survivors of the lost expedition. But they were more than five hundred miles south of Pond Inlet, where the white men were said to have arrived, and it was by now several years after the event. In addition, they were somewhat sceptical of Pakak's reliability. It was difficult to get the facts from him, Margaret noted, and her husband observed that he "contradicted himself frequently." In the end, they attached little importance to the report.

On 17 October the *Lady Franklin* and *Sophia* got under way again for Kekerten to take up winter quarters. There is no doubt about the location of the place because it is clearly described in the ships' logbooks, and many relics of a half-century of whaling activity are still visible on the ground. Today, it is officially called Kekerten Harbour and is situated between the islands of Kekerten on the south and Akulagok on the north. Kekerten Island is the largest and most southerly of a large group called the Kikastan Islands off the mouth of Kingnait Fiord (map 3). On a map, Kekerten resembles a harpoon head flying southward, with all the smaller islands strung out behind it for a distance of about twelve miles. According to the arctic navigational guide *Pilot of Arctic Canada*, "Many of these islands are surrounded by rocky ledges, reefs, or sand flats and the channels between them appear to be encumbered with rocks. They are … rugged and sombre in appearance, and almost destitute of vegetation; in altitude, they range up to about 500 or 600 feet" (Canada 1959, 185). The geography sounds forbidding, but within this small archipelago Penny had discovered on his first voyage into Cumberland Sound what he later described in his logbook as "one of the finest harbours to be found in the Gulf," and he intended to winter there in 1857–58.

One is certain to be confused by Margaret's description of the trip from Kingaite to the winter station because she uses the name Kekerten (or Kikertyne as she usually spells it) to denote two separate places – first, a harbour in the northern part of the group and, later, the winter harbour itself. She describes leaving for Kekerten on 17 October and arriving at Kekerten the next day, yet she then mentions boats sailing from there to Kekerten on several occasions up to the twenty-fourth, and it becomes clear that the ships do not in fact reach the station until the twenty-seventh, at which point she calls it Warmow Haven!

This confusion is not so much a result of an error or misunderstanding on Margaret's part as a symbol of the confused, evolving status of name giving in a frontier region where two languages were in use.

In the summer of 1857 the Scottish whalemen had probably not yet started to use the name Kekerten for the harbour in which they intended to winter or for the large island that embraces the harbour (both of which bear the name Kekerten today). The ships' logbooks show that they used the name Kekerten in two ways. First, they referred to the entire group of islands as the Kekerten Islands. On 17 August, when Penny sent the *Sophia* off from Sophia Harbour to survey the unfamiliar harbour in which they had decided to winter, Captain Cheyne wrote in his log, "Received orders to proceed to the Kekertian Islands and land the house and some coals on the south most island of the group where there is a harbour pointed out to me by Cpt. Penny where he thinks the ship can lay in saftey." Second, they used the name for "an excellent harbour" in the *northern* part of the island group. After Penny took the *Sophia* in pursuit of Captain Stewart and the *Alibi* in September, he collected about sixty dogs from Nuvujen and sailed back across the Sound "to Kikartine harbour," where he landed half the dogs before continuing on to rejoin the *Lady Franklin* in Kingaite.

A detailed system of place-names did exist among the native inhabitants of Cumberland Sound and adjacent regions. The anthropologist Franz Boas recorded almost a thousand of them a quarter-century after Penny's whaling voyage (Cole & Müller-Wille 1984, 52). But native names were learned by oral transmission rather than through the medium of maps and charts, and the whalemen's lack of fluency in the Eskimo language impeded their access to the native system and sometimes resulted in errors or ambiguities. When informants were on hand, the whalers might manage to learn the Eskimo names for places of particular prominence or interest, and they adopted some of them. Margaret's journal, Warmow's letters, and the logbooks of the two ships contain more than a dozen native place-names (appendix 4). More often, however, the whaling masters simply applied English-language names that seemed appropriate or convenient – including the names of ships and captains. Some of these, such as American Harbour, Blacklead Island, Bon Accord Harbour, Brown Harbour, and Quickstep Harbour, achieved permanence because they were widely used by whalemen, were later transcribed onto published charts, and were eventually given official status; others, including Margaret's Island and Sophia Harbour, vanished after limited use. It is thus hardly surprising that some ambiguities and contradictions occur in the journals and logbooks.

The move from Sophia Harbour to the winter harbour can be summarized as follows. The two ships left at eleven o'clock on the morning of 17 October for what Warmow called "another harbour, nearer our winter quarters." After "dodging" off the large island of Kekertukdjuak during the night, they dropped anchor at eight the next morning in the "fine safe harbour" they knew as Kekerten, where they saw the dogs Penny had left there more than a month before. It was, as Warmow recorded, "about nine miles from our winter-station." While gales confined the ships to harbour, bay ice began forming around them, threatening to trap them before they could continue to their designated winter quarters. They used whaleboats to break up the young ice but suspended work for the sabbath (25 October). On Monday, while a "keen frost" continued to strengthen the ice around the vessel, the crew managed to shift the *Lady Franklin* to a better position upwind, take a warp ashore, and put down two anchors "to prevent her driving on shore." The next day, with winds moderating, they weighed anchor, reached open water, and after three hours' sailing came at last to their destination. The ships anchored in an "outer harbour," which Warmow described as "only about a mile from our winter-quarters." The men ferried the Eskimos and their gear to the land and helped them erect their tents. The following day, they shifted both ships into the "inner harbour," where they were to spend the next three-quarters of a year – the place that is officially called Kekerten Harbour today (map 4).

If they used the name Kekerten for an island nine miles to the north, what did they call the winter harbour? Writing in his logbook in late November after the ships had taken up quarters there, Captain Penny called it Warmow Haven (Margaret had already used the name several times in her diary). Brother Warmow, on the other hand, referred to it as Kekertat. Was Warmow too modest to employ his own surname for a geographical feature, especially in letters to his superiors? Or had he learned in conversation with the Eskimos that the previous Scottish usage had been wrong and that the name Kekerten really belonged to the southernmost island and its adjacent harbour? By 3 December, when Penny sent some men to fetch dogs from the northern island, he no longer called it Kekerten. The place where he had left the dogs temporarily had been demoted to a nameless state – "the norther most island of the Kikertine group" – and the name Kekerten had been transposed nine miles south to their winter harbour, where it has subsequently remained, although it has been given the redundant form Kekerten Island. (As Warmow certainly knew, the name Kekerten [*qikiqtaq*] meant "island.")

Penny had first noticed the harbour in 1854. He had intended to winter there in 1855–56 with Captain Martin of the *Sophia* but had not

The harbour of Kekerten, looking southeastward. In the background
is the island group of Miliakdjuin and beyond it Wareham Island,
with the mountainous Cumberland Peninsula on the left
(photo by the author, September 1976)

done so. In 1856 he had pointed the place out to Captain Stewart and
instructed him to winter there, but Stewart had perversely chosen
Niantilik instead. In mid-August 1857, Penny had landed on Kekerten,
walked across the island, examined the "splendid haven" again, and
sent Captain Cheyne to survey a channel and erect a house at the
place. Cheyne noted some of the characteristics of the harbour in his
log book after completing a preliminary survey of depths in August.
He wrote, "[I] went away with the boat to survey the entrance into the
harbour pointed out by Cpt. Penny and found tow [*sic*] fine safe harbours with a passage of about 150 fathoms [900 feet] in length and
about 150 feet in breadth between them. At noon returned on board,
made all sail and proceeded for the harbour. At 4 PM came to anchor
in 4 fathoms [24 feet] water with 20 fathoms [120 feet] of chain,
furled sails and cleared the decks up and got all ready for discharg-
ing." Penny later elaborated on Cheyne's description: "Our haven is
formed by two island[s,] south and north, open to the west, having an
entrance about 80 feet wide to the NE from the Kingite side. The ships
are brought up about 200 yards from the land on which the house is."

The northeastern channel, although convenient for whaleboats sailing to and from Kingaite, was probably too narrow for use by the ships,
but the western entrance provided easy access from Cumberland

Kekerten Harbour. A panoramic mosaic looking northward at low tide:
left, the western entrance; *centre*, Akulagok Island with Tuapait Island behind;
right, the northeastern entrance; and *far right*, the lofty island of Kekertukdjuak
(photos by the author, July 1976)

Sound to an outer harbour, beyond which the sinuous configuration
of Kekerten's northern coast provided a more enclosed inner harbour,
in which ships could obtain greater protection against wind, waves,
and drifting floes. The s-shaped passage between the two islands was
between a half-mile and a mile wide, but scattered islets and reefs
made the navigable ship channel much less – only 150 feet according
to Cheyne. Although both ships had sailed separately into the harbour
during the summer, Penny was more cautious when they arrived in
late October; he had the whaleboats tow the ships "through the pass."
It was probably low tide, and he was well aware that their knowledge of
the bottom contours was still sketchy.

The ships anchored abreast of the house in ten fathoms of water
on a sand bottom. Owing to the gently shelving shoreline, the intertidal zone was wide. Archaeologist Marc Stevenson, who has studied
the site of the whaling station, reports a distance of between 150 and
200 yards between the extreme limits of high and low tide (Stevenson

1984, fig. 14). According to Penny, the ships had to anchor about two hundred yards offshore. Certainly, this was a disadvantage before freeze-up, making the unloading of cargo arduous, but the ships would soon be connected to the shore by a highway of landfast ice.

The first consideration in choosing a winter harbour was the safety of the ships. The inner harbour, located at one point of the zigzag channel between Kekerten Island and Akulagok Island, was partly en-folded within the protective embrace of Kekerten's rocky ridges. Shel-tered in this way, it promised to be a comparatively tranquil anchorage in which the ice surface would be stable, rendering the ships secure from disruption by autumn gales. Once the fast ice had formed solidly around the ships, the crews would hoist the anchors through holes in the ice, and from that moment on the vessels would be held by the ice alone. In the remarks that Penny and Cheyne made about the har-bour, the notion of ship security stands out. It was a "splendid haven," with two "fine safe harbours," where "the ship can lay in saftey."

In selecting Kekerten for a winter harbour and the site for one of his whaling stations, Penny must have considered other requirements as well. There had to be some level terrain close to the shoreline where boats could be hauled out and where native tents and, later, igloos could be built, a house erected, casks assembled, and blubber processed. In fact, only one locality on the rocky island was suitable, and that lay along the shore of the inner harbour. Today, from the air, this area in summer stands out like a green oasis in the desert, a flat meadow of luxuriant grasses, sedges, and lichens about four hundred yards long, backed by rugged outcrops of barren rock rising towards the interior of the island.

Water supply was another important consideration. In Hudson Bay, wintering crews cut slabs of ice out of ponds in the fall before the ice grew inconveniently thick; they then sledged these slabs to the vessels, stacked them alongside, and later melted them into water as needed. The routine at Kekerten was to cut and haul pond ice regularily. On 20 November the men obtained ice from a pond half a mile inland and about 200 feet above sea level. A month later the logbook reported that they were getting ice every day from a pond 100 feet high. Whether this was the same or a different pond is not clear. Air photos show several small ponds south of the station site, the two largest being approximately 600 and 1,300 yards away.

Kekerten's insularity, while providing an excellent harbour within convenient reach of the floe edge in spring, had two major disadvantages. It possessed little in the way of animal resources, and during the periods of freeze-up and break-up it was cut off from the mainland, where game was more abundant. This was especially serious in the fall, the season in which the Eskimos normally concentrated on the caribou hunt in order to obtain skins and meat for the winter. Although Captains Penny and Cheyne could help out with ships' provisions, their resources were far from inexhaustible, and their food did not possess the antiscorbutic qualities of fresh meat. When the *Lady Franklin* and *Sophia* arrived in late October, they carried a total of seventy Eskimo men, women, and children according to Margaret's count on 26 October, and eighty according to the ship's log. With approximately one hundred and twenty people living at the winter harbour, restricted access to hunting grounds was likely to pose a problem. There were many mouths to feed.

On Terra Firma

29 October – 25 November

The ships are now at Kekerten, where they will spend the winter.

Oct. 29th   Mr. Penny ashore in the forenoon. Mr. Cheyne out at the north point but saw nothing. We had a number of Esquimaux on board & amused ourselves in the evening by taking a game of the Tottem with them, having nuts for our counters. With what anxiety they watched the turn of the game & expressed their pleasure or disappointment as they gained or lost.

Oct. 30th   It is getting colder every day & the ice making fast. People busy cleaning the snow off the decks.

Oct. 31st   A fine frosty day. Saturday is always a buisy day, being that on which the mens stores are served out ‡ and the ship cleaned up. ‡

Nov. 1st. Sunday   A calm day & very frosty. Three Esquimaux boats were dispatched to day to Sophia harbour to bring down food for themselves & their dogs. Divine service at 2 o clock, men all most attentive.

Nov. 2nd   Ice now nearly surrounding the vessels. In the evening Billie & some of the men walked across it to the land.

Nov. 3rd   I have been ashore today for the first time for nearly two months. I felt very warm with the exertion of walking on the rough ice, but there is a pleasant feeling in being on Terra Firma & the air is very different from that on board ship, so refreshing & pleasant. I saw all the natives busy making snow houses. They do them very quickly by cutting the snow into large blocks.

Nov. 4th   A fine clear day. I have been walking about on the ice all day. The moon has not set today & the sun is shining bright, making the hills look purple. The scene altogether is very beautiful. The Esquimaux have returned with their boats today.

Nov. 5th   Not so cold to day. I have been on shore & into the natives houses. They make them with an outer & inner apartment. I could live in one very well. They are very warm & large. Sometimes two or three families live in the same hut. I never see any disagreement amongst them & they are all very fond of children.

Nov. 6th   Little doing. Men employed making roads in the ice that we may get to the house easily. A sort of influenza has broke out amongst the natives. The Dr. & Mr. P. are constantly assisting them & they seem very sensible of their kindness. I have now got on my winter clothing, that is a large great coat of Mr. Penny's lined with young deer-skin, a seal-skin bonnet lined with very fine deer skin, also trows-ers of deer skin & boots to match, all of which I find most comfortable. As yet I have never felt cold & thank God I am enjoying excellent health.

Nov. 7th   Fine weather. Men all buisy making a road to the land & get-ting their stores weighed out. A number of the natives on board in the evening.

Nov. 8th. (Sunday)   Fine weather. Divine service, after which Mr. Penny gave the seamen a short address with regard to the arctic winter, that they should live in harmony with one another, take plenty of exercise in the open air, have great regard to cleanliness, for which every facility will be given, & when they went at any time to take a walk they were to say where they were going & not fewer than three or four together for fear of storms or frostbite; each man to possess himself of a clasp-knife in case of being overtaken in one of the sudden & terrible gales prevalent in these regions, in which case he was told to burrow under the snow as no man could live in it for an hour.

Nov. 9th   Men beginning to prepare for houseing in the ship as it is now very cold.

Nov. 10th   I have been confined to my cabin to day with ear-ache.

Nov. 11th   Mr. Penny & some of the men went to the top of the hill, 500 feet, to look if any whales were in sight, but none seen.

Nov. 12th   Still very frosty. Men making roads. Nothing particular doing.

Nov. 13th   Esquimaux all very ill with some sort of disease like the influenza. The steward is also very ill with a wry-neck & muscular pains in his body. Indeed I may say that the whole ships company are affected with cold more or less.

Nov. 14th   The carpenter's mate has been much annoyed by some of the men putting disagreeable things into his food, at which Mr. Penny was very angry & had all hands called on deck to reprove them. They have even put in bread dust, as we suppose, amongst our tea.

Nov. 15th   A very heavy fall of snow has taken place since last night. Mr. Penny & the Dr. went on shore to visit the sick, & had to walk up to their waists amongst it. Few Esquimaux on board today for they do not like snow. Divine service as usual.

Nov. 16th   A fine day. Men busy cutting a road between the ships & house. Snow too deep for me to go on shore.

Nov. 17th   A beautiful, clear, frosty day, only a little wet. The salt in the ice melts the snow, but it makes a fine smooth flaw when it freezes again. I enjoy this frosty weather very much & have been visiting my Esquimaux friends to-day. They are always happy to see me.

Nov. 18th   Still fine. I have not felt cold although the thermometer is 10 below zero. The steward is now better. The Dr. says it was not

cold, but some spasmodic disease. 10 P.M. I have just been on deck
to see the bright arctic night. It is almost as light as day with the
Aurora Bor[ealis] arched from one side of the firmament to the
other.

Nov. 19th   I have been on shore the most of the day. Weather fine.
Sailors away for mactac. One party found the snow very deep, which
made them late of returning.

Nov. 20th   Wind strong from the east, To day weather not so pleasant.
We have had Pakak on board tonight. Mr. Penny has been questioning
him again. He tells us he saw a sledge at Pond B., the same
as one we have here made after the pattern of the Government ones.
When asked how they got it he said they had bartered it with the
English.

Nov. 21st   A very strong wind, water nearly up to the ships. No work
on shore going on today. People on board variously employed. Some
Esquimaux on board at tea; we had a song from them. Some of them
have sweet voices & all are fond of music. I trust Mr. Warmow is doing
his duty amongst them for they seem very teachable & anxious to
learn.

Nov. 22nd. Sunday   A fine day but a good deal of water on the ice,
which prevents my going on shore. Divine service, which is always
numerously attended. In the evening Mr. Warmow read the 1st chap.
of St. Matthew & explained it to some of the Esquimaux. With what
eager attention they listened to him.

Nov. 23rd   The wind has changed to the N.W. so we have a strong
frost again. I really thought we were to be afloat on Saturday evening,
for I could feel the ship moving up & down with the swell. Hadlaw,
one of our Esqui. sailors, came on board this evening in breathless
haste to tell us that his wife had born a son. He seemed quite overjoyed at the event. The child was named Warmow – in compliment to
Mr. Warmow. This is the first addition to the colony. The father &
mother are both excellent, industrious, quiet creatures. Mr. Penny
told Hadlaw to make choice of what he would like best & he would
present it to him, so he at once chose a large knife & was sent away
very happy in possession of it.

Nov. 24th   This has been a fine frosty day. I went on shore to see young Warmow. He is a fine healthy child.

Nov. 25th   A dull sort of day. On shore in the afternoon.

Within a few days of dropping anchor in Kekerten's inner harbour, the ships had been encircled by a delicate skin of flexible young ice, which steadily grew thicker and firmer as the cold intensified. By winter's end it would be a solid, stable platform about six feet thick, a natural highway to the shore. In the first few days, however, it was incapable of supporting human weight and was also impervious to boats, so all the people crowded together on the ships were isolated, yet tempted by the enticing glassy sheet extending to the island. The Eskimo men, with their superior knowledge of sea ice, were the first to reach the land, on 2 November; the whalemen, with young Billie Penny an eager accomplice in the adventure, ventured across soon afterwards. The very next day, Margaret Penny walked over the ice and set foot on land "for the first time for nearly two months," enjoying her unaccustomed liberty. She was delighted by the sight of Eskimos busily carving out blocks of firm snow and placing them end to end in tilted courses that spiralled gracefully inwards to form the symmetrical domes within which they would live for the next half-year. The sailors, too, after many long summer days of pulling oars in whaleboats and carrying out repetitive jobs on the cramped ships, must have been very glad to stretch their legs on the ice and land, even though (unlike the captain's wife) they were not entirely free to amuse themselves. With snow already mantling the island and ice covering the harbour, there was plenty of work to do.

The first task was to build a "road" from ships to shore. Around the two vessels the new ice surface was relatively smooth, but with each cycle of tides it rose and fell a vertical distance of about twenty-five feet, raising and lowering the ships frozen into it. Closer to shore, in the broad intertidal zone, the ice was disrupted because each ebb tide lowered the ice onto the shallow, uneven, rocky sea bottom, where it bent, fractured, and tilted before the flood tide elevated the distorted fragments again. Continued low temperatures would gradually consolidate the shoreward part, where the water froze to the sea bottom, into a rampart called an icefoot. Travelling the two hundred yards from ship to shore was therefore not merely a Sunday stroll across a smooth and immobile horizontal plane of snow-covered ice. It involved traversing a rough zone of deformed ice, which probably incorporated floes and bergy bits from outside the harbour and was interlace by tidal cracks. Some vigorous landscaping could make life much easier for casual pedestrians and, more importantly, for the men who had to carry or haul building materials, whaleboats, blubber, spare gear, and food to the shore and bring ice for drinking water back to the ships. The crews began cutting "a road through the grounded ice to the shore" as soon as it was safe, and the work continued for almost three weeks, by which time the changeable topography of the near-shore zone had been more or less stabilized by cold weather and thickening ice.

Another important task was to house in the ships for the winter. Following the example of naval expeditions, whaling masters enclosed the upper deck of their ships within a "house" of lumber and cloth to provide a sheltered space in which the men could exercise and work without exposing themselves to the biting arctic winds. A sketch of the *Lady Franklin* and *Sophia* wintering in 1850–51 (Sutherland 1852, 1: frontispiece) shows a boxlike enclosure extending along the length of each ship, with vertical walls and a sloping roof. These "houses" consisted of heavy windproof cloth stretched over a wooden frame, strong enough to withstand the pressure of winds on the sides and the weight of snow on top. Penny had planned to use the same housing cloths that had served so well on former occasions, but those for his own ship had been used by Captain Stewart on board the *Alibi* during the previous winter, and in August Penny had discovered that "the expensive housing cloth of L. F. [*Lady Franklin*] had been broken down to make sleeping bags and blankets." Nevertheless, by late November a housing cloth was rigged over the main deck of the *Lady Franklin*; it was probably the one from the *Sophia*, whose crew lived in the house on shore.

The crews had already unloaded building materials, coal, wooden staves and iron hoops for casks, some provisions, and various articles to be used during the winter and in the spring whaling. They next unbent the sails and stored them with spare sails in the loft of the house ashore. The boats, which at sea hung from davits or rested on cranes along the gunwales, had to be removed to permit the housing in of the upper deck. They were hauled out and stored on land, where they would be available during the spring whaling. In addition to the house constructed on shore by Captain Cheyne's men in late August, there

ASSISTANCE BAY 24ᵀᴴ FEBRUARY 1851, THE COLDEST DAY MERCURY FROZEN

The *Lady Franklin* and *Sophia* wintering in Lancaster Sound near
Sir John Ross's ship *Felix* during the Franklin search expedition of 1850–51
(Sutherland 1852, vol. 1, frontispiece)

was now a workshop (whose windows were installed by the carpenter
on 4 November) and a "fishing plant," or "boiling house," in which
whale blubber would be rendered into oil. To facilitate this operation,
Penny had brought out from Scotland a "boiler," or "copper," which
could hold more than two hundred gallons of oil. It was now hoisted
out of the hold and set up in a small hut ashore. During November the
men rose at seven and worked from eight until four. While the seamen
performed unskilled tasks such as cutting the road and hauling pond
ice, the carpenter and cooper built the workshop and boiling house,
installed the boiler, set up casks for whale oil, and constructed special
"boat-sledges" on which the whaleboats could be hauled over the landfast ice to open water in spring.

Normally, wintering whalemen lived on their ships, but the existence of the house at Kekerten provided an alternative. As the *Sophia*
was uncomfortably small, her crew was divided between the house and
the *Lady Franklin*, and some of the men from Penny's ship were also

moved to the land. Those selected for the luxury of shore living were
men who, in Penny's judgment, were "likely to take scurvey." How
Penny determined in advance their degree of vulnerability to scurvy
and what advantages he saw in living on land are not explained; but as
it was commonly believed that the cramped, poorly ventilated living
quarters on ships contributed to the disease, Penny evidently considered the house ashore a healthier place in which to spend the winter.

If there was no conclusive evidence that exercise could prevent, alleviate, or cure scurvy, it had other undeniable benefits. No less than military commanders or expedition leaders, whaling captains needed men
who were healthy and strong. The tasks that seamen performed at
sea on sailing ships not only required muscular strength, coordina-
tion, and stamina, but also tended to reinforce these characteristics.
The men's work kept them fit. But during the winter there was no hauling on halyards, sheets, braces, and mooring lines; no walking round
the capstan or ratcheting up the windlass; no climbing aloft to man-
handle the heavy canvas sails; no pulling at whaleboat oars for hours
at a stretch or even flexing the legs to meet every roll and pitch of the
deck. Most captains therefore compelled the men to undertake some
daily exercise on the ice or on land during the winter months, and
some encouraged games such as football. Captain Penny, as Margaret
noted, had the men take two one-hour walks around the deck each day
within the shelter provided by the deck covering.

Outdoor activities required precautions. The combination of low
temperatures and high wind speeds in a landscape devoid of shelter-
ing trees was a serious hazard. The land and ice surfaces were exposed to the vicious sweep of wintry blasts and could quickly produce
a stratum of swirling snow in which a person could easily become dis-
oriented. On the relatively featureless sea ice, direction finding was
extremely difficult when visibility was obscured, and the long periods
of darkness in winter made matters worse. The road between ships
and shore was intended not only to make walking easier but also to
help the men find their way when the weather deteriorated. Although
almost half of the men on board the two ships had wintered in the
Arctic before, Penny wisely "gave the seamen a short address with regard to the arctic winter," as Margaret recorded on 8 November, to
establish a few guidelines for their safety.

Warm clothing was essential when anyone left the shelter of the
ships or house. To the very few whalemen who wrote private journals
or kept ships' logbooks, the clothing was too familiar to need description, but some surviving lists of the possessions left by men who died

Eskimos of Foxe Basin wearing traditional winter clothing made
from animal skins and fur. Whalemen came to appreciate the effectiveness
of such garments against cold (Parry 1824, facing 163)

during a voyage give a good idea of what they wore. A seaman on the
Alibi was drowned on the night of 30 July 1856. According to the ship's
logbook, "Alexander Gardiner, standing on the rail drawing water, lost
his hold by some means and fell overboard. Hove one of the life buoys
to him, cut the quarter boats lashing and lowered her very immediately, using every possible means in our power to save him but all to
no avail, being very dark." Next day, an inventory of his belongings
included the following articles of clothing: five pairs of drawers, five
shirts (three blue flannel and two cotton "ship shirts"), two pairs of
trousers, three worsted "cravats" (neckcloths), one moleskin vest, two
woollen "frocks" (sailors' sweaters), one jacket of pilot cloth, four
pairs of mitts, two hats (a fur cap and a sou'wester), five pairs of worsted stockings, two pairs of footgear (sea boots and shoes), and "1 new
cloth Cip" (cap?). Gardiner's only other property consisted of a mat-
tress, a sheet, a blanket, a rug (woollen coverlet), a pillow, two "shawl
napkins" (scarves?), a towel, a pound of soap, a razor, a pair of scissors,
one canvas bag and a smaller bag, and a small chest.

From a modern vantage point, Gardiner's outfit appears rather in-
substantial (no Lifa underwear, polypropylene socks, fibre-fill trousers,
Polartec vest, Thinsulate parka, Supplex nylon shell, Gore-Tex mitts,

Neoprene face mask, or Sorel boots). But in relation to the textile technology of the day, his wardrobe was probably considered adequate if a bit sparse. Warmth was provided by the insulating quality of the woollen fabrics – flannel, pilot cloth, and worsted – and by air entrapment when more than one layer was worn. Wind was blocked by tightly woven material, such as the pilot cloth and moleskin. In rain and spray, head and feet were kept dry by the wide-brimmed, waterproof sou'wester and the sea boots (probably gutta-percha), but the middle portions of Mr Gardiner would have become somewhat soggy in wet weather.

Whalemen were not issued with uniforms. They wore what they could afford to purchase in advance or what they could obtain on credit from the ship's slop chest as the need arose during the voyage – and, occasionally, what they could buy when the clothes of a dead shipmate were auctioned. Inevitably, some men were inadequately prepared for the intensity of arctic cold and wind. They simply had to make the best of it. Young men on their first voyage, lacking money and experience, were usually the worst off. Their outfits tended to improve with successive voyages. The logbook of the *Alibi* contains an inventory of the possessions of one of the ship's tradesmen, who died of scurvy at Niantilik on 27 January 1857. "At 0010 AM John Brown the ship's cooper having been assisted out of bed & sat on a night stool fell suddenly down upon his knees & expired without a struggle in a few moments time." Having risen through apprenticeship and accumulated enough experience to serve as a cooper and earn wages appropriate to his position, John Brown had been able to purchase a more generous assortment of shipboard clothing than seaman Alexander Gardiner. When his possessions were auctioned a week later, they included five pairs of cloth trousers (rather than two), six shirts (rather than five), three waistcoats or vests (rather than one), six frocks (rather than two), two comforters or mufflers, three jackets (rather than one), twelve pairs of stockings (rather than five), six pairs of boots and shoes (rather than two), four hats (rather than two), and seven pairs of mitts (rather than four). In addition, he left a pair of oiled (waterproof) trousers. His footwear included not only two pairs of sea boots but also a pair of "snow boots," which unfortunately are not described. His personal effects were also more varied. Appropriate to his elevated position on board ship, Cooper Brown carried twice as much soap as Seaman Gardiner.

On wintering voyages, whalemen usually had the opportunity to see Eskimo clothing. If they had had the foresight to bring along a few manufactured items to barter, they could usually acquire skin boots, mitts, and, sometimes, parkas made up by native women living at the winter harbour, who coveted imported articles such as red handkerchiefs, bright buttons, coloured beads, metal needles, knives, and cooking pots. The advantages of the native garments were not difficult to appreciate. Anyone who had tried them found that they were lighter, looser, more comfortable, and warmer, and the footgear was waterproof. But the availability of native garments at winter harbours depended largely on the Eskimos' success in their hunting for caribou, ringed and bearded seals, and other animals. The fact that the cooper John Brown apparently possessed no Eskimo clothing, even though there were native hunters in the employ of the *Alibi* during the winter, suggests that skins may have been in short supply at Niantilik at the time, though perhaps it was simply that Brown preferred the British clothing to which he was accustomed. What Captain Penny wore in 1857–58 is not recorded, but Margaret's description on 6 November of her own winter outfit makes it clear that her husband appreciated the advantages of Eskimo clothing, for he had outfitted her from head to toe in garments of skin and fur. One hybrid article, a greatcoat of his own lined with fur, embodied the Eskimo technique of wearing fur facing inwards to trap air near the body and utilized the excellent insulating properties of hollow caribou hairs. Margaret was well served by her fur clothing and seldom had occasion to complain of being cold.

Many nineteenth-century arctic explorers, especially naval and military ones, were blind to the advantages of Eskimo methods and equipment. Their unshakable belief in the superiority of European technology clouded their vision, and their unquestioning adherence to the traditions of their services limited their innovation. Where they might have adopted the use of dog teams, they had men haul the sledges. Where they could have obtained Eskimo clothing, they continued to wear apparel of standard issue. Where they could have learned much about the geography of the Arctic from the native people, they trudged onward with compass and distance wheel. Whalemen were less constricted by rigid regulations and tended to be more openminded and pragmatic. They were prepared to observe how the original inhabitants of the Arctic did things. They were ready to experiment with those methods and willing to adopt them if they worked better than their own. This is reflected in their close relationship with Eskimos at winter harbours, their use of native clothing and dogsleds, and their consumption of fresh meat to prevent scurvy. Penny's advice to the men that if caught out in winter gales they should "burrow under the snow" to survive was certainly a technique learned from the Eskimos.

From their very first attempt to winter on the whaling grounds, whalemen had experimented with native clothing. And Eskimos had experimented with European garments. In his autobiography, the famous Hull whaling master William Barron told an amusing story about arriving in Cumberland Sound in 1852 on the lookout for men from an American whaler who had spent the winter ashore. Excitement reigned when Barron's crew sighted a whaleboat manned by men in European garb, but they turned out to be Eskimos. Soon afterwards, they encountered a boat whose occupants were dressed in Eskimo fashion. These proved to be the Americans.

The appeal of European clothing to the Eskimos is less easy to understand, because in general the garments were not as effective against cold. But they had other attractions. There is a souvenir hunter in all of us and often a desire to identify with another culture or to flaunt a real or imagined association with exotic places or institutions. Our T-shirts may proclaim "I (heart symbol) New York" even if we have never been there; or they may say "Vuarnet" even if we never wear sports goggles, or "Buffalo Bills" even if we don't know a nose guard from a split end. Similarly, a woollen shirt or jaunty cap on an Eskimo of Cumberland Sound could excite admiration or confer prestige by suggesting larger horizons of experience and culture. The element of fashion, so much a part of our outlook today, was also of considerable importance then. Foreign coins, buttons, and spoons added gaily clinking fringes to Eskimo amautiks. Brightly coloured glass beads expanded the boundaries of needlework creativity. A pocket watch and chain proclaimed one to be a stylish man of means.

Although whalemen had begun wintering in Cumberland Sound only half a dozen years before, the Eskimo use of European garments had become common enough to upset a somewhat straight-laced Brother Warmow, who wrote to his superiors, "I am always sorry to see the Esquimaux wearing European clothes, and, in short, imitating the European in all respects. They were undoubtedly better off in their original state, and more likely to be gained for the kingdom of God. But when they begin to copy our mode of life, they are neither properly Europeans nor Esquimaux, and will speedily die out, in consequence of the change" (*Periodical Accounts* 1858, 23:89). Warmow's outlook had been conditioned by his previous missionary experience in western Greenland. Although the aboriginal people there had been living within a colonial framework for more than a century, the Danish

administrators had restricted their contact with foreigners and controlled their access to European goods. On the opposite coasts of
Davis Strait, Warmow was exposed to an entirely different situation,
in which no European government exercised colonial power, and the
whalers hunted, traded, and employed Eskimos as they wished. Unlike
the Greenlanders, the Eskimos of eastern Baffin Island had experienced only irregular contact with Europeans, and for less than forty
years. Not a single trading post or mission existed among them. Whalers had first entered Cumberland Sound only seventeen years before
Warmow's visit, and the first overwintering had occurred a mere half-
dozen years before. The native people were only in the initial stages of
contact and cultural change. It was Warmow's first experience of an
abriginal society so unaffected by European value systems and goods.

Many changes had occurred during whaling's brief tenure, and not
all of them had been good. Warmow was shocked at the "wretched"
and "miserable" condition of the first people he encountered at Niantilik in early August and at the "poverty" he later saw among the residents of Kekerten. He must have anticipated something like this,
because Captain Penny had been pleading with the Moravians for several years to send a missionary to Cumberland Sound to counteract
the harmful influence of whaling. It was precisely because of the
wretched conditions among the Eskimos that Warmow was there. Yet
the reality confronting him appeared harsher than he had expected.

Warmow held that whereas in "other heathen lands" it might be
appropriate to "cast the natives in an European mould," at Kekerten
"the evil results of such attempts are too soon visible." He did not spec-
ify exactly what evil results he had observed, nor did he explain the
difference between the Eskimos of Cumberland Sound and indigenous people elsewhere. But he firmly believed that if the natives took
up Christianity, "true … Christian civilisation will follow, and that,
withal, in such a manner, that they will remain what they are, namely
Esquimaux." The paradox is that he did not consider Christianity to be
part of the European mould he sought to avoid.

Were European and American whalemen really attempting to "cast
the natives in an European mould," as Warmow asserted? Although
they did instruct them in whaling methods, hold them to schedules of
work when employed, provide them with some food and material
goods, and – at least in Penny's case – tell them to respect the sabbath
when working for the ship, they had no reason to destroy their traditional activities or fundamental beliefs. The very things that made Eskimos useful partners in whaling were their knowledge, experience, and

skills, which the Europeans lacked. Whalemen therefore tried to change Eskimo behaviour only where it promised to improve whaling success or where it seriously conflicted with their own practices. But to turn Eskimos into Europeans? This was not their objective. Warmow was closer to the mark when he observed that the Eskimos were "imitating the Europeans in all respects" and had begun "to copy our mode of life." When two soluble liquids are united and stirred, they mix and relinquish their uniqueness. Cultural change was inevitable, and although some changes were imposed on the Eskimos by the whalers, others were adopted voluntarily, as they usually are when any society is exposed to a dazzling array of entirely new goods – some useful and others merely flashy – imported from another region along with new modes of behaviour.

It is not entirely clear whether Captains Parker and Penny had encouraged the Moravians to send a missionary to Cumberland Sound to alleviate the harmful conduct of whalemen or to elevate the spiritual condition of the Eskimos and thereby enable them to resist those destructive influences. Either intention would have been praiseworthy because the objective was the welfare of the aboriginal population, but both overlooked the fact that the introduction of Christianity would threaten the natives' religion, the king post of their culture. The shaman's role of linking people with deities was central to Eskimo life, and the imposition of an alien system of worship, administered by foreign missionaries, would inevitably undermine his authority and disrupt the belief system. But what was the alternative? Penny and Parker felt that in less than two decades of whaling contact, the native population of Cumberland Sound had experienced a severe decline in numbers and a significant moral retrogression. As whaling masters, they could exercise some control over the conduct of their own crews, but they could not regulate the behaviour of men on other vessels. Perhaps the influence of missionaries would have a beneficial influence on all whalemen and would soften the adverse effects of contact.

With whaling operations suspended for the winter and the ships united to the land by ice, Brother Warmow was at last able to devote himself to work among the Eskimos. He visited their tents and snow houses daily to teach them about Christ, and he accompanied Dr Grant when the latter tended the sick. Everyone welcomed Warmow, listened with interest to his words, and urged him to repeat phrases such as "Jesus Christ, have mercy upon me" so that they could memorize them. He was a favourite with "those who are poor and shy, and who are not made so much of on board the ship," but he also managed to gain the trust of "the younger and more lively individuals, with whom the sailors frolick a good deal." His fluency in the Eskimo language was a great advantage. "With what eager attention they listened to him," exclaimed Margaret after Warmow had explained passages from the Bible on Sunday, 22 November. The following day, the first child born at Kekerten was named Warmow in appreciation of his work.

For the benefit of the Moravian Brethren in Europe, Warmow described a typical scene in one of the snow houses at Kekerten.

Imagine an entire family, old and young, in such an abode. The whole furniture consists of a lamp, often very dim and scarcely burning, and a few well-worn reindeer-skins. Upon these latter, the members of the family sit, in a posture similar to that which the ptarmigan assume in very cold weather, namely, with the head drawn down between the shoulders. The mistress of the house is engaged trimming the wick of the lamp, and carefully dropping it on the scanty supply of oil, lest the light should be altogether extinguished, – a piece of frugality, of which they know nothing, when better times come. Beside her sits another female member of the family, chewing at a skin, destined to be made into boots or clothing, a domestic employment which is here perhaps equivalent to washing clothes with us. The master, if not out hunting or fishing, occupies a place beside his wife, and is busy trimming some of his implements, or boring holes in the pieces of a broken stone-vessel, in order to repair it, – an operation which he will perform very skilfully.

They have nothing to eat, except occasionally a handful of seaweed, which they dip in hot water and consume with a good appetite, unsuitable for food as it may appear to us. With all this poverty, we must not imagine discontented looks. In such circumstances, many Europeans would murmur against God and man. But these people are quite contented, and seem to know nothing of misery. When I go in, the man takes up his pipe, with the remark, that it is old and much used, but he could use it still, if he had but tobacco, and adds, 'Matiuse ibet tubakakangilatat,' that is, 'Matthew (for, like the Greenlanders, they call me by my first name,) have you not any tobacco?' If I take a present out of my pocket, they receive it with smiling faces. (*Periodical Accounts* 1858, 23:91–2)

On 6 November Margaret wrote in her journal, "A sort of influenza has broke out among the natives." Three days earlier, in the ship's logbook, Captain Penny had reported, "A good many of the Esquimaux

sick," and Warmow had mentioned the fact as well. Their remarks reveal that the illness was serious and that many individuals were affected. The epidemic raged for about two months, during which time Penny, Grant, and Warmow visited the tents and snow houses daily to tend the sick. Unfortunately, the doctor's diagnosis is not preserved, but Warmow thought that "severe colds" were unavoidable because the Eskimos often became overheated while visiting the ships during the day and then returned perspiring "to their freezing abodes" in the evening; he recorded that "several of the natives lay dangerously ill of pleurisy and affections of the chest" (*Periodical Accounts* 1858, 23:91). Penny mentioned "inflamation blisters."

The whalemen were sick too. Margaret wrote that all of the *Lady Franklin*'s crew were "affected with cold more or less" and that the steward was suffering from muscular pains (which cleared up several days later). But whereas there are several references to the doctor, the captain, and Warmow visiting sick Eskimos, there are none indicating that they tended sick sailors. No seamen were reported off duty during November; the men appear to have been employed as usual on various tasks. If the whalemen and the Eskimos were experiencing the same illness (as Captain Penny believed), only the latter were seriously affected by it. Indeed, this was the usual pattern when diseases were introduced by Europeans to the native peoples of North, Central, and South America, beginning with the voyages of Columbus. Pathogens to which Europeans had long been exposed, and to which they had built up some immunity, often found fertile "virgin soil" in aboriginal populations. The most deadly diseases, such as smallpox and cholera, which were still ravaging European society in the mid-nineteenth century, had an even more disastrous impact when they reached the New World. But in addition to these killers, some comparatively innocuous diseases, such as measles and influenza, which usually affected Europeans only slightly, could cause serious illness and even death among people who had not been exposed to them. The arctic regions of North America were late in coming within the sphere of European exploitation, and as a consequence the Eskimo population was highly susceptible to alien diseases. As late as 1949, almost a century after Margaret Penny's arctic voyage, influenza introduced to the settlement of Cambridge Bay spread to virtually all the Eskimos within hundreds of miles and killed eighteen individuals, while fifty whites living in the region were hardly affected at all (*Polar Record* 1953). The introduction of disease was an inevitable concomitant of European and American whaling activities in the Arctic.

Fortunately, the epidemic at Kekerten in November and December 1857 – a common cold, influenza, or some similar infection – ran its course without incurring serious damage. One child died, but its death cannot certainly be attributed to the illness. But the ingredients of a major disaster were there: a number of whalemen who had recently been in contact with the crews of several other ships; a community of Eskimos living nearby for the winter; frequent visits of native men and women to the ships, where they congregated in cramped, stuffy spaces; daily contact between individuals while at work; and crowded, poorly ventilated Eskimo dwellings. A serious illness at a whaling harbour could spread to other areas when a ship shifted its location, when native hunters travelled on hunting trips, or when hired Eskimos and their families returned home at the end of the season. Penny's labour force included individuals from around Kingaite and Nuvujen, from Saumia and the region around Niantilik, so Kekerten could have dispersed the illness throughout most of Cumberland Sound. Perhaps such an event had occurred in the past; Penny and Warmow believed that the native population of that vast region had fallen from 1,000 to 350 during the brief span of whaling activity (Holland 1970, 40).

November was a month of settling into the winter harbour. The whalemen and Eskimos worked at their appointed tasks. Dr Grant tended the sick. Brother Warmow provided Christian instruction to the natives and officiated at the Sunday church service. Margaret occupied her idle hours by strolling on the ice, visiting the snow houses ashore, entertaining her "Esquimaux friends" on board ship, and playing totum, or teetotum, a game of chance in which the players spun a square-sided top and counted the letter on its uppermost side. Young Billie Penny's activities are not on record.

Ill Supplied with Food

26 November – 31 December

Nov. 26th   During the night a strong gale came on from the E.N.E. It shook the vessel until I thought she would fall over on her side. In the evening it became rather more moderate. We are now housed in for the winter. Everything on deck is cleared away & we have a good space for a promenade when there is nothing going on, on shore. The men have a walk of an hours length twice a day round the deck. It is very pleasant to see them & hear their cheerful voices keeping up the merry song.

Nov. 27th   It has been very cold to day, but nevertheless the men have all been able to work on shore. Some of them had their faces frost bitten a little. It is beginning to get very dull & hazy all day, something like the sort of light we have at home about 5 o'clock in the end of Novr.

Nov. 28th   Saturday is always a busy day & we generally have a visit from the Esquimaux to see if there is any bread dust, as that is divided amongst them. They are at present very ill-supplied with food on account of the open winter which prevents them travelling to the places where they stored it in summer.

Nov. 29th   It is very cold today. I have been obliged to keep below all day for fear of getting frost bitten. Several of the men have had slight touches in their faces. Divine service in the afternoon.

Nov. 30th   The boats have been taken on shore for the winter. The boiler for the oil is now set on shore. It was filled with snow today, a fire lit in the furnace & found to answer well. I have had a walk on deck today.

Dec. 1st   The first copper of oil has been boiled today – everything has answered well. We have full moon today & full moon again on the 30th, making two full moons in one month.

Dec. 2nd   I went on shore early today to see the dogs fed from the refuse of the oil. They were like a pack of wolves. The man was obliged to throw the tub from him or then they would have trampled him down, so hungry were they.

Dec. 3rd   I had a fine walk to the top of the hill behind the house & was rewarded for my trouble with a sight of the sun shining in all his glory. The prospect was truly beautiful. We had the water calm & lovely at a short distance, the hills covered with snow except here & there, a large black rock standing out in releif, & in the valley below we saw all the little colony carrying on their different occupations with spirit & alacrity. William has been away about 8 miles with two Esquimaux & their dog sledge. He enjoyed his trip very much. I have just got a present of 4 part[ridges] from the Esquimaux.

Dec. 4th   A fresh breeze today. People employed cleaning out the boiler from which 184 gallons of oil had beeen drawn off.

Dec. 5th   I am always amused on Saturday watching the weighing out of the provisions to the Esquimaux. In the afternoon I had a drive in the sledge drawn by twelve dogs. It was very pleasant but rather cold.

Dec. 6th. Sunday   I have had a severe headache all day, which I attribute to my being out so late last night on the sledge. About midnight a native woman & boy arrived at the ship from Kingite. They had been obliged to leave behind them an old man who had got himself frost-bitten in his feet. She had taken off his [boots?] & tried to restore the circulation, but could not. It had taken her ten days to come down, making for herself & boy a snow hut every night. All the food they had was five salmon, three of which she left with the man. As soon in the morning as possible Mr. Penny dispatched two native sledges with pro-visions to try & bring the man down, but if they found him dead they were to proceed farther up the inlet & bring some of their summer-stored salmon.

Dec. 7th   The men commenced today cutting blubber again to get another copper boiled, as there is nothing to feed the dogs with but the refuse which comes from the oil. Indeed, the natives eat of it themselves, although they do not like us to think so. It does not look so bad as one would suppose, being boiled with fresh snow. It does them no harm & looks like turtle soup for all the bits of fat float about & the water turns into glue.

Dec. 8th   It is rather cloudy today. I have been on shore as we all are everyone about his own business. The Dr. visits the sick twice every day & is always anxiously looked for, as he is generally provided with something for them to eat. Mr. Warmow also visits the huts daily, but has much to contend with as food is very scarce with them at present & they have no idea of listening to spiritual consolation when hungry. Another copper of oil boiled which yielded 200 gallons.

Dec. 9th   The second mate with William & an Esquimaux set off with a sledge to go down to Middleaktuak Islands for some seals as also to see what property belonging to the Arctic Co. had been left by Messrs. Martin & McKinnon & which had been neglected by the Alibi. The distance is only 15 miles, but after going two thirds of the way they were obliged to return, not being able to cross for water.

Dec. 10th   I was unable to go on shore today, it was so cold & windy. The people could not boil their copper for cold.

Dec. 11th   Still very cold & a strong wind blowing from the N.E. I went on shore, but had some difficulty in finding the road, the snow was blowing so thick. However, I did not find the cold too much.

Dec. 12th   This being my birthday, Mr. Penny gave the men a half Holy-day & they had the two vessels decorated with their flags. I had a number of kind congratulations on the occasion & twice was saluted with three hearty cheers by all hands. The Esquimaux seemed also much taken up & one had a flag displayed on the top of his snow house. Dancing commenced at 4 o clock & was kept up until 10. Every body seemed very happy. It was a beautiful day & I took a walk to the top of the hill to get a look of the sun. But I must not conclude this day without mentioning the neat & appropriate speech made by the

Dr. when he proposed my health after dinner, although I must not for a moment suppose I was entitled to all the compliments he paid me.

Dec. 13th   It is windy to-day & I have not been on shore. Some of the people had a long walk before Divine service. Some natives have gone to Tongite & some to Shoumea for their stores of deer & one of them has caught a large seal which was divided skin & all amongst them, it being their usual custom to do so to the first one they catch in the season.

Dec. 14th   Strong wind. People unable to work on shore for the cold.

Dec. 15th   People all employed cutting up blubber & boiling oil. Weather cold. I was on shore in several of their edloos [i.e., igloos]. It is really wonderful what one can get accustomed to for I can now crawl out & in as well as any Esquimaux & eat mactac with pleasure.

Dec. 16th   I had a pleasant walk today on the flaw out nearly as far as the sealers. The Dr. & Mr. Penny accompanied me. We met Mr. Warmow who informed us that two seals were caught, at which we were very glad as oil & food is very scarce with the natives. Mr. Penny walked on & joined the natives, but the Dr & I felt too tired to do so. Having [walked] three miles over hummocky ice we were almost done up before we reached the vessel again. Mr P. returned about an hour after us, bringing William home with [him]. He generally goes out to the sealing with the natives & is a favourite with them.

Dec. 17th   The natives & William set off again today [to] fish. I took a walk to the hill head to take a look of them & get a glimpse of the sun. There was another seal caught today. William was second harpoon & was quite elated at his luck.

Dec. 18th   I had a walk to the opposite side today. Weather very fine. I enjoy excellent health. One of the sledges returned to day, bringing a load of deer with him. He gave us one newly shot. It is a great treat.

Dec. 19th   The second mate, William, & two natives set off today to complete their journey to Middleeaktualik. It is a very fine day. I had a walk to the top of a hill to get a glimpse of the travellers. Mr. Penny & the Dr. accompanied me. We saw them with the telescope about ten miles down & expect them to return tonight.

Dec. 20th. Sunday   A soft blowing day. Mr. Penny & the mate walked
to the top of the hill to look if they saw the sledge returning, not
having done so as expected last night. Mr. Penny was much alarmed
for their safety as he saw some of their dogs returning & the water
almost surrounding the islands with no appearance of the sledge. We
looked for it most anxiously all the evening. A boat had been taken
down to the flaw by Captn. Cheyne & the men, who were all most
active. One of the dogs was found to have his leg tied up, which
enabled us to judge that they had reached the land. That gave us hope
& we could trust in God for his protection to them if it was his Divine
will. We had our church service in the evening, but, the wind getting
very strong, I spent a most anxious & sleepless night.

Dec. 21st   Capt. Cheyne, who is a most active man, was on board
by 5 oclock after calling all the natives who were to go down with
Mr. Penny & the Dr. taking with them the boat & three sledges. They
all started at 6 oclock after having breakfasted & great was their joy
when they met the missing sledge about half way up. They had been
unable to return, the ice being so rough although still attached to the
back of the island beyond our sight. They had visited two of the
islands, the mate & William to look after the property of the Arctic
Copny & the natives to bring up food. They had driven until late the
preceding evening & had been obliged to make a snow house on the
ice & remain all night. I went ashore about 11 oclock to take a look
from the hill head & was overjoyed to see Mr. Warmow come running
towards me with his handkerchief tied on the top of his walking stick,
which I knew was a signal that all was right & I from my heart thanked
God for his great mercies to us sinners.

Dec. 22nd   The wind is blowing very strong today & increasing every
hour. The sledge which was dispatched for the old man has returned,
bringing him down. He has lost all his toes, but is wonderfully well otherwise. They have also brought down with them several bags full of
salmon. They gave Mr. Penny five bag fulls. We had one today, which
was a great treat.

Dec. 23rd   People employed boiling oil. Mr. Penny went to the hill
head & saw nothing but water both up & down the inlet, the strong
south-east wind having carried away all the ice.

Dec. 24th   Still windy & cold. Oil drawn off & copper cleaned.

Dec. 25th Christ-mas day was kept as a holiday. We were all very happy & had a splendid dinner. In the evening one of the natives came to anounce to us the birth of a son. Mr. Penny named him John Barrow.

Dec. 26th I was awoke this morning by a suffocating feeling & had I remained in bed a little longer I beleive I should have been so, had I not [gone] out to the air. It was caused by something on the wood by which the fire was kindled. The funnel is copper & that having got red hot, combined with something noxious on the wood, caused such a pernicious gas to generate that the pain in the lungs was excessive. I got a severe headache & a pain in my chest all day. Fortunately the mate came to our assistance & also experienced much difficulty in breathing.

Dec. 27th. Sunday It still keeps cold & windy. A sledge came along late last night from Noualaktalik [i.e., Niantilik]. It proved to be Newbooligar. He informed us that the Alibi had got another fish killed by Tessiwine, who the master of the Alibi had by falsehood induced to go on board the Arctic. He had also harpooned 2 whales for her, one he lost. He likewise informed us that Capt. Stewart had not landed any provisions for [us] as he had been instructed to by the Directors & Mr. Penny. I think he is about the worst man I ever met with. This is the Esquimaux who harpooned the fish in dispute between the owners of the Alibi & Clara. Mr. Penny requested Mr. Warmow to ask him to describe the circumstances connected with it, which he did most distinctly. He had harpooned the whale while in the boat belonging to the Clara. He attached his [illegible word] to her but the line broke & the Alibi boat then came up & fired into her & secured her. There can be no dispute about her, only a dishonourable action in Capt. Souter in trying to claim her. Divine service in the afternoon.

Dec. 28th I had a walk on shore today & found it very cold. We brought out some malt with us & one of the men commenced to brew this morning in the house ashore. I would feel much at a loss for amusement were it not [for] the natives. They are constantly coming & going. I generally make out about 20 cups of tea every evening for them after we are served. Poor things, they are very happy & contented with little.

Dec. 29th I could scarcely sleep last night for cold & today could not face the land so great is the cold. The thermometer stands 20 below zero.

Dec. 30th   This has been a fine calm day. I had a walk on shore in the after noon. The moon is full & was shining bright, making everything as clear as day. The natives & William were off at the fishing, but did not succeed.

Dec. 31st   This being the last day of the year, we all sat up until 12 P.M., when the sailors came aft & wished us a happy new year, each one getting a glass of gin & a bit of cake.

The illness affecting the native community lingered until the second half of December. Food scarcity at the harbour may have contributed to the severity and duration of the outbreak. As with clothes, there was usually some exchange of food between wintering whalemen and Eskimos. The ships contained enough provisions to feed the crews during the voyage of about fourteen months, but because their food lacked the antiscorbutic benefits of fresh meat, whaling masters depended on their hired Eskimos to supply carcasses, quarters, or joints of caribou and other game, and fish. The ships' natives and their families normally subsisted on their own food – the meat, fish, and eggs obtained by hunting and gathering – but because wives and children were sometimes left at the harbour when the men were off hunting, and because the hunts were not always successful, whaling captains often distributed some of their shipboard provisions, such as soup, biscuit, coffee, and molasses, on a daily basis. Thus, each group relied primarily on the food to which it was accustomed but supplemented its diet with food from the other group, either for nutritional reasons or of necessity.

Before European whalers began wintering in Cumberland Sound in 1853, the Eskimos had obtained all they required for life from the resources of land and sea. Their hunting activities were carefully attuned to the seasonal variations in climate and animal life. Winter was always a critical time because many of the animals that provided them with meat, oil, skins, furs, ivory, antlers, bones, and baleen had migrated south. In addition, winter imposed some severe climatic challenges, including extremely low temperatures, reduced light, and blowing snow, which tended to make hunting the few species that remained in the Arctic more difficult and dangerous. To prepare for winter food scarcity, therefore, it was customary to establish caches of food during the summer and autumn. Carcasses of caribou, walrus, and fish, naturally frozen and protected from marauding animals by heavy boulders, would last until needed several months later.

The annual hunting cycle also had to take into account the interruption to travel and hunting caused by the freeze-up and break-up of ice. The unstable young ice surface of fall and the rotting old ice surface of spring could not be safely crossed by dogsleds or on foot, or penetrated by skin boats. During these environmental transitions, it was best to be on the mainland, where terrestrial game could still be pursued and food caches visited if necessary. But when Eskimos accepted employment with a wintering whaleship, they had to be available at the winter harbour chosen by the captain at the time when he needed them. This meant that their usual cycle of migration and hunting was certain to be disrupted. The whaling ship had to arrive at the winter harbour before freeze-up, and if the captain had selected an island as his winter base, the Eskimos and whalemen were isolated from the mainland, its terrestrial resources, and their food caches until such time as a solid ice cover connected the island to the mainland.

Climatic and oceanographic factors affected the length of the freeze-up period. In Hudson Bay, where American whalers began wintering a few years after Margaret Penny's voyage, a strong current running between Marble Island and the mainland retarded the formation of an ice bridge. When unusually mild temperatures delayed freeze-up even more than usual, whalemen and Eskimos on the island might be isolated for most of the winter, unable to reach the mainland to secure caribou and musk oxen. In such seasons, scurvy took a dreadful toll.

At Kekerten the two ships were encircled by landfast ice in early November, but the eight-mile-wide strait separating the island from the nearest point of Cumberland Peninsula was still unfrozen. Three native whaleboats that had been sent to retrieve meat cached on the mainland sailed back to the island with food and some dogs on the fourth day of the month, but after that date no voyages are mentioned, and at the end of the month the whaleboats were stored on shore for the winter. The first crossing over the ice between the mainland and the island occurred on 6 December, when the starving woman and boy arrived on foot at the harbour, having left a man crippled by frostbite ten days' travel to the north. Penny sent out a rescue party the next morning – the first reference to sled travel across the strait. For a full month, Kekerten Island had been completely cut off from the mainland as sea ice formed, became thicker, and consolidated into a continuous surface – a month during which the eighty Eskimos on the island were unable to hunt caribou or collect the meat stored in caches on the mainland. As Margaret noted on 28 November, the whalemen considered it to be an unusually "open winter."

Entries in journals and logbooks during the month of enforced isolation reveal the seriousness of the food crisis and the measures taken to alleviate it. Warmow mentioned a family with nothing to eat but seaweed, and Margaret reported people coming to the ship to receive "bread dust" – the crumbs left in empty hardtack casks. According to Penny, the Eskimos were "very ill off for food and useing our food." He felt "obliged to supply them with provisions just as much as keep their lives in," but even the sparse daily allotment of soup, tea, sugar, and bread was beginning to strain the resources of the ships. "I wish they had some food," Penny wrote a few days later, "for they come very hard upon us."

Adding to problem were the sledge dogs. In addition to those at the harbour, thirty had been left on the island farther north to scavenge for food until they were needed for winter travel, but twenty of these turned up in late November having "sented out the ships some 8 miles off" and reached them over the ice. By the beginning of December there were between sixty and seventy dogs at the harbour. Six more were retrieved from the northern island a few days later; the rest had died from hunger. Penny decided to have oil rendered out of the blubber of the whale they had captured in September so that the leftover bits of shrivelled skin and meat could be fed to the dogs. Using the large copper cauldron already set up in the small boiling house ashore, the men started work on 1 December. The irresistible aroma of heated blubber created a frenzy among the ravenous animals, some of which repeatedly forced their way into the flimsy hut and had to be beaten back. So desperate were they to get hold of something edible that they struggled to get into the cauldron of boiling oil, which the men had to cover with a weighted lid and then tie down with ropes. "What a scene with the poor dogs when the refuse was emptyed out," commented Penny, while Margaret compared them to "a pack of wolves."

Persistent efforts to catch seals at their breathing holes in the ice were unsuccessful, even when the whalemen made up nets and metal-shafted harpoons to help. Day after day the hunters returned empty-handed, and all of November passed without a single seal being killed. And athough some dogsleds reached the mainland in December, surprisingly little appears to have been brought back from hunts and summer caches. The hunger continued at Kekerten, and Penny's men boiled twice a week to keep the dogs alive. But the scraps from rendering blubber, known to British whalemen as "fenks," provided more than dog food; they also constituted a desperation diet "for the Esquimaux," as the logbook recorded. Penny noted that the boiled shreds of meat and skin were "very good indeed," but one wonders whether he meant good to his own taste, good to the Eskimos' taste, or merely adequate to keep the people from starving. Margaret, perhaps more sensitive and perceptive than her husband, and keeping a personal record rather than an official logbook, remarked, "Indeed the natives eat of it … although they do not like us to think so." It is hardly surprising that there was a stigma attached to consuming what was scarely fit for dogs.

The food crisis was compounded by the shortage of sea mammal oil, the usual fuel for the soapstone lamps that provided heat and light within the snow houses. Penny noted that "the poor Esquimaux have neither food nor fuel but [are] still very happy and an example to civilised men." At the end of November, they were "both cold and hungry." The whalemen extracted almost a thousand gallons of whale oil from blubber during the month of December, enough to heat all the snow houses for a long time, but none of it was used for this purpose. Oil had commercial value, and the two crews would share in the profits when it was sold at home port. To allocate part of the oil to the Eskimos in time of need was apparently too big a sacrifice to make, even though the native helpers had assisted in the whaling effort.

Through November and December the native community was locked in the grip of a self-reinforcing cycle. Undernourished and weak from illness, the men were less effective in the hunt and failed to obtain the meat, blubber, and skins required for winter food, heat, and clothing. Poorly fed, heated, and clothed, they were less capable of making long sorties to secure food and were more susceptible to infections.

Although interrupted repeatedly by gales, the process of freeze-up continued through November and December. The ice that had formed first in protected bays extended outward to meet the frosty fringes around other islands and then continued to expand until eventually it formed a continuous cover over most of Cumberland Sound. The enlarging ice surface allowed for extensive travel on foot and by dogsled.

Seal hunters went out daily; some parties crossed to the mainland; two
small expeditions tried to reach the island of Miliakdjuin, almost fifteen miles to the southeast (to retrieve whaling equipment left there a
year or two earlier); and on 27 December a dogsled arrived from Niantilik, more than sixty miles away on the opposite coast – the first settlement Margaret Penny had visited in the previous summer.

The news brought from Niantilik by Newbullygar concerned the Aberdeen Arctic Company's whaler *Alibi*, commanded by the recalcitrant
Captain Stewart. In early September, just before the *Alibi* departed for
Scotland, Penny had chased the ship across Cumberland Sound to confront Stewart and remind him to leave surplus provisions for the use of
his two ships during the winter. But Newbullygar now reported that
Stewart had left nothing. He also reported that the expert harpooner
Tessuin, whom Penny had employed before and wanted to hire again,
had been persuaded by Stewart – "by falsehood," Margaret wrote – to
work for the *Arctic*, a non-company ship. Tessuin had struck two whales
and secured one of them before the *Arctic* sailed for Scotland, thus
putting money in the pockets of rival owners.

More than a year earlier, Captain Stewart of the *Alibi* had been involved in a dispute with Captain Sutter (also spelled Souter, Soutar,
Soutter) of the Peterhead whaler *Clara*, probably the same captain who
had shipped all the able-bodied men from Niantilik in August 1857,
leaving the women, children, and infirm to shift for themselves. At
issue was the ownership of a whale harpooned in 1856 by boats from
the two ships and lanced by a boat from a third, the *Sophia*. Both Newbullygar and Tessuin had been involved, the former working for the
Clara and the latter for the *Sophia*. Penny now took the opportunity of
interviewing Newbullygar about the event, and as Margaret recorded
on 27 December, the report convinced him that Stewart's claim had
been justified and Sutter's was "dishonourable."

Disputes occasionally arose when boats from more than one ship
pursued the same whale or when a harpooned whale broke free and
was later harpooned by a boat from another ship, or when a captured
whale went adrift and was picked up by another whaler. Enough incidents of this sort during two and a half centuries of arctic whaling had
led to the formation of rules by which arguments could usually be
settled on the whaling grounds without costly and time-consuming
recourse to courts of law at home. In 1820, when Captain William
Scoresby, Jr, outlined the tacit code of law governing British whalers,
he recognized two underlying principles. The first was that a captured
whale, or "fast fish," whether alive or dead, remained the property of

its captors only as long as they retained a connection with it. The usual connection was a harpoon and line from the whale to an occupied whaleboat or whaling ship, but the principle could be extended to cover someone merely holding the whale with a boat-hook or even a man in the water touching the whale (Scoresby 1820, 2:319–21). If the line broke on the boat-hook slipped out or the man floated away, the connection was severed and possession ceased. The second principle, a corollary to the first, was that a whale not so connected, termed a "loose fish," belonged to no one and was "fair game" to all.

A strict application of these principles sometimes seemed unfair. Suppose, for instance, that a whaleboat crew had harpooned a whale and played it for several dangerous hours and that just when the animal was tiring and the men had drawn their boat up closer to make the kill, the whale dived beneath the pack ice, forcing the crew to leap into the frigid water and attempt to save themselves from destruction; and that when the wounded whale later emerged, trailing harpoon, lines, and whatever remained of the boat, it was lanced and killed by a fresh crew from another ship. The latter crew could lawfully take possession of the whale, while the crew that had laboured so long, taken so many risks, and exhausted the animal (thus making its killing easier) had no claim on the whale or even on their own lines and harpoon still attached to the carcass. The instant they abandoned their boat, they had severed their connection with the whale and lost possession, turning a fast fish into a loose fish. In practice, however, the letter of the law was not always applied. A decent and considerate captain sometimes offered to share the prize that was lawfully his with the ship that had first harpooned it.

The dispute in 1856 turned on the question of whether the whale harpooned for the *Clara* by Newbullygar and his native crew had become a loose fish by the time the boats from the *Alibi* planted their harpoons and a native boat from the *Sophia*, headed by Tessuin, began to lance the dying animal. What made the case interesting was Captain Sutter's contention that a different concept of a loose fish had evolved in Cumberland Sound because the native whaleboat crews employed by British ships used a different method of catching whales. Although they operated in whaleboats with European harpoons, lines, and other gear obtained second hand from whaling ships, the Eskimos had retained from their ancient tradition of sea mammal hunting the effective technique of employing inflated sealskin drogues. Instead of connecting the whaleboat to the harpooned whale with a long line – as the British and Americans did – they simply attached a few drogues to a comparatively short line and threw them overboard in order to tire the animal until it could be killed. Their method was much less dangerous.

Captain Sutter pointed out that, in Cumberland Sound, British whalers not only employed Eskimo crews who whaled with drogues, but often carried drogues in their own boats. He argued that it was ludicrous to say that a crew that had attached harpoons, lines, and drogues to a whale and was still actively pursuing it, waiting for the opportune moment to make the kill, had no right to the whale simply because it was not connected to it all the while. He contended that British whaling law had been modified in Cumberland Sound to take into account the Eskimo method of fishing, and that a whale with harpoon and drogues attached remained the property of the boat that had affixed them. Captain Stewart of the *Alibi*, on the other hand, claimed possession of the whale on the basis of the usual British concept of a loose fish. He conceded that Newbullygar's crew from the *Clara* had been first to harpoon the whale, but insisted that they had relinquished their right to the prize as soon as they tossed the line and drogues overboard, breaking their connection with the animal. Crews from the *Alibi* had then harpooned with lines attached to their boats, thereby gaining possession of the loose fish.

Captain Sutter and the co-owners of the *Clara* decided to press charges against Captain Stewart of the *Alibi* and the Aberdeen Arctic Company in the Scottish courts. In the summons of 13 February 1857 they sought compensation of £1,200 for the *Alibi*'s "illegal seizure ... of a whale" (Scotland 1859–60, 3). Captain Penny, whose role in the Aberdeen Arctic Company gave him a special interest in the case, may have wondered about the reliability of the account of events provided by his irascible colleague, Alexander Stewart. Now, at Kekerten, he was able to hear the story directly from Newbullygar, the harpooner who had first struck the whale on behalf of Captain Sutter's non-company ship *Clara*. Newbullygar's report convinced Penny that Stewart had been right in claiming the whale for the *Alibi*. Penny's conclusion is, in a way, surprising. Considering his concern for Eskimo welfare, his dependence on Eskimo labour, and his willingness to adopt Eskimo methods (including the use of drogues), one might expect him to have initiated – or at least approved of – changes in the whaling regulations pertaining to Cumberland Sound so that native crews harpooning whales with drogues in their customary way would not be penalized. But Penny appreciated the simplicity and wisdom of the loose fish concept and realized that to abandon it would open the door to countless difficulties of interpretation. He advised his own crews not to rely solely on drogues if boats from other ships were in the vicinity, knowing that they risked losing their whale.

Margaret reveals that the dispute had not simply been one of native drogue fishing verus European line fishing. According to her understanding of the event, Newbullygar had been "attached" to the whale with a line but the line had broken. However, Captain Sutter's court testimony a year later, based on what the Eskimo had told him on the day of the dispute, was slightly different. Sutter conceded that Newbullygar's crew had controlled the line from the boat but stated that the line had run completely out, whereupon Newbullygar had let it go with drogues attached. Whether the line had broken or run out is unimportant. The point is that if Margaret's information was correct, Newbullygar had not in fact been whaling in native fashion with drogues alone but in European fashion with the line connected to the whaleboat; and then, at the last moment, before the line ran out, he had attached the drogues. There would not have been any justification, therefore, for relaxing the loose fish rule. Captain Sutter's assertion that "a drogged whale was the property of the crew who first put a harpooon with drogs attached into the fish" (Scotland 1859–60, 19) appears to have been a smoke screen or perhaps wishful thinking. Margaret called it "a dishonourable action."

Winter was steadily closing in. During the short days approaching the solstice, the feeble sun climbed half-heartedly into the bottom of the sky, then steadily sank again. The cold became more intense, making outdoor work uncomfortable and decorating whalemen's cheeks and noses with insidious grey patches of frostbite, which the natives helpfully pointed out. On the tenth, Penny suspended the boiling of blubber because it was too cold, but this was a rare concession. Most of the time, work and recreational activities continued as usual. The lowest temperatures occurred in the last few days of December, when the mercury dropped to minus twenty-six degrees and even Margaret admitted that she could "scarcely sleep" at night. The coal-burning galley stove provided heat during the day, and there may have been coal fires in the forecastle and in the cabin as well. But coals were evidently in short supply; they had been distributed among the two ships and two shore stations, and several months of cold weather lay ahead. A few entries in the *Lady Franklin*'s logbook dispel any impression that all was warm and snug in the sleeping quarters. In mid-November Penny wrote, "No fires at night sleep at zero in cabin," and a few days later he remarked that although the men living in the house ashore "would like a fire all night, this we can not afford yet." Whether the luxury of night-time fires had been allowed by late December we cannot know. If any stoves burned on the *Lady Franklin*, they certainly fell a long way short of providing Margaret with a decent sleep.

A number of enjoyable activities offset the deepening gloom associated with decreasing sunlight and increasing cold. Margaret visited the snow houses, rode in a dogsled, walked on the landfast ice, watched the hunters stalking seals, shared their maktak, entertained women on board ship every evening ("they are constantly coming and going," she wrote), and celebrated festive occasions with enthusiasm. On her forty-fifth birthday both ships, the house, the workshop, and even a native snow house were festooned with signal flags ("a plesant sight it was on the lonly waste of snow," the ship's logbook recorded). The sailors gave her three cheers, not merely once but twice, as Margaret noted in her journal with evident satisfaction. At dinner, Dr Grant, with all the eloquence one expects from a university education, paid Margaret many compliments as he proposed a toast to her health. Dancing continued for six hours. Two weeks later, Christmas Day seemed to take on a special significance when the wife of Noodlook gave birth to a son. Captain Penny provided presents for each of the parents. Then, on New Year's Eve, Margaret, William, and the ships' officers stayed up until midnight to welcome the year 1858, and offered gin and cake to the sailors.

Penny gave the name John Barrow to the boy born on Christmas Day. It seems somewhat doubtful that Noodlook and his wife had ever heard of John Barrow, Jr, whose father – one of the founders of the Royal Geographical Society and second secretary of the Admiralty for almost four decades – had played a dominant role in guiding British arctic exploration up to 1845. Penny was a friend of John Barrow, Jr, and corresponded with him for a quarter-century, hence the choice of name for Noodlook's son. It may seem presumptuous for a whaling master visiting Baffin Island to bestow an alien name on an Eskimo baby in much the same way that he would assign a European name to a geographical feature that already possessed a native name; but for linguistic convenience, whalemen used their own system of names for both places and people. For ease of pronunciation, they applied Euro-American names to many of the Eskimos they hired in northern Canada. These might be ordinary names such as Ben, Billie, Gilbert, Harry, Joe, Mary, Paul, and Suzy; descriptive (though not always complimentary) names such as Molasses, Shoofly, Scotch Tom, Starboard Eye (a one-eyed man), Fatty, and Pie-face; or names commemorating people either dead or living, such as John Ell (for John L. Sullivan), Santa Anna, Stonewall Jackson, and – in Penny's case – Warmow and John Barrow. Of course, the Eskimos used their own names among their own people and continued to assign native names to their children, but when associating with the whalers they reverted to the European nicknames. On the other side of the coin, the Eskimos had their own nicknames for many of the whalemen, though they were discreet enough to keep these largely to themselves.

The early months of winter contained a few unfortunate episodes as well as the seasonal festivities. The arrival on 6 December of the woman who had been forced to abandon her starving, frost-bitten, disabled husband and walk with her son for ten days to the winter harbour to get help was a vivid reminder that the arctic environment was harsh and unforgiving. When the rescuers reached the scene, they found the man miraculously alive after two and a half weeks alone in an unheated snow house with only three fish to eat. For another week he was on a sledge before reaching Kekerten, where Dr Grant was able to dress his rock-hard feet. The frost-bitten parts sloughed off and the feet were soon "taking on a healthy appearance." The man appeared to be cheerful.

Margaret's journal mentions her son Billie only three times in the first four months of the voyage and infrequently afterwards. His two birthdays pass without remark. She does not seem to have been greatly concerned about his activities, his safety, or his upbringing. But children were "older" then. Many boys embarked on seafaring careers in the whaling trade or in the Royal Navy at Billie's age. The most famous British whaling master of all time, William Scoresby, Jr, first sailed to the Greenland Sea in his father's ship when only ten (Stamp and Stamp 1976, 8). Horatio Nelson, hero of the Battle of Trafalgar, joined his first naval ship at the age of eleven (Walder 1978, 9). At the age of thirteen, young Billie Penny was already in full training for adulthood and possibly for a career at sea. He therefore came more under the authority of his father, the commander of the vessel, than of his mother, who was a mere supernumerary on board. On a ship worked entirely by men, lavish displays of motherly affection would have embarrassed him and undermined his stature. Even so, one wonders at Margaret's seeming indifference to his welfare.

Billie often went walking on the land with Captain Cheyne, Brother Warmow, Dr Grant, or his parents. On some of these outings he shot birds and small game; proficiency with a fowling piece was expected of

men of rank, authority, or class. His father recorded in the ship's logbook one small adventure: "Mr. Warmow and William away hunting he
lost sight of the boy who nearly lost his life in the face of precipice however he lost not his presence of mind, not so Mr. Warmow."

After the ships took up their winter quarters at Kekerten, Penny
often entrusted Billie to the care of Eskimo hunters who were setting
off by dogsled to hunt seals at the floe edge, and on one occasion the
boy distinguished himself by hitting a seal with a second harpoon.
Twice Billie accompanied the second mate John Lucas and one or two
Eskimo men on sledging trips towards Miliakdjuin, an island group
about fifteen miles to the south. On the first try they were stopped by
open water and turned back the same day. Ten days later they tried
again. Margaret, her husband, and the doctor watched by telescope
from the island's summit as the party receded in the distance. Patches
of open water were still visible, and when the travellers failed to return
that night or the next and when two of their dogs made their way back
to the harbour, it looked as if a disaster had occurred. Captain Penny
set off with three rescue dogsleds and a boat, and happily found Billie
and the others making their way homeward after an eventful trip. The
episode was serious enough to provoke some signs of motherly concern at last. Margaret wrote two unusually long journal entries and admitted to spending "a most anxious & sleepless night." Penny simply
noted in his logbook, "Mother anxious about her boy," without admit-
ting to any anxiety on his own part.

I Had My Usual Tea Party

1 January – 1 February 1858

January 1st, 1858   The new year has commenced with fine, bright weather. The sailors have had a holiday & we all dined in the seamans apartment along with them & about 70 natives. We had a splendid dinner, the greatest delicacies being contributed by the natives, consisting of 6 fine large salmon & 2 quarters of deer. The evening passed off very pleasantly & everyone seemed to enjoy themselves.

Jan. 2nd   I feel rather out of sorts today with my late hours. Weather still fine.

Jan. 3rd   Every body on land today. Divine service in the afternoon, at which all attended.

Jan. 4th   The mate (Mr. Birnie), the Dr., Billie, & 11 natives started today for Newbuian & Nouiactalik to try to bring over Tessiwyne, who had been left there & had his mind poisoned by the falsehoods of that bad man in the Alibi.

Jan. 5th   Rather cloudy today, but not so cold. Several more of the natives have started today for deer hunting. I had a long walk on shore & made some calls.

Jan. 6th   Still cloudy today but calm. We feel rather dull for want of our three travellers. I hope they are getting on well.

Jan. 7th Wind blowing very strong today from the s.e. People unable to work on shore for cold.

Jan. 8th Wind still high & very cold. I feel anxious about our young travellers, but must comfort myself with the knowledge that God can protect them everywhere & earnestly pray that He may guide them on their way.

Jan. 9th One of the natives, that old man who got his feet frosted, died last night. He told my husband he had no wish to live for all his children were dead that he loved, & he wanted to go to them that he might again be happy. "This was a heathen's testimony of a hereafter." Mr. Penny made the sailors assist to bury him.

Jan. 10th. Sabbath The weather is very cold, but I always manage to keep myself warm & comfortable. I have likewise plenty of amusement with the natives & I seldom find them forward or ill disposed of their own accord. I, every evening after we are done with our cabin tea, fill the kettle with water & make out about from 20 to 30 cups for the natives who come to me in rotation. Divine service in the after noon read by Mr. Warmow.

Jan. 11th Very cold & windy. Nothing doing today on shore except by the trades people, who always attend their regular hours in the work-shop.

Jan. 12th Oil drawn off today. Weather very cold. No seals getting.

Jan. 13th I took a short walk on land but found it too cold to go far. Natives all on board cutting up the whales tail, which is to be boiled for them in the copper, food being so scarce.

Jan. 14th We have had a very strong gale all night. I could feel the ship shakeing very much. Weather most boisterous all morning. The natives who were away deer hunting have returned today, having shot three deer. One of them brought a nice peice & a tongue for me. I feel very anxious about our absent ones.

Jan. 15th People busy cutting up blubber to fill the copper. I have not been on shore today, the weather being cold & windy. Two of the natives were made very happy to night by a present of a bonnet box each. I had my usual tea party.

Jan. 16th   Weather very cold. Provisions served out as usual. Natives always happy when they get the bread dust.

Jan. 17th. Sabbath   A fine day. We can again see the sun from the deck, which makes it very pleasant. Divine service always attended by the men with great apparent sincerity.

Jan. 18th   This being Mr. Warmow's birthday, the colours were hoisted on both vessels & we had a bottle of wine to drink his health after dinner. (I saw today a beautiful [triluminae?].)

Jan. 19th   Our hunters have set off again for the hills.

Jan. 20th   People all busy today filling the copper & boiling oil. I had a long walk on the shore & a treat of mactak when I returned.

Jan. 21st   Fine bright weather. About 8 oclock the Dr. returned with the first sledge from Newbeouen & announced that Billie & my old friend New Lairlaw would be up in about 2 hours more, which they were, all well & in good spirits. Billie & Mr. Birnie had been down as far as Neouaktalik to see Tessiwine. They also called upon the Americans who were very kind to them; in all they travelled about 200 miles. The ice being so bad, at one place it was too thin to bear the weight of a person & the poor Dr. fell through & would have been unable to extricate himself had it not been for the assistance of Billie, all the natives having run off whenever he fell in. Notwithstanding, they were were quite well pleased with their journey & had executed it well.

Jan. 22nd   This is a very cold day. I feel very happy that our young travellers returned last night for it looks very lowring now.

Jan. 23rd   Weather bad & very cold. Little doing today.

Jan. 24th   I feel so cold today that I am unable to go on deck. Divine service.

Jan. 25th   Still very cold & a strong wind blowing from the S.E.

Jan. 26th   The gale still continues. Thermometer varying from 30 to 35 below zero.

Jan. 27th   The gale a little abated today. I have been able to venture on deck, which I always like to do if possible.

Jan. 28th   A sledge should have gone down to Medleaktuak Islands ‡ but for some cause not known to us the natives had not obeyed the command ‡

Jan. 29th   I had a walk on shore today with Mr. Penny. He went in to Pillouseak's edloos ‡ and found him much out of spirits. Some evil disposed person had caused him to beheave very ill. Certain it was that they had rendered the poor creature very unhappy and deprived him of the advantages which that [*sic*] Mr. Penny intended. ‡

Jan. 30th   Mr. Cheyne & Alex Ross started today for the Salmon Lake, ‡ having collected some 12 dogs for their sledge, as the distance was some 60 or 70 miles. Temperature was low but fine weather and clear, so having provided themselves with a week provision they started upon their voyage of exploration for the future advantage of wintering parties. ‡

‡ *Sunday, 31st Jan. 1858*   Continued keen frost and clear weather. At noon had Divine service and a walk on the land ice. The natives generly put on their best deer skin dresses and come on board to tea, beheaving very politely and never fail to add when they finish with many thanks for your kindness. ‡

‡ *Monday, Feb. 1st*   This month and the former is generly the most severe in the Arctic climate, the thermometer ranging from zero to −30, −35, and unless blowing strong we are enabled to go about our ordinary duties, though Jack often gets light frost bit by his carelessness. We call all the people out at 7 A.M. The work people go to the workshop, the blacksmith, carpenter, cooper light their fires and prepare for work. Sailors go 200 ft. high with a sledge to a lake for fresh ice, which they bring down in a [ravine?] over the snow. The surface is hard frozen and down it comes at a great rate but not to quick for Jack. Breakfast waits his return. At 9 A.M. clean ship down, the Esquimaux busy assisting. Some half-dozen of them live constantly on board, widows sons or orphans very happpy to be employed by cook or steward,

cheerful & kind to one another & never quarrel. The Esquimaux sealers generaly wait to get a cup of coffee and then start off with his
pointer in [tracking?] that is if he is going only a short distance without his sledge. If he returns successful the little one[s] spy him from a
distance and off they are to meet him and drive the dog on shore who
is harnest on to the seal's head, the Esquimaux hunter paying a visit to
the cook to see if any soup or a cup of tea can be procured to refresh
him after an absence of 8 or 10 hours watching. This he never fails to
be supplied with if anyone be moving about on his return. The seal to
the Esquimaux are food & clothing and his summer housing, for their
tents are made of the skins. The [frame?] to clean the skins this is to
them a tedious process. Every [female?] has as part of her establishment some fifty wooden pins about 6 inches long. With them she pins
skins tight out in winter on the frozen snow. As the oil oses out of the
skins she scrapes it off with her half moon knife. This generaly takes
three or four days if keen frosty weather. After this date they are rolled
up. If coarse they are kept for a summer tent, which requires 15 skins,
as they generaly have a new tent every year, the old tent being taken to
line the inside of the snow eddloo or hut. The form is a dome in fact a
perfect arch so the summer tent has to be converted into the shape of
the dome, therefore little remains in another season. If sealskins are
used for atagois [i.e., parkas] or trowsers the prosiss is more tedious,
has to be scraped and softened with their [teeth?] untill they become
as pliable as doe skin. The boots again ... [sentence incomplete] ‡

With six months of the arctic voyage completed, a new calendar year
under way, the days slowly lengthening, and the cheerful rays of the
sun once again beaming upon the ice-bound ships, Margaret Penny
and the men on the two whalers could begin to look forward to the
summer of their return to home port. Months of cold blustery weather
still lay ahead, of course, but somehow the prospect now seemed more
bearable. And continued low temperatures, it had to be admitted,
would actually confer some advantages. By thickening and extending
the ice cover within the sound, they would create better conditions for
sled travel and seal hunting. In a few months, female seals would be
bearing pups in snow dens beneath the wind-packed snow, where they
would be vulnerable to crafty, dog-guided hunters. Early in May, bowhead whales would reappear among the floes in the southern part of

the sound, initiating the hectic but exhilarating period of floe-edge whaling. And during the long sunny days of June, the hunters would be able to stalk basking seals on the landfast ice.

For the Scottish whalemen, the winter months were little more than a long cold interlude between the periods of intense whaling effort in fall and spring. The object of wintering with their ships and enduring six months of comparative idleness was simply to be on hand in May when the whales returned to the sound. The seamen's daily routine, summarized in the journal entry of 1 February, was more relaxed than in the whaling season. They could sleep in until seven instead of being roused at four-thirty; and their chores, which included cutting and hauling pond ice for water supply, rendering blubber into oil, and keeping the gear in good shape, were neither demanding nor dangerous.

The ships' natives and their families viewed the winter very differently. Unlike the whalemen, who relied mainly on preserved food brought from Europe and who received regular meals as part of their employment, the Eskimos depended largely on animal food, which they had to secure by hunting and fishing even though they were working for the whalers. And whereas most sailors saw whaling as a lifetime career, the Eskimos considered it a windfall economic opportunity of uncertain duration, to be exploited concurrently with their traditional activities for as long as it remained profitable. Because they did not possess the range of food preservation techniques available to Europeans, they were less able to store food for future use and therefore had to secure it steadily throughout the year, according to the seasonal availability of each species. To the Eskimos, the winter was not a period of idleness but an integral part of their annual cycle of food procurement. During the winter months, their principal quarry was the ringed seal.

For Margaret Penny, the winter had a somewhat different meaning. Doubtless she shared some of the concern expressed by her husband and the officers regarding the financial outcome of the voyage and wished – as they so fervently did – for outstanding results in the floe whaling of spring. At the same time, her journal entries suggest that she was sensitive to the Eskimos' need for food and eager for them to achieve success on their hunts. Yet, to her, the winter was not primarily an interlude between whaling episodes or a season of native seal hunting. In this section of the journal we sense that, for Margaret, the winter was an opportunity to establish a closer relationship with the Eskimo women and to learn more about their way of life, thereby enriching her own cultural awareness.

She herself must have been an object of considerable curiosity to the Eskimos, the first white woman they had ever seen. Her appearance, clothing, and behaviour were surely given close scrutiny. "It was quite amuseing to see them examining my dress," she had written on 11 August at Nuvujen. We cannot know whether Margaret measured up to the descriptions of British ladies recounted many times by Tackritow since her return from England in 1854. Having met Queen Victoria and lunched at Windsor Castle, she had acquired standards of dress and deportment that Margaret Penny – a mere whaling captain's wife – may have found difficult to match.

Another woman in Margaret's position might have remained aloof from the native community, strutting importantly about the ship of which her husband was master, disdaining to recognize that Eskimo culture could be of any interest to a person of her station in life, and regarding the native people as curiosities rather than social acquaintances. Such attitudes were all too common in the annals of British exploration in remote regions. An arrogance nourished by centuries of colonial aggrandizement and the powerful transformations of the industrial age had closed the minds of many individuals and blinded them to the admirable achievements and impressive qualities of other cultures. Fortunately, whalemen were less burdened with these prejudices than men of wealth, education, power, or class. They were practical men of the sea who judged others by their actions. The Scots in particular showed a special aptitude for getting along with native people. Among the arctic whalers, Captain William Penny stood out for his ability to recognize valuable traits and capabilities in the Eskimo population and for his eagerness to learn from their knowledge. Clearly, Margaret was of similar mind. After ten days at Nuvujen early in the voyage, she had referred to the native residents as "my Esquimaux friends," and during the subsequent months her fondness and admiration for the people had intensified.

In establishing social connections with the Eskimo women at Kekerten, Margaret took the initiative and assumed the role of hostess on board ship. She spearheaded her entry into the Kekerten social whirl with that potent British weapon, the tea party, entertaining so many visitors that they had to attend in rotation owing to the cramped quarters on the vessel. The parties were held in the evening, after the ship's crew had eaten, and they evidently took place every night. "I generally make out about 20 cups of tea every evening for them," she wrote in late December, and two weeks later: "I, every evening after we are done with our cabin tea, fill the kettle with water & make out from

20 to 30 cups for the natives." It was a lavish and elegant scale of hospitality for an arctic whaling harbour.

What the hostess wore on these occasion is not recorded, but an entry made by Captain Penny on the last day of January explained that "the natives generly put on their best deer skin dresses and come on board to tea." By "dresses" he probably meant the traditional women's long-tailed, hooded amautik, though he may have been referring to a garment of native make but European style. In September 1857 the surgeon of the Hull whaler *Anne* had called Tackritow and her friend Mary (wife of the harpooner Tessuin) "the two *belles* of Niatoolak." His description of their attire leaves no doubt that impeccable standards of haute couture were already securely established in Cumberland Sound, probably as a result of Tackritow's visit to England in 1853–54, and that an interesting blend of native and imported fashions was developing:

They are both young, and the best looking of any I have seen. Mary had on a beautiful skin dress made in the English style, with a row of pearl buttons in the front, reaching from the neck to the waist. The skirt hung a little below the knees. She also wore wellington boots made of seal skin, and a most warm-looking bonnet made from a young deer's skin – the first and only bonnet I have seen in this country. Anne [Tackritow] had on a faded silk dress (the last of the gifts of her kind friends in England), and a skin tunic, wellington boots of seal skin, and a Glengarry cap. To do them justice, both looked exceeding well, all things considered. (*Hull Advertiser* 1858b)

Like Eenoolooapik and other Eskimo visitors to Britain, Tackritow had returned to Baffin Island with an assortment of European clothes, some useful and others merely fashionable. As these wore out, local materials were used to make replicas. The dresses, skirts, and bonnets of caribou skin were therefore hybrid garments reflecting both European and Eskimo cultures. Tackritow's sojourn in England had stimulated a demand for imported items of clothing, which the whalemen could only partly satisfy. The women were also eager to get hold of rings, brooches, and brightly coloured cloth and ribbon. American whalemen later took ball gowns, fancy hats, and even foundation garments into Hudson Bay so that during the winter the native women could appear at shipboard dances dressed like the girls back home. These articles had a strong purchasing power as well. They could be traded for souvenir items of skin and fur, such as slippers, mittens, and tobacco pouches, and were doubtless also offered in return for sexual favours. As Eskimo women acquired European garments or incorpo-

Tookoolitoo (Tackritow in Margaret Penny's journal).
She met Margaret in Britain in 1853–55 and in Cumberland Sound
in 1857 (Nourse 1879, facing 448)

rated aspects of European design into the clothing they made from animal skins, some aspects of their traditional dress began to atrophy. The surgeon of the *Anne* quoted above noted, "The long-tailed coats are in nearly every instance discarded by the junior females, their hair is neatly done up, and their seal-skin clothing is clean, and made in the English mode."

A few years after Margaret Penny's reunion with Tackritow in Cumberland Sound, the American explorer Charles Francis Hall had a surprise visit from the same woman (whom he called Tookoolito, or Hannah) in a harbour north of Frobisher Bay. As he sat writing in the cabin of the American whaler *George Henry*, the refined tones of a "soft, sweet voice" fell on his ears: "Good morning, sir." A lady stood before him dressed in "*crinoline*, heavy flounces, an attenuated toga, and an immensely expanded 'kiss-me-quick' bonnet." Then, a second surprise: her features revealed her to be not a European lady but "a *lady* Esquimaux" (Hall [1864] 1970, 133). Hall was so impressed by "the exceeding gracefulness and modesty of her demeanor" and by the sterling qualities of her husband Ebierbing (or Joe) that he more or less adopted the young couple, taking them on a five-year expedition to Hudson Bay and later on his polar expedition to Greenland, as well as settling them in a house in Groton, Connecticut, where the belle of Niantilik died in 1876 at the age of thirty-eight (Nourse 1879, 445).

At one of her soirées, on 15 January, Margaret Penny presented gifts of "bonnet boxes" to two of her callers. A hat box seems an absurd article to give to Eskimo women, and one wonders whether they were later put to some totally different use, such as storing sewing gear or other domestic paraphernalia (for useful containers were always in great demand); but judging from the descriptions of Eskimo fashions above, it seems quite possible that they were actually used to store bonnets.

Each fall the formation of landfast ice in arctic regions creates a solid barrier between the aquatic habitat of mammals such as seals, narwhals, walrus, and whales, and the air which they need to breathe. In most species the response of the animals is either to migrate southward to oceanic regions beyond the ice zone or to concentrate in polynyas (areas of open water within the ice cover). For the native people of the arctic, the outmigration of most sea mammals, as well as birds and some terrestrial mammals, meant nothing less than the departure of their principal sources of food and other essential resources at the beginning of the coldest season. Winter was their "period of hardship" (Weyer 1932, 113), and if it had not been for a species of seal that is capable of remaining in the ice zone, some arctic regions would probably have been uninhabitable before the modern system of importing food from southern agricultural regions. The ringed seal adapts to winter ice by breaking breathing holes through young ice in the fall and keeping them open all winter by scratching with its claws. This is more difficult than it sounds, because the ice grows steadily thicker as the cold weather continues until, by May, it measures about six feet from top to bottom. Nevertheless, each seal manages to maintain several holes and rises repeatedly in one hole or another to take in air. In March the females enlarge the breathing holes and excavate birthing dens beneath snowdrifts on top of the ice in which to produce their young. These techniques, along with a thick insulating layer of blubber to withstand the cold, enable the animal to remain year-round in the Arctic.

In their pursuit of the ringed seal, the hunters had to employ methods appropriate to each season. In the open-water conditions of summer, they used harpoons from kayaks. In the fall, they hunted from the edge of the growing coastal fringe of landfast ice when it became strong enough to support their weight. In winter, they sought the seals when they rose for air in their breathing holes. In late winter, they hunted the females and newly born pups in their snow dens. And in June, they stalked seals that lay on top of the ice basking in the sun. Each situation demanded different techniques and equipment. More than any other hunting method, breathing-hole sealing epitomized Eskimo ingenuity, determination, and patience. The hunter was faced with several problems. He could not see the breathing holes because they were hidden beneath a blanket of snow. He could not predict when a seal would rise to breathe or which of its several holes it would use. He could not see the animal as it approached a hole or even when he tried to harpoon it. The slightest noise or human smell would frighten it off. If wounded, the seal would attempt to dive and swim away. If the hunter succeeded in killing and retrieving it, he would have to lift the heavy animal onto the ice through a hole that was often smaller than its body.

Captain Penny's statement on 1 February that a hunter might wait for a seal for eight or ten hours is not an exaggeration. Richard K. Nelson, a careful observer of Alaskan Eskimo hunting methods, wrote that during periods of extreme food scarcity, Canadian Eskimos had been known to wait more than twenty-four hours at seal holes (Nelson 1969, 238). De-

Eskimos hunting seals at breathing holes (Parry 1824, facing 173)

spite the piercing cold, such a wait could not include foot stomping or arm thrashing, for the slightest noise would alarm the seal. It had to be a silent and almost motionless vigil, during which the solitary hunter huddled inside his fur clothing, trying to remain alert. One can well believe that at the end of a day's hunt, a hot cup of tea or soup in the galley of a wintering whaler was greatly appreciated.

Usually, the hunter used a single sledge dog (the "pointer" in Captain Penny's description) to sniff out a seal hole. After leading the dog away, he built a seat and sometimes a windbreak out of snow blocks, lay down pieces of fur beneath feet and buttocks, and placed his harpoon and coiled line close at hand; he held the looped end of this line in one hand as he sat patiently awaiting the seal. To detect the seal's arrival, he could either listen for its exhalations or place a feathery in-

An Esquemaux sealing, in Cumberland Inlet

Eskimo seal hunter in Cumberland Sound (sketch by Timothy Packard,
by permission of the Houghton Library, Harvard University)

dicator on the snow over the centre of the hole and watch for its slight
tremor to reveal the presence of the animal below. When a seal arrived
in the hole, the hunter would stand up quietly and plunge his harpoon
vertically downward through the snow and into the animal, using the
line to prevent it from escaping or being carried away by under-ice currents. With the snow knife he would then enlarge the hole, draw the
seal up onto the ice with a seal hook, and use his dog to haul it away.

Breathing-hole hunting was exceedingly time consuming. A hunter
might obtain only one or two seals a day (Nelson 1969, 235). The seals
tended to be most abundant within a mile of shore in the protected
fiords and bays of indented coastlines, where the ice cover was comparatively stable (McLaren 1961). Around the island of Kekerten,
where ice conditions fluctuated greatly until the end of December and
perhaps longer, ringed seals probably did not occur in large numbers.
Margaret's several references in January to rendering oil from the
whale's tail for the Eskimos and distributing bread dust leave no doubt
that hunting was still not providing enough meat and oil for the native
community.

The Scourge of the Sea

Unfortunately, there is a gap in Margaret's journal between 2 February and 12 May, and the official ships' logbooks were not kept up during this period either. With the exception of a few remarks by Brother War-mow, there is virtually no information about events at Kekerten during these three and a half months. This chapter contains some general observations about the arctic winter and how it affected Europeans who committed themselves to what a newspaper once called a "long and tedious imprisonment in the ice" (*Whalemen's Shipping List* 1858). In particular, it discusses scurvy, the disease that claimed five of the *Alibi*'s men at Niantilik before the *Lady Franklin*'s arrival. The chapter ends with a description of Warmow's activities among the people at Kekerten, based on extracts from his letters.

As January gave way to February, Warmow wrote of "violent winds and exceedingly cold weather" and remarked on the discomfort caused on board ship. After eleven years at Greenland missions, he was no stranger to cold, but in Cumberland Sound temperatures drop lower than on the opposite coast of Davis Strait, and the degree of cold at Kekerten may have exceeded anything Warmow had experienced at Lichtenau and Lichtenfels. In addition, he was accustomed to dwellings of European type with a reasonable level of warmth inside. Half a year in England must have exposed him to the British antipathy towards interior heating, yet he may have been unprepared for the spartan conditions on board a Scottish whaler, especially one commanded by William Penny. It was not simply a question of attitude or tradition, however.

With two ships and two shore stations to look after, Penny was using his limited supplies of coal sparingly. The result was a shipboard environment of which even the Eskimos would disapprove. Warmow wrote on one occasion: "The thermometer, which hung about eight feet from the stove, in the cabin, seldom indicated more than 21 °F. Once it sank to 10°. At another time, when laid on the floor, it fell to 2° below zero. At night, when the fire was out, it was almost as cold in the cabin as outside" (*Periodical Accounts* 1858, 23:132). Whether conditions were better for the men living in the house ashore is doubtful.

Although frostbitten feet led to the death of one native at Kekerten, no Europeans perished from exposure or from the indirect effects of cold during the voyage. When proper precautions were taken, the cold did not present insurmountable problems for human health. In fact, it probably contributed to sound health among the Europeans by restricting the aerial spread of bacterial and viral infections and breaking the chain of transmission of parasitic diseases. On British naval expeditions the incidence of illness and mortality from disease was far lower in arctic regions than in the tropics, owing chiefly to the lower temperatures, and the same was probably true on whalers.

The men knew that cold could kill them, but warning signals sent out by the body enabled them to take measures to prevent mere discomfort from turning into a dangerous threat to survival. They could generate more body heat by consuming food and hot beverages or by doing physical work. They could restrict heat loss from the body by donning additional clothes or finding shelter from the wind. They could create additional environmental heat by lighting a fire if they had stove and fuel. Made aware of the hazards of the arctic climate, they could use foresight and common sense to avoid situations in which these measures would be impossible. Whaling captains normally ordered their men not to leave the ship alone or without announcing their destination, and usually gave them a few tips on emergency survival, as Penny had done in early November.

For arctic whalemen, safety lay at the ship, where shelter, warmth, food, clothing, and medical attention were available. The ship itself was at considerable risk while navigating in the vicinity of ice floes, and the destruction of a vessel sometimes meant the death of the crew. But once a vessel was securely frozen into stable ice in a sheltered harbour, there was less likelihood of being holed or driven ashore by encroaching floes or crushed by advancing icebergs. Secure within the wooden-walled refuge, her crew had little cause to fear the cold, as long as they took the necessary precautions whenever they left their vessel to go ashore. Cold was still a threat to be reckoned with during the arctic winter – unquestionably so – but because the tactics of the foe were known, appropriate defensive measures could be taken.

There was another enemy, however, also recognized as potentially fatal, and it was a far more serious threat than cold and exposure. Its cause was unknown, its early symptoms were deceptively benign, and effective protective measures were not entirely clear. It was a guerrilla enemy, evading early detection, waiting in ambush, resisting traditional methods of detruction. Scurvy vaulted vigorously into human experience during the long sea voyages of the Age of Discovery. It ran like a thread through the great maritime adventures of succeeding centuries, disabling and killing sailors on expeditions led by many of the great navigators, including da Gama, Magellan, Drake, Hawkins, Anson, and Bougainville. Hawkins called the disease "the scourge of the sea" (Carpenter 1988, 29), a designation so vivid that it is still used by modern writers (Baynham 1972, 35; Lloyd 1968, 259).

It is common knowledge today that scurvy results from a lack of vitamin C. The consumption of about ten milligrams per day is regarded as sufficient to avoid coming down with scurvy, and between thirty and forty-five milligrams per day are considered optimum for general health (Sharman 1981, 23). If we think we are not getting enough in our diet, we can pop into the drug store and for a few dollars purchase a small bottle containing enough vitamin C pills to keep scurvy away for a dozen years. It is as simple as that, but largely as a result of relatively recent research. The existence of vitamin C was unknown during the whaling period. Today, the principal natural sources of the vitamin – fresh fruit, vegetables, milk, and meat – can easily be bought at the supermarket, but they were notably absent from the traditional shipboard diet of earlier centuries, and this was the cause of the scurvy problem. Even if these foods had been universally recognized as antiscorbutics, it would have been impossible to preserve their freshness and vitamin C content with the traditional methods of drying, salting, and pickling. Up to the late eighteenth century, the standard diet of sailors on Royal Navy ships consisted of biscuit, beer, salted beef and pork, dried peas, oatmeal, and butter (Lloyd 1981, 10). These were all foodstuffs that could be transported easily without spoiling, but unfortunately they were all deficient in vitamin C.

A few months at sea on such a shipboard diet could produce signs of scurvy. As time went on, the symptoms became unmistakable: dizziness, lethargy, swollen gums, loose teeth, foul breath, tender and blackened legs, painful and stiff joints, purple spots and blotches, and a general physical weakness. Steadily, one's vitality and strength ebbed, and without treatment death inevitably followed. But long before death, a sailor's capacity to perform his task was impaired. Declining strength and mental acuity made him less and less reliable in the various functions of making decisions, working the ship, and fighting battles. It became clear that the disease could seriously undermine the success of discovery expeditions and influence the outcome of naval engagements. In 1780 a British fleet returned from a six-week cruise in the English Channel with 2,400 men affected (Lloyd 1981, 12), and the following year almost 3,000 cases occurred in six months in Admiral Rodney's West Indian fleet (Carpenter 1988, 1). During the eighteenth century, scurvy killed more British sailors than enemy action. Nor were soldiers on land exempt from the scourge; scurvy was a serious problem during the American War of Independence, the Crimean War, and the American Civil War. For more than four hundred years, scurvy exacted a heavy toll among sailors, soldiers, urban poor, prison dwellers, and even hospital patients.

One surprising aspect of the story is that during an era characterized by scientific and industrial progress, European knowledge about the nature of the disease retreated instead of advancing. Da Gama learned in 1498 that fresh oranges cured men badly afflicted with scurvy, and in the sixteenth century Drake and Hawkins fed their sick with fresh lemons, oranges, and a plant whose very name, scurvy grass, reveals an awareness of its antiscorbutic effect. Practical knowledge led in time to scientific interest, and in 1734 the Dutch physician John Bachstrom correctly recognized scurvy as a disease caused by some dietary deficiency and recommended fresh vegetables as preventatives. A dozen years later James Lind, a Scottish surgeon in the Royal Navy, put six pairs of scurvy-ridden sailors on different experimental diets. Within six days, the two men who had been consuming two oranges and one lemon per day in addition to the basic diet were well enough to nurse the others. Lind thus confirmed scientifically what da Gama and other sea captains had discovered a century and a half earlier (and what inhabitants of the tropics may have known all along), namely, that fresh citrus fruit cured scurvy (Carpenter 1988, 51–3). But despite the publication of Lind's book *A Treatise of the Scurvy* in 1753, another forty years passed before the Royal Navy adopted the practice of issuing each sailor with three-quarters of an ounce of lemon juice every day. The unnecessary delay has been called "a notorious scandal in medical history" (Lloyd 1981, 13), but at least the measure came in time to keep British tars relatively scurvy-free as they blockaded the coast of France and won victory at the Battle of Trafalgar.

During the nineteenth century, however, the issue was complicated by numerous other theories that were put forward. Scurvy was variously attributed to the hot air of the tropics, the presence of salt in preserved meat, the use of copper cooking vats, lack of exercise, poor ventilation, and uncleanliness. Many more preventive measures were suggested, and in the resultant morass of ideas and recommendations, the most reasonable policy for ship captains was to take along a variety of provisions that might be antiscorbutic, to stop for fresh food whenever possible, and to implement a number of measures that were said to discourage the disease. This was the "shotgun approach" adopted by Captain James Cook in his circumnavigations of the 1770s, and although it proved very successful it did nothing to reveal which of the various measures really worked.

The problem of how to combat scurvy in the Arctic was especially difficult because edible plants and cultivated crops were absent. In 1819, after the Royal Navy had resumed the search for a Northwest Passage, two ships commanded by William Edward Parry sailed into the heart of the extensive archipelago lying west of Baffin Bay and wintered near Melville Island. To forestall the dreaded scurvy, Parry expanded on Cook's approach, taking lemon juice, sauerkraut, vinegar, pickles, herbs, essence of spruce, essence of malt and hops, unsalted tinned meat, tinned soups, flour for the baking of fresh bread, and the seeds of mustard and cress to grow on board ship for fresh salad. Innovative measures were taken to heat the ships, and Parry also took steps to keep the crews mentally alert and physically fit. The ships' hunters secured musk oxen, caribou, hares, ptarmigan, geese, ducks, and even lemmings, and almost two tons of fresh meat were served to the crews (Savours and Deacon 1981, 134). Whether the lemmings actually got as far as the table is not absolutely clear. (If they did, one wonders what culinary extravagances might have been concocted in the galleys of HMS *Hecla* and *Griper.* Rôti de lemming à la béarnaise? Extremely spare ribs chinoise?) Only four men came down with scurvy during the winter and all were cured. Subsequent Admiralty expeditions adopted the Parry model, taking lemon juice and other supposedly antiscorbutic food, hunting for fresh meat when feasible, and keeping the crews active.

Unlike ships of the Royal Navy, for which there was a regulation standard of victualling, whalers and other merchant ships sailed with whatever provisions their owners saw fit to supply. Consequently, there were striking differences from one vessel to another, though in general the basic diet was similar to that of the navy's ships. On arctic whaling voyages between 1812 and 1823, the ships commanded by Captain William Scoresby, Jr, carried the usual salt beef and pork, potatoes, oatmeal, peas, barley, soup, bread, beer, and ale (Stamp and Stamp 1983, 33), supplemented with some meat, eggs, and other fresh produce purchased at the Shetland Islands on the way north and a few seals, birds, and fish caught in the northern seas. This diet, which apparently contained no lemon juice, kept scurvy at bay during one-season voyages, which lasted six months or less, but it proved inadequate when whalers were detained for longer periods, as the disastrous events of 1835–37 vividly demonstrated. In two successive years, early ice formation prevented some of the ships from leaving Baffin Bay and forced them to spend several winter months beset among ice floes and bergs. Aside from the terrible cold which the men had to endure with inadequate bedding, clothing, and fuel, as well as the constant threat of destruction from ice pressure, there was desperate hunger and malnutrition as the paltry supplies of food (intended to last only for the summer) dwindled steadily. Scurvy inevitably made its appearance among the crews and, assisted by cold and hunger, snuffed out the lives of many men before the ships managed to reach the Atlantic Ocean and sail home. The *Dee* arrived in Aberdeen in early May 1837 with forty-seven dead (Cooke and Ross 1969, 590), and when the *Advice* reached Stromness in the middle of June, only seven men were alive out of the forty-nine originally on board (Lubbock 1955, 333).

The owners of whalers were harshly criticized for failing to equip their vessels with contingency supplies of food and antiscorbutics in case they were trapped for the winter. Nevertheless, it was not until 1854, almost a century after James Lind had proved experimentally that lemon juice cured scurvy and sixty years after the Royal Navy had introduced the daily ration of lemon juice, that British merchant ships were required to carry antiscorbutics (Troup 1987, 34). Evidently, whaling and trading interests were not quite in the vanguard of preventive medicine! And even in the merchant shipping act of 1854, an exception was made for ships bound for islands in the Atlantic or ports on the east coast of North America if their latitude exceeded thirty-five degrees north (Great Britain 1854, 929), an exemption that appears to have included arctic whalers.

The beginning of intentional wintering on the whaling grounds made it necessary for whalemen to come to grips with the scurvy problem. Whereas a normal one-season voyage lasted about half a year and an accidental ice-drift voyage up to a year, wintering could keep a ship away from home port for a year and a half. Whaling masters were certainly aware of the measures usually taken by discovery expeditions to prevent scurvy, and they could hardly have failed to notice when a dozen men from the American whaler *McLellan* wintered ashore in Cumberland Sound in 1851–52, subsisted largely on a diet of meat and fish, and emerged in perfect health. Associating with Eskimos at winter harbours from 1853 on, whaling captains learned firsthand about the value of a meat diet in the arctic regions, and for the rest of the century they generally placed greater confidence in fresh meat than in any of the other supposed antiscorbutics. The problem was how to get it.

In the Pacific, whalers could stop at the Galapagos Islands, capture dozens of the defenceless giant tortoises, keep them alive and immobile on deck for months simply by turning them onto their backs, and kill them for meat when needed. Examining the logbooks of seventy-nine ships for the period of 1831–68, the zoologist Charles Haskins Townsend (1925, 57) documented more than thirteen thousand captures and considered this a "mere fraction" of the total number of tortoises consumed by the American whaling fleet. But no comparable wild food source existed in the Arctic. Most of the arctic animals could be caught only with sophisticated hunting techniques, and some species were not available at all during winter.

One approach used by whaling captains was to leave port with some domestic livestock on board, a practice that made for a cluttered and decidedly messy deck. Pigs were the most popular choice, but goats, sheep, and poultry also travelled to the arctic seas. On wintering voyages, captains would often keep the animals alive long after fresh meat and vegetables had run out, if possible until Christmas, when a celebratory feast of fresh pork was a sure way to boost sagging spirits. With proper care, some animals could be kept until even later, in case hunting failed to produce enough meat to counteract scurvy, but as one captain admitted on 21 December one year, "The cold punishes them sorly" (*Ocean Nymph* 1866–67a). The whaler *Glacier* left New Bedford, Massachusetts, in late June 1864 with four pigs on board, reached the west coast of Hudson Bay in early August, and took up winter quarters at Marble Island in mid-September. Two pigs fell to the butcher's knife just before Christmas. The two that remained proved useful, along with some caribou obtained by hunting, when scurvy appeared a few months later. Some entries from the ship's logbook (*Glacier* 1864–65) record the efficacy of this treatment:

Headboard at the grave of a young Scotsman who died of scurvy
at Niantilik a few years after Margaret Penny's visit
(photo by the author, August 1976)

8 April. "A few of the men got a slight touch of the scurvy."

10 April. "7 men have a light touch of the scurvy give them raw deer meat for it."

11 April. "Killed a hog weighing 217 lbs."

12 April. "Scurvy men are better."

14 April. "The scurvy men about well."

17 April. "The men are getting better."

25 April. "The scurvy men all well."

Another approach on arctic voyages was to take on some freshly butchered domestic meat just before departure and rely on the cold air to preserve it. Captain Scoresby explained the procedure when he departed from England in March 1814: "Took on board fresh stocks consisting of the beef of one and a half oxen, the legs were retained uncut and the finer part in large pieces for the purpose of preserving fresh, which can be effected for several months by immersing a few times in sea water and then suspending them in air." If temperatures rose above freezing, putrefaction was mainly confined to the surface of the meat. When Scoresby feasted on a leg of mutton that had been hanging in the rigging for almost five months, he found that "the taste was excellent, well gravied, sweet and of a delicious flavour" (Stamp and Stamp 1983, 34).

The principal source of fresh meat for wintering arctic whalers, however, was neither live nor frozen domestic stock but wild game secured by hunting. Many captains, surgeons, and mates – and even Brother Warmow and twelve-year-old Billie Penny – liked to go out shooting birds, hares, and other small game; and some occasionally accompanied Eskimos on hunting trips of several days' duration for larger game such as caribou and – in Hudson Bay – musk oxen. But the bulk of the meat used by wintering whaling crews was provided by hired Eskimo hunters. The amount obtained was sometimes impressive. In Hudson Bay, American whalers received an average of thirty caribou per vessel in the 1860s, and this increased to approximately ninety in the last decade of the century (W.G. Ross 1975, 107). In the western Arctic, the average consumption of each American vessel wintering at or near Herschel Island during the period 1890–1908 has been estimated as 169 caribou (Bockstoce 1980, 83).

When scurvy occurred, it was usually because game could not be obtained at the right time or in sufficient quantities. Warm winters could prevent ice formation between islands and mainland, thereby isolating wintering ships from both Eskimo hunters and wildlife. The break-up of fast ice in winter gales could impede sealing. Freezing rain could increase caribou mortality and reduce herd size. Deep snow could restrict the sled travel of hunters. There were countless reasons why hunting might fail. In utilizing the biological resources of land and sea to sustain life and combat scurvy, the whalemen, like the native inhabitants of the North, had to face the uncertainties of a "land of feast and famine."

Despite widespread recognition among whalemen of the antiscorbutic properties of meat, there was still plenty of room for a variety of opinion about the prevention and cure of scurvy. Some captains advocated preventive and curative measures that in retrospect seem not merely implausible but patently ridiculous. But even in the British medical and scientific communities and the Royal Navy, the theories about scurvy became chaotic after 1850, and it is hardly surprising that some of the confusion spilled over into the whaling fraternity. Most whaling masters organized regular exercise periods and encouraged games, not simply to keep the men fit during the comparatively idle winter months but also because they thought activity would help keep scurvy at bay. The belief that lack of physical vigour contributed to scurvy persisted through the nineteenth century, because observers tended to confuse cause and effect. Seeing scurvy patients who were weak, they concluded that weak men developed scurvy (Carpenter 1988, 241).

At Kekerten a few years after Penny's voyage, when an American captain sent his men ashore to run on 3 February, the ship's log recorded, "Them that has got the schurvy is better by good attendance all the auther men thinks that plenty of runing is very good to keep it off" (*Ansel Gibbs* 1866–67). In Hudson Bay a British captain wrote in late January, "I got some of our men to work at the game of football today as an amusement and exercise to prevent scurvy" (*Ocean Nymph* 1866–67b). If sailors were sometimes reluctant to participate – as they understandably were when they were already weakened by the disease – many commanders nonetheless felt it was their duty to enforce exercise. A logbook entry in Hudson Bay reads, "Tha men all taking thare daly walk, some of them quite lame" (*Ansel Gibbs* 1860–61, 13 Feb.), and one captain admitted that to get the men to take exercise he had to "drive them out" (*Orray Taft* 1866–67, 1 Jan.). It was not until half a century after Penny's voyage, by which time arctic whaling had ceased, that Vilhjalmur Stefansson, the great proponent of Eskimo methods in the Arctic, stated categorically, "Exercise does not prevent scurvy" (Stefansson 1918, 1718).

Ship captains hate to see sailors with nothing to do (as I myself learned as a naval cadet). Keeping the men busy keeps them out of trouble, the argument goes, and if there is nothing useful to be done, then put them to work doing something useless, such as chipping paint off recently painted metal surfaces with unnecessarily small hammers and chisels. On ships wintering in the Arctic during the nineteenth century, idleness was opposed with special vigour because it promoted "mental disquietude" and "melancholy," and these conditions were thought to contribute to scurvy or even cause it. In conjunction with cold, confinement, and partial darkness, idleness could demoralize men and undermine their alertness, so mental activity was encouraged as well as work, exercise, and sport. On most arctic expeditions the officers became what we might today call "social animators," taking the lead in putting on amusing plays and concerts, printing comical newspapers, organizing sports and games, teaching classes, arranging festive celebrations for special occasions, and doing whatever they could to combat boredom among the crew. At Marble Island in Hudson Bay, Captain George Parker of Acushnet, Massachusetts, wrote on 18 December 1864:

Quite a number of cases of scurvy in the fleet. It seems hard to be shut away from the whole world and this dreadful scourge coming on slowly and steadily and we are not able to do any thing for the men. It is not to be cured by medicine. It is brought on by depression of the mind, mostly, and the question arises how can we as we are situated, affect a cure? We have the theater, which employs some twenty-five men. They are clear from it I think as their minds are busy. Then we have dances. Out of door exercise is bad as we have not skins to wear, and it does more harm than good. (*Orray Taft* 1864–65)

If "depression of the mind" caused scurvy, then let the play begin! The crews of the five ships wintering at Marble Island combined to erect oil casks into a building that measured forty by thirty-two feet, and in mid-November the "Marble Island Theater" opened to a full house with songs by the "Hudson Bay Minstrels" followed by a play called *Pizarro*. Musical and theatrical evenings were held regularly through the winter, as were dances and "Grand Fancy Balls."

When there was no access to fresh meat or vegetables and when entertainment, exercise, and fresh air failed to improve the health of scurvy victims, some captains tried the earth cure. This involved taking the lame ashore and covering their legs with earth. "We think it helped them," a logbook reported (*Ansel Gibbs* 1860–61, 16 May). On the *Syren Queen*, after fifteen men had come down with scurvy by 1 February and one had died, earth was somehow chopped out of the frozen tundra and hauled over the ice to the ship as part of a more elaborate treatment. From the ship's logbook:

Our ship is a complete hospital and the captain's [cabin?] is full. Mr. Atkins, and Mr. Lee, are constantly occupied through the day. The mornings from 5 A.M. to 6 are devoted to bathing the limbs of the patients with spirits to relax the mussels, and immediately after breakfast commences the dirt process, which is by putting the limbs into a barrel and filling it up with warm moist earth. In this earth the patient commonly remains three hours, but at times they become faint, and then they require to be taken out, and other patients take their places, and so through the day until 8 P.M. when bathing with warm water commences and after thougherly bathing, poultices of beans are applied to them that are the worst off. Nearly all of the men have very sore mouths, for which bottles of wash are at hand to be used every few minutes and oft repeated, ennemas are needed, for the bowels. Salt meat is prohibited and has been for one month. (*Syren Queen* 1860–61, 23 Feburary)

Unfortunately, the dirt treatment did not halt the progress of the disease. Another man died a week later, and a third in early April when the logbook reported in desperation, "At this date there is [one?] forward and one in the steerage able to walk alone or doe any thing for themselves. This is a dark looking ship all hands [know?]. The Lord Pitty us and help us is our mindful prayers" (*Syren Queen* 1860–61, 6 April).

Scurvy sometimes occurred on vessels or expeditions that were well provided with antiscorbutics, for the simple reason that some individuals refused to consume them. Captain James Cook, who earned a fine reputation in the late eighteenth century for keeping his crews healthy, noticed that some men had a strong aversion – "an obstinate prejudice" – to the scurvy grass and celery that were added to their wheat and peas (Carpenter 1988, 80). His officers had to force men to take their antiscorbutics, and once he ordered two seamen flogged for refusing fresh meat (Milton-Thompson 1981, 29). British sailors often objected to unfamiliar food such as sauerkraut and even resisted the introduction of tea (Lloyd 1981, 9). The conservatism of seamen was a barrier to scurvy prevention, and some men paid the ultimate price for their obstinacy. During the first two years of Parry's second expedition in search of the Northwest Passage several men, including Parry himself, developed scurvy but were cured. During the third summer the ominous symptoms appeared again with greater severity, but an increased ration of lemon juice effectively cured all but one man – Mr Fife, the "Greenland master" of the *Hecla*, an experienced arctic whaleman. As Parry later explained, "Mr. Fife had taken so great a dislike to the various antiscorbutics which were administered to him, that he could seldom be induced to use any of them. The disease, in consequence, reduced him to a state of extreme disability." Fife died in September (Parry 1824, 479–81). Parry's antiscorbutics consisted of lemon juice with rum added to prevent it from freezing, "carrots preserved in tin cases," and "crystallized lemon acid, cranberries, lemon marmelade, tamarinds, pickled walnuts and cabbage, essence of malt and hops, essence of spruce with molasses, dried herbs for tea, and a quantity of the seed of mustard and cress to be grown as circumstances required" (Parry 1824, viii). Were these antiscorbutics really so repulsive that a man would refuse the means of sustaining life?

Sand-blasted headboard at the grave of a man from the American brig
Georgiana, who died of scurvy at Niantilik in April 1861
(photo by the author, August 1976)

Food prejudices and preferences usually defy rational explanation.
While some sailors turned up their noses at lemon juice or sauerkraut,
others happily ate ship rats (a logical way to get protein and vitamin c
from a renewable resource on a sustained-yield basis while at the same
time achieving a degree of pest control at no cost to shipowner or
consumer). Many sailors in the arctic regions would pass up a hearty
Eskimo meal of slightly cooked seal meat, blubber, and blood in
favour of some salted pork that had been stored in wooden casks for
months or even years. Early in the twentieth century, a few of Vilhjalmur Stefansson's sledging companions ignored his advice to eat fresh
meat, preferring what Stefansson contemptuously referred to as "gro-
ceries." They soon developed severe scurvy, and he cured them – with
fresh meat. Food prejudice is not simply a thing of the past. Today,
I find that my own liking for liver, heart, sweetbreads, tongue, and
brains is not shared by many of my acquaintances. I draw the line at
ship rats, however.

Arctic whalemen were not immune to the phenomenon of food prejudice. Many refused to eat the meat of sea mammals. "The only difficulty will be to get them to eat seal, as some of them refused it before,"
wrote a frustrated captain in Hudson Bay (*Ocean Nymph* 1866–67a,
12 Jan.). Five men affected by scurvy on the *Isabella* in 1879 would not
eat walrus or seal meat (*Isabella* 1878–79, 9 Feb.). Frederick Schwatka,

an American explorer well known for his readiness to adopt native diet and travel methods, observed when visiting whalers wintering in Hudson Bay that the foremast hands were "firmly wedded" to the traditional shipboard diet of "hard tack, salt junk, and bitter coffee" and that they found the fishy taste of seal, walrus, and polar bear repugnant (Stackpole 1965, 45).

Some even objected to a small ration of citrus juice – a mere ounce or two per day. Several scurvy patients on a whaling ship sent out by the Hudson's Bay Company in 1866–67 could not break the grip of the disease because, according to the captain, "they do not drink enough lemon juice" (*Ocean Nymph* 1866–67a, 1 Feb.). On the *Abbie Bradford* (1884–85, 26 Feb.) three seamen "refused to take there lime juce," and at least one of them came down with scurvy within a month. The frustration experienced by ship captains faced with the irrational reluctance of sick men to consume antiscorbutic food or beverages is apparent in a few of their short entries in logbooks and private journals. One wrote, "I have only my one case [of scurvy] and he is nearly well, but I have to stand over him and cure him against his will, (so it seems)" (*Orray Taft* 1864–65, 1 Jan.). Several years later, the same captain complained about the crew, "They think they have the best doctors amongst themselves," adding a week later, "It is not pleasant to be doctor as they will not be doctored" (*Orray Taft* 1872–73, 24 Jan; 2 Feb.).

Captain Penny's ideas on scurvy prevention were based largely on his own experimentation with a variety of food during three winters in the Arctic, as well as on what he had been able to learn from the Eskimos. Peter Cormack Sutherland (1852, 1:223), who served as surgeon with him in 1850–51, noted that on the coast of Greenland the raw skin (maktak) of narwhal was "highly prized" as an antiscorbutic. Whenever Penny's men killed a few narwhals, they preserved the skin in vinegar in order to have some on hand in case scurvy occurred later. When they fried some for afternoon tea on 30 July, it was decribed as "most delicious eating like so much firm turbot" ([Stuart] 1850–51). The whalemen later encountered three hungry Eskimos at the ice edge near Cape York and offered them a feed of boiled maktak – an interesting turnabout.

In 1850 the *Lady Franklin* and *Sophia* had carried vegetables (including carrots) preserved by the relatively new process of canning, as well as lime juice. The officers grew mustard and cress on board ship, in the Parry tradition, and potatoes as well. In March 1851 they ate the last of the potatoes, whose ancestors had been harvested in Scotland almost two years before. Penny's technique is described in an account of his 1849 whaling voyage on the *Advice*. On that occasion he had shipped fresh potatoes at Dundee, stored them in "mould" (soil or compost) underneath the stove, and watered them regularly. New potatoes had sprouted and grown to the size of eggs (Goodsir 1850, 93). During the winter of 1850–51, scurvy appeared among the crew of Sir John Ross's small schooner *Felix*, which was frozen in nearby. Ross was a seasoned arctic explorer who had survived four years in the Arctic during his expedition on the *Victory*, but on this occasion his outfit and provisions were woefully inadequate. Penny sent over several batches of antiscorbutics, including potatoes, carrots, and porter, which helped to cure the men.

To keep the men alert and cheerful at winter harbour on the search expedition, Penny's surgeons had organized the "Royal Cornwallis Theatre" on board the *Lady Franklin*. Drawing actors from both ships and also from Sir John Ross's nearby vessel, the company distributed printed handbills and performed in front of an audience of fifty, wearing calico costumes and accompanied by music that was described – possibly with some exaggeration – as "tolerable" (Sutherland 1852, 1:428). At about the same time, the "Arctic Academy" got under way, also under the direction of the surgeons. Its classes ran for three hours a night, four nights a week. Reading, writing, and arithmetic formed the basis of the curriculum, but geography excited the men's interest in a special way because some of them had sailed on merchant voyages to various parts of the world. Despite a limited supply of educational materials (slates, some paper and pencils, an old world map, and one copy of *Johnston's Physical Atlas*), the seamen (some of whom were barely literate) eagerly participated in discussions of global physical and human geography. The brightest men on the ships showed promise of learning elementary navigation by winter's end.

In 1857 Penny may have taken the same sort of antiscorbutic food that had served him so well during the Franklin search expedition, including fresh potatoes, tinned carrots, tinned meat, lemon juice, and possibly watercress. But as some shipowners are said to have regarded canned meat, preserved fruit and vegetables, and lemon juice as "expensive novelties" (Troup 1987, 35), the Aberdeen Arctic Company may have considered them too costly to include among his provisions. If in fact Penny's ships were inadequately supplied with antiscorbutics, as many whalers unquestionably were, scurvy could still have been prevented by the regular consumption of fresh meat. But as we have seen, caribou-hunting excursions to the mainland had to wait until after freeze-up, and winter sealing around Kekerten was generally disappointing. In the spring, all the men were so busy with floe-edge whaling that they had no time for hunting.

One of the most interesting antiscorbutic measures on Penny's voyage of 1857–58 was his use of wild plants. In August 1857 he sent the men ashore to "eat a small sour plant which is an excellent preventative for scurvy and I would strongly advise all those who intend passing a winter in the 'Arctic' sea to take every opportunity to allow their crew on shore for the above purpose." This may have been the plant which the surgeon Peter Sutherland had learned about on the Greenland coast in 1850 and which the Danes used to make an infusion. They had called it "bukoblather," and Sutherland tentatively identified it as *Pyrola media* (Sutherland 1852, 2:116), a member of the wintergreen family (Porsild 1957, 129–30). In addition, Penny often sent his men ashore to collect and "eat their pot" of crowberries and blueberries (probably bilberries), which he considered "very good for preventing scurvey," noting that "precautions are always best." But berries and other plants were not available during the winter.

In accordance with the prevailing notion that exercise helped prevent scurvy, Penny required the men to walk round the ship's deck for an hour each day within the canvas shelter, and he encouraged them to take walks ashore on Sundays. He appears to have paid less attention to nourishing their minds, however. Although celebrations marked the birthdays of Margaret and Warmow, and festivities were held on Christmas Day, New Year's Eve, and New Year's Day, neither Margaret's journal nor the ships' logbooks mentions plays, concerts, or classes. It seems curious that Penny did not arrange cultural activities of this sort, considering the importance he had attached to them during the winter of 1850–51, but on that occasion he had been accompanied by surgeons Robert Goodsir and Peter Sutherland, two well-educated and energetic individuals who had sailed with him before and who took the initiative in organizing entertainment and education. Sailing under Admiralty orders, Penny might have been criticized if he had neglected to follow the naval tradition of keeping the men mentally stimulated. He may have been ill suited to directing such activities on his own; and his surgeon in 1857–58, Erskine Grant, who was only twenty-one years of age and had never been to sea before, may have been either incapable of acting as drama director, concert master, and teacher or simply unwilling to do so. In any case, the lack of intellectual activities is unlikely to have contributed to the occurrence of scurvy.

Since Penny had fed maktak to starving Eskimos and had supplied antiscorbutics to the crew of a famous arctic explorer, he clearly knew how to avoid the disease, and he expected the captains under his authority to take appropriate measures to prevent it. He blamed Captain Stewart for the five scurvy deaths on the *Alibi* in 1857 because Stewart had wintered at Niantilik instead of Kekerten. But there is no obvious reason why Niantilik should have been more prone to scurvy than Kekerten, and Penny's aversion to the former place may have had more to do with the fact that it had become popular among American whalemen, whom he suspected of harbouring territorial ambitions. Then why was the *Alibi* so badly affected by scurvy? Before leaving Aberdeen for Cumberland Sound on 22 June 1856, the ship had made a three-month arctic sealing voyage to the Greenland Sea. If some of the men had participated in both voyages, their reserves of vitamin c might already have been depleted by the time they left on the whaling voyage. But half the men serving on the *Lady Franklin* and *Sophia* in 1857 had also completed Greenland Sea voyages shortly before leaving for Cumberland Sound, and none of those men died from scurvy. According to an article in the *Peterhead Sentinel* (1857b), based on information from the mate of the *Alibi*, the deaths had been "occasioned by living on salt meat, and the want of suitable provisions." This appears to place the blame on the owners who outfitted the vessel, though lack of hunting success may also have been a factor.

The *Alibi*'s logbook first mentioned that several men were affected by scurvy on the last day of November, only eight weeks after arrival at Niantilik. Captain Stewart then organized daily walks on the ice before breakfast, but these did nothing to halt the progress of the disease, and by mid-January some men were incapable of walking. On 27 January, John Brown, who had been "quite lame" for a month and a half, became the first to die. The other deaths occurred much later: James Moir on 17 April; John Dunnet on 24 May; Fraser Davidson on 1 July; and George Allan the next day (*Peterhead Sentinel* 1857a).

Considering Penny's criticism of Stewart, it comes as quite a surprise to learn that one of the *Lady Franklin*'s crew died of scurvy on 1 May 1858 (during one of the gaps in Margaret's journal). In the first summer, John Falconer, a forty-one-year-old cooper, and Andrew Lindsay, a thirty-five-year-old spectioneer, had been left at the new station at Nuvujen. On whalers, the cooper assembled staves, headings, and iron

Part of a headboard at Niantilik commemorating the death of a man
from Shetland (photo by the author, August 1976)

hoops into casks to hold blubber or oil, and the spectioneer directed
the flensing of whales. The two men were to take charge of the processing of any whales taken by native crews in the fall and to supervise
the storage of blubber. They were to remain at Nuvujen for the winter
(coals had been left to heat the house) in order to be on the spot
for floe-edge whaling in spring. But Falconer died there eight months
later (*Aberdeen Journal* 1858), leaving his shipboard possessions – "one
chest and sundries" and some clothes. The fact that only one of the
pair died suggests that Falconer may have been one of those stubborn
individuals who baulked at taking the recommended lemon juice, vegetables, and fresh meat. Living far from the two ships and the watchful
eyes of Captains Penny and Cheyne, it would have been easy enough
to avoid taking the antiscorbutics which the men at Kekerten, under
close supervision, were required to take. Yet even at Kekerten there
were signs of scurvy. In late May, Margaret noted that some men were
"complaining a little" and had to be sent ashore for berries, and a
month later she reported two men affected by the disease.

Whatever the cause of the scurvy that killed John Falconer – inadequate provisions, insufficient fresh meat, or the man's rejection of antiscorbutics – Penny's record against scurvy was probably well above
average. On some arctic whalers scurvy was epidemic. In 1855–56 the
American whaler *Georgiana*, wintering in or near Frobisher Bay, lost fifteen men to the disease (Starbuck 1964, 2:532–3). The *Daniel Webster*

(1860–62), after wintering at Kekerten in 1861, had ten men suffering severely from scurvy by May, one of whom died, and at least six deaths from scurvy occurred among the other ships wintering in Cumberland Sound. In Hudson Bay the *Ansel Gibbs* and two other ships lost fourteen men to scurvy at Marble Island during the winter of 1871–72 (Tuttle 1885, 113).

Margaret's attitude towards certain antiscorbutics is very interesting. The Eskimos greatly enjoyed maktak, the raw skin of such sea mammals as beluga, narwhal, and Greenland whales, and Captain Penny was aware of its antiscorbutic properties. But eating the uncooked skin of dead animals was not something that British whalemen queued up to do. They approached the consumption of maktak with absolutely none of the enthusiasm they demonstrated for overcooked Brussels sprouts, bangers and mash, bubble and squeak, or Scotch eggs. The idea did not initially appeal to Margaret either, but she was willing to try it, perhaps on the suggestion of her husband or, more likely, on that of the native women with whom she passed so many enjoyable hours. "I have managed to overcome prejudice & eat a bit of the skin, which is a preventative for scurvey," she declared with a hint of pride in late September. By mid-December she was able to write, with evident satisfaction, "I can … eat mactac with pleasure," and a month later she called it "a treat." Thus was prejudice set aside and scurvy prevented by the enlightened attitude of a woman.

The period of more than three months for which neither Margaret's journal nor the logbooks of the ships provide any information was for Brother Warmow a time of close contact with the Eskimos at Kekerten. During the previous summer the ships had been on the move, encountering Eskimos only sporadically. He had spoken with the people at every opportunity, had gone on a hunting trip up Kingaite, and had accompanied hunters on a week-long boat trip to Kingua, the region around the head of Cumberland Sound, but it was not until November, after the ships had taken up winter quarters at Kekerten, that he was able to visit a large number of families on a daily basis. This he did throughout the winter until the beginning of floe-edge whaling in April, after which "their whole attention was devoted to this pursuit, so that there was but little hope of missionary activity" (*Periodical*

Accounts 1858, 23:134). The details of Warmow's activities at Kekerten presented below and all the quotations are from the *Periodical Accounts* (1858, 23:130–2).

Warmow made regular visits to the Eskimo dwellings, consoling those who were ill and teaching about Jesus. The people were attentive and eager to learn. They listened not only because he was a European, an authority figure, a man who had been recommended by Captain Penny and who spoke their language, but also because he discussed topics that had always been close to their daily existence, such as supernatural spirits and life after death. At this initial level of communication, Warmow told Gospel stories and introduced Christian principles without intruding on the Eskimos' traditional practices. But as time passed, he assumed a more assertive role among them. The first opportunity came on 6 December with the sad death of his namesake, Hadlaw's two-week-old son Warmow, the first child born at the winter harbour. At the funeral the next day, it was not the shaman or the parents but Brother Warmow who "bore the little corpse wrapped in its clothes, and laid it in its resting place," then "covered the grave with stones."

A month later, Warmow temporarily took on the duties of Dr Grant, who was away on a sledge trip to Nuvujen and Niantilik, along with the mate Mr Birnie, young Billie, and eleven natives. Warmow's most critically ill patient was the old man who had been left on the trail with frost-bitten feet, rescued by sledges from Kekerten, and brought to the harbour. The man's toeless feet, now gangrenous, had become "offensive." On 7 January, when Warmow changed the dressings, there was nothing to indicate that a crisis was near, but later in the day a woman brought the surprising news that the man would soon die. Warmow and Captain Penny went immediately to the man's snow house. Warmow's description of what followed reveals a confrontation between missionary and shaman, between Christianity and the traditional religion, and between the European and Eskimo cultures:

As I hurried forward, I heard already at a distance the shouting and howling of an angekok, which however ceased, as soon as I entered the house, and began to speak. I rebuked the people for making such a noise, and advised them rather to be quiet, and to attend to the wants of the sick man. They had already begun to carry the things belonging to the patient out of the house, as, according to the custom prevailing among them, all which is not removed while the sick person is still alive, must be buried with him.

Words such as "crying," "moaning," and "wailing" are often used to describe the way people express grief out loud. Warmow's choice of "howling," a term usually associated with animals, seems loaded with disapproval and suggests contempt for the shaman and his authority. Warmow clearly disapproved of the behaviour of the people present, whom (according to his own admission) he "rebuked ... for making such a noise." As we look at this episode from a distant time and place, it seems astounding that Warmow could intrude unhesitatingly into this sensitive scene without respecting the time-honoured rituals of the people. Was it not their custom and their right to lament in their own way? He usurped the authority of the shaman, a man greatly respected in native society, and took charge of the proceedings: "I now spoke of the hope of everlasting life, as resulting from faith in Christ, who by His death conquered death and hell; but they did not seem to comprehend much of it."

The man with the frost-bitten feet was still "quite conscious and able to speak." Warmow, Penny, and others from the ship seem to have been intent on saving his life, and perhaps they thought that the shaman and other people present had the same object in mind. But in fact the man had decided to die, and they were giving him the best of all send-offs until rudely interrupted by the Europeans. The following day, the man was not only still alive but, as Warmow observed, "he was cheerful and seemed to have no fear of death, but rather to rejoice at the prospect of going to be with his [dead] children." When the missionary asked him where the children were, he said he thought they must be "in another world, where they were happy."

That night, the man embarked at last on the journey for which he had been preparing. When Warmow learned that the funeral had begun, he hurried ashore – not to watch respectfully from the side but to officiate:

I found the Esquimaux engaged in dragging the corpse, – which was wrapped in skins and tied up with thongs, – over the snow to a distance from their habitations, while the articles used in the chase by the deceased, were carried with the corpse. When we had arrived at the appointed place, I set to work to make the grave, requesting the Esquimaux to help me, and to gather stones to cover it, that the dogs might not devour the body. They replied, 'the poor animals are so hungry, let them devour it if they like.' They also gave me to understand, that it if was covered over at all, this must be done by an angekok and his pupil. At length they consented to let the ship's crew, who had meanwhile come to the spot, give their assistance. At the request of the Captain, I took, from among the weapons, one or two very neat bows and arrows, stating that the Captain desired to have them, as a remembrance. At this, the Esquimaux expressed great surprise, and said that the dead man would come to me and demand the articles. They also insisted that some of the arrows should be placed in the grave.

Undeterred by the objections of the people, Warmow then took the opportunity to give a sermon "on the perishing state of our mortal bodies, and the eternal destiny of our souls." Afterwards, the widow and the boy were confined in the dwelling by themselves for three days of secluded mourning, but Warmow interrupted their vigil with daily visits.

It is not difficult to detect an undercurrent of conflict. The Eskimos take the body and grave goods to the place of burial; Warmow intervenes and tells them to fetch stones to cover the body. They insist that this must be done by an angekok; he persuades them to let the sailors help. Without asking permission, he helps himself to some of the grave goods; they warn him that the man's spirit will demand them back. The family go into the traditional period of seclusion; Warmow intrudes insensitively upon their mourning.

All the aspects of Eskimo behaviour noted by Warmow during the death and burial of the frost-bitten man were part of their traditional culture: the shaman's performance at the bedside of the sick man; the lamentation by relatives and friends; the man's willingness to die; his eagerness to be reunited with dead relatives; the binding of the body; the dragging rather than sledging of it to the burial site; its interment beneath rocks along with the man's belongings; the lack of concern about protecting the corpse from animals (without flesh, the soul can escape more easily); and the three days of seclusion and mourning for members of the family (Boas 1888; Weyer 1932). Although the fundamental beliefs underlying their attitude towards life and death had much in common with those of the Christian religion – a supreme being, the existence of body and soul, the transmigration of souls, life after death, and a final, happy resting place – Warmow saw it as his mission to oppose the authority of the shaman, discourage the native religion, and introduce Christianity.

His description of the events was later submitted to his superiors in the Moravian Church, so it is clear that he felt he had acted in a manner that would please them. Apparently, the church believed that Christianity could not coexist with the native religion. It had to replace it. This put the missionary in the unfortunate position of an adversary who had to suppress many aspects of native belief and behaviour in order to impose those of Christianity. Warmow noted that because these "natural men" were "not aware of their sin and misery," they did "not feel their need of a Saviour"; therefore, the concepts of original sin and guilt would have to be taught to them.

The Eskimos believed that breaking taboos would be counted against them when the final resting place of their souls was decided. Was this so different from Christian belief? They were quite willing to respect the whalemen's taboos, such as not working on the sabbath. As Margaret observed one Sunday in October, "The Esquimaux seem to understand very well that they are to respect this day, for they go about very quietly & forego their usual occupations." In general, the whalemen respected Eskimo practices, but the missionary could not.

Captain Penny was involved in the episode of the frost-bitten man. He accompanied Warmow to the man's dwelling with the same good intention of curing the patient. He was present at the burial and may have asked Warmow to take some of the grave goods (although this seems out of character). He had worked hard to promote the introduction of Christianity because he believed it would benefit the native people. But one senses that he was not as overbearing as Brother Warmow.

After a special dinner in honour of his fortieth birthday on 18 January, Warmow left the ice-bound flag-festooned ships and walked alone to commune with Christ and reflect on his work. "I had recently been often cast down, when contemplating my circumstances, and the work to which I was called," he admitted, "but I was now enabled anew to believe, that, although I can of myself do nothing, He would effect His gracious purposes concerning me." With renewed vigour he continued his work through the winter months, consoling the sick, teaching about Jesus, celebrating the Resurrection on Easter Day, explaining the significance of hymns, and leading prayers.

Fish in Every Direction

13 May – 30 June

Whaling at the edge of the landfast ice has already begun.

May 13th   A strong southerly gale blowing. Mr. Cheyne went to the floe lead at 4 A.M. to look if the boats were all safe & found they were. Little doing as there is no water to be seen.

May 14th   Still no water to be seen & blowing a strong gale from the south.

May 15th   A little water to be seen this morning. Breakfast at 4 A.M., 7 boats in the water by 10 oclock, one or two whales seen. I went to the hill to look at them. It was very warm & the water as smooth as a mirror but no whales caught.

May 16th. Sunday   A beautiful warm day, the snow dissolving very fast. All the natives removeing into their tupiks [i.e., tents], the sun having dissolved their snow huts. Some of them are left without any covering at all. Out of humanity Mr. Penny was obliged to go on shore with all his forces & errect a tent for them.

May 17th   The boats left at 6 A.M. It is very foggy. Some white whales, but no black ones, seen. Hauled up the boats at 4 P.M. The ice is disolving so fast that Richard the cook, who goes down with the mens dinner, fell throw in crossing a crack.

May 18th   Boats all in the water at 6 A.M. Still very foggy. Only one whale seen today. The weather is very warm & the female natives seem to amuse themselves in little excursions to gather the berries that have been buried under the snow all winter. I have had many presents of them & find them very good & fresh. I have also had some fine wild ducks brought by the natives.

May 19th   The boats all in the water. No whales. One of the natives shot an ouktuk seal [i.e., bearded seal]. They are valuable to them, being the seal they use for soles for their camines [kamingit, or skin boots]. Still foggy. A large sheet of ice came down from Kingua on which was a number of seal-skins & other things belonging to the natives here & had been left by them. It was very fortunate they were seen & secured, the ice breaking away much sooner than was expected.

May 20th   Eight boats again in the water this morning. A whale came up a few minutes after. Lucas fired & got fast in her. In about an hour she was killed. I took a walk over to the edge of the ice to get a look of her. She proved to be pretty large, her bone measuring 7 feet 4 inches. It was very enlivening to see the men & natives so actively engaged in cutting up the immense creature & getting the dog sledges loaded & sent to the ship, a distance of [blank space]. I, along with two female natives, seated ourselves upon the top of the first sledge for I was quite unable to walk home & when I did reach it I was obliged to go to bed, completely tired out, the snow being so soft that you sink to the knees at every step.

May 21st   The boats are all out today, the sun bright & warm, & the natives engaged bringing up the bone & blubber on their sledges, which will be all accomplished tonight.

May 22nd   A fine day but no whales yet. I had a walk on the land. It is very pleasant to smell the earth again.

May 23rd. Sunday   Rather thick & foggy today. Several of the men who are complaining a little were sent to gather berries on the hill. Divine service in the afternoon.

May 24th   Fine weather. Whales anxiously looked for. None seen, but I have observed that they always make their appearance with the full moon.

May 25th   I have been at the hill-head all forenoon but have seen no whales. There is much to like about the natives. They are so kind if left to themselves but I am sorry to say they have been taught much evil.

May 26th   Mr. Penny unable to set off this morning with the pain in his knee. It is much swollen. Mr. Warmow came down from the hill with the intelligence that they had got a fish, but he could not think what sort of a one as it did not present the usual appearance of a whale, so we came to the conclusion that it was a dead one picked up. In a little time a boy came to tell us that they had got another fish. Mr. Penny immediately made the natives set off with their sledges to bring up the blubber & went down on one himself accompanied by Mr. Warmow. On their way they met a sledge coming up full of natives who explained that what Mr. Warmow took for a whale was a boat bottom up. An Esquimaux having fired & got fast, it proved that the harpoon gun had been overloaded & a kind Providence had preserved them from death, having escaped with the loss of the gun & two rifles. The second whale was [here?] secured so we were thankful.

May 27th   People all set off for the boats at 5 A.M. I went to the hill head at 10 A.M. & had the pleasure of seeing 9 boats moveing about in a sea of glass with the sun as warm as a day in July at home. I also saw fish in every direction, but it was very difficult to approach them, being so calm. After watching until 2 P.M. I saw one boat get fast to a small fish. I then came down to allow Mr. Warmow to go up & have the plea-sure of a look. He had no sooner reached the top than up went the signal that another whale was captured. As soon as the small fish was towed down by five of the boats they returned again to assist in getting the other fish down. She proved to be a large one & had been shot by Mr. Cheyne. She was very little trouble, having gone to bottom at once under a floe, close by where she was shot. Mr. Penny directed the men to go on the floe after she had been down a long time & draw in the lines carefully as the least [jerck?] would have broke them. When she came up she was found, as Mr. P., had supposed, dead. The 9 boats then bent on to her & towed her away down towards where they flinch the fish. Mr. Penny went in the first boat that he might pick a good lead, as there were a number of streams of loose ice. When he had brought them through these into clear water he saw a fish rise near his boat so he loosed her & went in pursuit, but she escaped him. Think-ing it quite needless to return to the boats he went to the floe & made the natives flinch the small fish, got the sledges packed, & started them for the ships: by this time it was midnight, quite calm, & the boats near

the land with the large fish. He felt his knee very painful & seeing no
difficulty in their way he left Mr. Cheyne & Lucas to bring her to land,
& arrived at the ship at half past 1 A.M. with all the news for us, but he
was ill pleased with Lucas & saw that he had not exerted himself or
then they would have been in [by?] that time. Mr. Penny was obliged to
lie down with his leg, Mr. Warmow waiting up to give Mr. Cheyne his
orders on arrival, which were to give the men 4½ hrs. sleep from the
time of their arrival at the ship. At 4 A.M. Mr. Warmow came to tell
Mr. P. (who had been obliged to get up with severe cramp in his leg)
he was surprised that the men were not come.

May 28th   A gale had come on in the morning before they had
brought the whale to land. On inquiry Mr. P. found that the cook had
returned at 2 A.M. & had gone to bed without informing him that he
had been unable to send off the mens dinner to them. By this time it
was 7 o'clock & Mr. Penny was very angry that he had not been informed on his arrival as that time he could have rendered them some
assistance to bring them to land. So we were in a state of anxiety all
day. Mr. Penny went to the floe to see what could be done. In the
evening part of the crew landed with the second mate saying that
Mr. Cheyne had stayed by the fish, but they could not yet land her.
They were ordered to take 6 hours sleep & then start again.

29th May   Mr. Penny ordered Lucas to go to the hill head to see what
the boats were doing. He came down & said that they were far off & a
great deal of ice. He was then ordered to go to the north head, where
five boats were lying, taking all the men & natives with him to launch
them, but although Mr. P. distinctly told him they were not to leave
until he [i.e., Penny] returned from the hill, he [i.e., Lucas] neglected
to do so & they had all set off for the south [*sic*] point. Mr. Penny was
then obliged to send him after them saying to save the fish if possible,
but the first thing to look to was the mens lives. In a short time back
came a native saying he had been sent by Lucas to say that the boats at
the N. point were all adrift; what was now to be done with only Mr. P.,
the cooper, cooks & two boys on board? We sent word on shore to the
females to see if they would help. They were no sooner told than they
set off, old & young, to lend their aid. Mr. Warmow was dispatched to
the hill to watch the boats & I was left in charge of the ship. When
Mr. P. with his assistants reached the boats he found they were not
adrift so he got one of them on to a boat sledge & got her into the
water, when he set sail, taking William, who had walked over to get

information to his father, a distance of 30 miles, & the cooper along
with him. The wind was so strong that they soon ran down & found
Mr. Cheyne with the other boats & fish in no great danger. She was
safely moored that night, & all the men came up to the ship to get a
rest & sleep, having been away three days. In the after noon a native
came running on board pointing to the boats & calling out that they
were in danger. When I went on deck I saw the floe covered with native
men, women & children flying towards them. Mr. Penny was on shore
& I ran to the mate of the Sophia (who was below weighing out provisions) telling him to run too. He said he could not do so without
orders, but I said they would be sent after him, so Mr. Warmow, William
& he, with the ship boys, all ran together & just reached in time to save
the five boats with all their whaleing gear, the ice having broken off at
our harbour mouth & the wind blowing a gale from the north.

May 30th. Sunday   Being the work of necessity, the men were obliged
to go & tow the fish up today as the wind was more moderate. I took a
walk with Mr. Penny to the lookout on the south hill & saw the 9 boats
towing up the great monster to get her flinched on the N. point at the
mouth of the harbour. When we turned the telescope to the N. we saw
two boats towing a fish down & surmised that it was the mate coming
down.

May 31st   Mr. Birnie arrived this morning with the intelligence that
in going up from Newbuean to Kingua with his boats & men to fish as
he had been ordered they had encountered a very severe gale which
broke up all the ice & brought it down upon them. They lost their
boats, but fortunately found them in the ice next day, along with two
other boats belonging to the Arctic & Enuite [i.e., *Innuit*]. They were
obliged to return to Newbuean to refit. The poor Dr. was along with
them. He used often to say he would like to see a storm at sea, but he
had little idea of the reallity.

June 1st   Sledges still driving up blubber & the last of the bone. It is
upwards of 11 feet long. While sitting below a native came & called for
Mr. Warmow to come on shore, two females having found a woman
dead on the hill. Poor creature, she had hung herself, for what cause
we cannot tell, but there appears to be some mystery about it.

June 2nd   The ice has gone off a little & the boats are away to try &
get the mate down with his fish. When about two hours gone, a gale

from the s.w. has come on & brocken up all the ice. Our two carpenters were down mending the boats damaged the other day & the swell came in so strong that they were carried away, boats & all, but the natives with their usual alacrity ran with what people we had at the ship & got them to land. I am most anxious about the other 10 boats as the ice is breaking in every direction & a strong wind along with a great swell, but God is great & He can protect them in every danger.

4 P.M.   Two boats are just in sight at 6 [o'clock]. Mr. Penny with the 8 men from Newbeuian & some natives reached the ship & gave us the intelligence that the 7 boats had been suddenly carried away in the pack, but the wind being from the s. there was no great danger, only delay, so about 10 in the evening we could see them off the mouth of the harbour, but they could not get in for ice.

May [sic] 3rd   The boats got round to the south point. Some of the people came home & the rest staid by the boats. They are all off again to look for the whale which they had abandoned. Mr. Penny has just seen her from the hill & dispatched a crew of natives to take hold of her until the other boats join to tow her down. I feel much for the poor native who lost his wife the other day. His sorrow is very great.

May [sic] 4th   Mr. Warmow & William are gone upon a shooting excursion & the boats have not yet got down, although we can see them coming with the fish. Another gale, but the boats are so near that we think they will reach about midnight.

May [sic] 5th   The boats & people with the fish once more all safe in harbour. Mr. Penny & the mate have gone down to the ice to flinch the fish & get her up to the ship for fear the ice break away.

May [sic] 6th. Sunday   All is quiet on board today. Divine service as usual. While sitting with some of the natives in my cabin that poor creature who is in such grief stretched out his hand & took up my bible, opened it, turned it over leaf by leaf. Althoug he could not read a letter he looked as if some inward instinct told him consolation was to be derived from it. I tryed to explain to him, as far as my imperfect knowledge of the Esquimaux language goes.

May [sic] 7th   All the boats off today, three of them in sight of the ship all manned by natives, Mr. P., Newbulligar, & Tshatluta harpooners.

I could see first Tshatluta get fast, Mr. P. killing her, & then towed off
by two boats. Bulligar then got fast & after an hour's work she shared
the same fate. By this time the other boats who had gone s. with
Mr. Cheyne came & Andrew Lindsay got fast. They then all came to the
floe where they are flinched. The people all came home & had dinner
& tea at once & then commenced to work, being about 11 o'clock P.M.,
finishing somewhere about 7 next morning. A number of the females
turned out & dragged up the blubber on sledges. They then all went to
bed & slept until 12 noon.

May [*sic*] *8th*   At 1 P.M. 5 boats started & were not long out until Ross
got fast & secured a fish. Three other boats then set off. Mr. Penny
fired & shot a fish but the lines being hard they started off the billet
head & in pulling them on again those behind drew the line too tight
which made him unable to get out his thumb & I am sorry to say got
the point taken off & otherwise much bruised, but I trust it will soon
get better. Lucas then got fast in a large fish which he succeeded in securing. A fog came on suddenly & the boats had a good deal of trouble
in getting to harbour.

May [*sic*] *9th*   People all off again to work at 12 noon. Two boats are
out to fish with Mr. Cheyne. Not long away when he got fast in a large
fish. It took about 4 hours to kill her. Mr. Birnie flinced the yesterday's
two & then started with 6 other boats. He also got fast in a large fish.
She nearly took the boat down with her, but the others came to his
assistance & she was secured. I went down with Mr. Penny to the floe at
2 A.M. to see them bring the Leviathan to shore, which they did about
4 A.M. The scene was most enlivening to behold & the morning sun
shining in all the splendour of a fine morning. I have truly great
reason to be thankful to my God for all the great mercies to me, for
they are numberless.

May [*sic*] *10th*   All engaged in flincing. Three boats out. New-
bul[lygar] got fast in a large fish. She was got to land at 6 A.M. The
people all came up, had breakfast, went to bed & had six hours sleep,
when they commenced again.

May [*sic*] *11th*   Mr. Cheyne & 2 other boats set off today. Mr. C. got a
fine large fish. It is so exciteing to see all the operations going on that I
can scarcely sleep any. My department is to feed the natives & pretty
hard work it is when you know that there are three hundred of them.

May [*sic*] *12th*   No boats away today as everything has to be cleared away for the Sabbath. At half past 11 the flag was hoisted to drop work. Newbuligar set off without leave this morning.

June 13th. Sunday   Everyone is glad of this day of rest. Divine service in the evening. At 12 midnight all hands called & work commenced.

June 14th   Nine boats out today. Mr. Penny from the hill saw a great many whales. George Findley caught one. I got a present of a half-do[zen] eggs from one of the natives.

June 15th   Mr. Birnie set off with 4 boats. In a few hours he got fast to a large fish. Mr. Cheyne & Lucas, after finishing the flincing of the yesterdays fish, also set [off] with 7 boats. I walked down to the edge of the floe about 10 oclock in the evening. O, how I wish I could discribe the beauty of the scene. The bright sun dying everything purple with his glory, while at the same time the moon with her silver light was distinctly felt. Then the calmness of the ocean, with large peices of ice floating about in the distance. Near the land the water is covered with various kinds of birds. I can with a telescope see all the boats, 4 towing in their fish, the other 7 lying watching a chance of securing some. I stayed until 1 oclock in the morning.

June 16th   Mr. Cheyne & Lucas got each a fish, about 12 feet bone. They went by Mr. Penny's directions a far way off for them, but they would not grudge trouble if they were to succeed so well. From the hill we can see the direction in which the [fish are?] better than those in the boats. Mr. Pennys thumb is very sore. An artery broke last night & bled very much. Mr. Birnie's fish is now flinched & sledged up to the ship.

June 17th   Mr. Cheyne & Lucas's fish are flincing today. They are 11 feet bone each. The natives are all busy helping, the females cutting at the ship & the males at the floe.

June 18th   Four boats are out today. No whales seen from the hill but we can see the one shot by Mr. Penny when he lost his thumb. The men see her from the boats & are bringing her in. The ship is now quite free from her icy bed & floating about in a pool of water. I got from a native today a beautiful northern diver.

June 19th   All hands at home, today being Saturday. The Sophia's lower hold filled up & all the week's work finished by a little past 11 P.M.

June 20th   Sunday, our day of rest. Divine service. All hands called at 12 midnight.

June 21st   All the 9 boats are out today. Tsiatlita got a large fish up the inlet. Mr. Cheyne & Findley one each down the inlet. They were so far out that it took them until 10 oclock Tuesday morning to tow them in.

June 22nd   We had a call from Mr. Quail, the American capt. He had had a very unfortunate season, no whales being seen at the side where he wintered [at Niantilik], but he is now come over & perhaps may soon get his ship filled, as she is small.

June 23rd   All hands flincing today, which is found very dificult on account of the ice breaking up. The more I see of these poor natives the better I like them for I cannnot express a wish to possess any thing they can procure, but everyone trys to be the first to bring it. Well may it be said "that these waters are teeming with animal life." We are supplied daily with varieties of delicious birds. This is now the season for their eggs & some of the natives have been down as far as fifteen miles to procure some for us. They are a great treat.

June 24th   The wind is blowing very strong from the south & the ice breaking up in every direction. The boats went all adrift but were secured before they got out side the harbour.

June 25th   Wind still blowing strong from the south. Boats unable to get out. Ice completely broken up & drifted out of the harbour without causing any harm or damage.

June 26th   We can now feel the ocean swell, which is not so pleasant as I could wish. Several of the men are complaining of colds & two are affected with scurvey. I do not feel so well myself, not having got on shore for the last week.

June 27th. Sunday   Weather rather better. All hands at rest. Divine service in the afternoon.

June 28th   We had a call from Mr. Quail & his mate today. They have not yet succeeded in securing any fish. Our boats were all out today, but obliged to return for the swell.

June 29th   Seven boats out today. We see them just off the harbour mouth & several whales near them, but still a strong swell. Tsiatita has shot a fine large one. It is a fine sight to see the 7 boats towing her to the ship. There is an iceberg in the entrance of our harbour & this afternoon just as Mr. Penny was passing it in a boat it fell in two with a noise which appeared to me like as if a thunder storm had suddenly arisen, the noise being re-echoed by all the hills around.

June 30th   All hands busy today making off the fish. The poor natives are all lamenting our leaving.

Spring comes quickly in the Arctic. Warming air works steadily upon the snow that mantles land and ice so that the firm, dry, wind-compacted material, which for months has been strong enough to support the weight of men, dogs, and sledges, and rigid enough to provide building blocks for dwellings, is transformed into a coarse granular mush, which yields at every step and finally turns into running water, surging seaward in swollen streams. Because the ground temperatures rise above the freezing point of water only at the surface, the permanently frozen layers below (permafrost) act as a barrier to the downward-percolating meltwater, forcing it to drain away over the land, thereby turning the tundra desert temporarily into a waterlogged morass. Plants emerging from their protective blanket of snow and responding to the available moisture, the increasing warmth, and the lengthening days, race to complete their seasonal cycle in the short summer ahead. After the snow on the coastal fringe of landfast ice melts, the ice itself gradually deteriorates. Meltwater ponds on the surface grow into a honeycomb of vertical thaw holes, weakening the ice. Fissures expand, and ice floes break loose and drift away. This process is slower than the frenzied ablation of snow cover on land. Intact portions of landfast ice may remain in place until July, and ice floes sometimes linger through the summer, companions for the long-lived icebergs that have grounded on shallow banks.

When Margaret's takes up her journal again in mid-May, she records some of the signs of early spring. The Eskimos' snow houses are melting; one day is "as warm as a July day at home"; walking on the soft snow of the landfast ice, she sinks "to the knees at every step." Eskimo women give her edible berries, preserved since the previous summer beneath the snow. She delights in the unaccustomed smell of exposed earth, and a spirit of reawakening pervades her entries, a feeling of sensory exhilaration after the confinement, cold, and gloom of sterile winter. The community at Kekerten is alive and vibrant. Everyone is caught up in the excitement of whale hunting from the floe edge.

In May 1858 the ice surface surrounding Kekerten Island was still thick and solid, enabling the whalemen to cross to its margin – the floe edge – and launch their whaleboats to pursue the whales migrating into Cumberland Sound. But by operating from a steadily deteriorating platform, they were putting themselves in an inherently risky situation. They considered it worth the risk because the whales, temporarily halted in their attempt to reach the upper regions of the sound by the barrier of landfast ice, were now concentrating at the floe edge and were highly vulnerable to the hunters. The open area beyond the floe edge was not entirely icefree, because it was receiving all the fragments broken off from the fast ice, and it probably contained a few icebergs and bergy bits as well. It was a region of unconsolidated floes drifting southeast towards Davis Strait, but the geographical distribution of drifting ice could be altered very quickly by the vagaries of winds. When winds blew strongly up the gulf, they drove floes against the floe edge like battering rams and created waves that helped dislodge more fragments of the deteriorating fast ice. At these times the waters near the floe edge were crowded by jostling, grinding ice floes, and there was no opportunity to launch boats. But winds blowing down the sound tended to disperse the ice floes and create more open conditions in which the whalemen could pursue whales.

Margaret's daily record shows how fast the ice conditions and whaling prospects could change. On 13 May, with a strong southerly gale driving ice floes against the floe edge, there was "little doing as there is no water to be seen." Two days later, after the wind had swung round, she observed "a little water to be seen" and "one or two whales," and the boats then began cruising. The most open conditions occurred in calm weather on 27 May, when from the summit of Kekerten Island she saw nine whaleboats "moving about in a sea of glass" and "fish in every direction."

As the weather systems were bringing about day-to-day fluctuations in the distribution of floating ice, the gradual seasonal warming of air and water was causing the floe edge to retreat everywhere towards the land. But the floe edge was the place where the whalemen launched their boats in pursuit of whales in the morning and where they left their boats and whaling gear overnight. It was the dock from which they flensed dead whales and sledded blubber and baleen back across the ice to the harbour. The floe edge, however unstable, was the focus of their operations, but they had to exercise constant vigilance in case segments of ice supporting men or equipment broke off and drifted away. Crises of this nature occurred four times within the two-week period beginning on 19 May, as well as at least twice after that. On one occasion, two carpenters went adrift with the boats they were repairing, but they had the good luck to be seen and rescued.

The gap in Margaret's journal from 2 February to 12 May hides the early stages of floe whaling. According to the *Aberdeen Journal* (1858), two whales were taken in late April, and probably three more were taken in early May. After resuming her journal on 13 May, Margaret recorded twenty-one whales killed between 20 May and 29 June, and a dead drift whale recovered on 6 July, an average of approximately one whale every two days. Most of them were captured by boats launched from the floe edge near Kekerten, within sight of the island's hilltop; but after 16 June, as the retreat of ice gave whales access to a greater area, boat crews had to cruise more extensively, killing whales "up the inlet" and "down the inlet." As ice broke away from the land, the men were able to beach whales at high tide and flense them as the sea level fell. Margaret reports an early example of this on 30 May at the north point of the harbour entrance. By 23 June, the disintegration of the landfast ice was making flensing at the floe edge "very difficult," and the two whales secured after this date were almost certainly flensed in the intertidal zone. On the twenty-fourth, Margaret reported that the ice was "breaking up in every direction," and on the following day the harbour itself – the last refuge of the landfast ice – cleared out. As Warmow described it, "The ice, by means of which we had maintained a communication between the ship and the land, for nearly eight months, was to-day broken up, and carried away by a strong wind" (*Periodical Accounts* 1858, 23:134). Margaret found the unfamiliar, slightly queasy sensation of the ship responding to the ocean swell "not so pleasant as I could wish."

Four years earlier, when Captain William Penny and his colleague Captain Brown had been among the first whaling masters to winter on

Covered whaleboats near the floe edge ready for spring whaling.
The photo is from Hudson Bay, but the methods were similar
in Cumberland Sound (photo by A.P. Low,
National Archives of Canada, PA-53596)

board ship intentionally, the *Lady Franklin* and *Sophia* had entered
Cumberland Sound in mid-September and had taken ten whales before freeze-up. Penny had chosen the harbour at Nuvujen for winter
quarters, and the following spring he had devised a system for floe-
edge whaling that in future years became more or less standard. A brief
summary of his 1854 operation may help us visualize the activities at
Kekerten in 1858.

The floe-edge whaling in 1854 had depended heavily on Eskimo
labour and skill, mainly for the tasks of sledging whaleboats out to the
floe edge and transporting blubber by dogsled back over the ice to
the ships for processing. When three boats were taken to the water on
1 May, the floe edge was an inconvenient twenty-one miles from the
ships. Penny reckoned that a return trip, including detours to circum-
vent rough ice, amounted to about forty-five miles. Three of his whaleboat crews camped in tents at the floe edge and managed to secure
eighteen whales. As many as twenty-two Eskimo dogsleds were used to
carry the blubber back to the harbour, and the total distance covered
by the dogsleds, according to Penny's calculation, was an astounding
fourteen thousand miles (*Literary Gazette* 1854, 23 September).

The floe whaling in 1858, based at Kekerten rather than Nuvujen,
was much closer to the wintering ships. Although Margaret leaves a
frustrating blank space in her journal for the distance between the harbour and the floe edge on 20 May, it is clear that it was far less than the

An Eskimo dog team in Foxe Basin. Whalemen relied on this mode
of transport to carry blubber and bone to the ships during floe-edge whaling
(Parry 1824, facing 290)

twenty-one miles that had separated the ships from open water four
years earlier. From Kekerten's hilltop lookout, Margaret could see the
whaleboats operating, and she walked out to the floe edge at least
twice. In 1858 more whaleboat crews were involved – usually from
seven to nine but occasionally as many as twelve, compared with only
three in 1854. Both Eskimo and Scottish boat crews participated in the
hunt, whereas in the initial venture the work of native men had apparently been limited to the transportation of blubber. By 1858 some Eskimos owned their own whaleboats and gear, and this gave them more
economic independence.

Another difference between the situation in 1854 and that in 1858
was the number of Eskimos attracted to the winter harbour. The fact
that there were twenty-two dogsleds used in 1854 suggests (assuming
one per family) that the native community at Nuvujen then comprised roughly a hundred individuals. Penny undoubtedly cemented
his relationship with the inhabitants of Cumberland Sound during his
next wintering voyage, and by the time he returned for his third winter in 1857 he was able to attract even more of them to live and work

at the whaling harbour. Seventy to eighty natives accompanied the two ships to winter quarters in October 1857, and more arrived later. By early May, Warmow reported one hundred and fifty Eskimos at Kekerten (*Periodical Accounts* 1858, 23:134), and on 11 June, Margaret wrote, "My department is to feed the natives & pretty hard work it is when you know that there are three hundred of them."

Were there really three hundred Eskimos at Kekerten? We could understand why a person charged with the task of handing out food for many hard-working men and their hungry families might tend to exaggerate, but nowhere else does Margaret's written record suggest any tendency to distort numbers or facts. If it was Margaret's responsibility to prepare, or at least distribute, food, she must have had a pretty good idea of the numbers involved. Her figure of three hundred, like Warmow's earlier hundred and fifty, was certainly not a precise head count; it would have been a rounded-off figure or even a rough estimate.

Margaret does not explain why it was her job to "feed the natives." There was a cook on each ship, of course, but during floe whaling the cooks were required not only to feed the whalemen but also to deliver the food to the boat crews camped out at the floe edge, several miles away. This was time consuming, arduous, and not without physical risks, as Margaret's entry of 17 May reveals: "The cook, who goes down with the men's dinner, fell throw in crossing a crack." Margaret had earlier demonstrated a capacity for entertaining large numbers of native women at tea in the evening, and she may have volunteered to help out by taking charge of meals at the vessel. Her mention of three hundred individuals suggests that she fed all the native people living at Kekerten – men, women, and children. Although she provides no details about the type of food or the frequency of meals, it is likely that she distributed only simple fare, such as ship's bread and a hot beverage once a day, to supplement what the Eskimos could procure by hunting.

If there were really three hundred Eskimos at Kekerten during the spring whaling, they outnumbered the Scots seven to one. To put the matter in a more revealing light, the economic activity of some forty Scots had dictated the place of winter residence and the seasonal livelihood of three hundred natives. Warmow claimed that the entire population of the Sound was only three hundred and fifty (Holland 1970, 40). Without knowing how Warmow obtained this figure, one cannot determine its reliability; but of all the people on board the ships, he was by far the most fluent in the Eskimo language, and his mandate to assess the potential for the establishment of a Moravian mission must have made it important for him to ascertain the size of the native population. In 1857 Warmow had visited Niantilik and Nuvujen on board ship and had travelled to the heads of Kingaite and Cumberland Sound by boat. After wintering at Kekerten, he revisited Nuvujen and Niantilik by ship in 1858. At every place, he talked with the natives and doubtless questioned them about the location and size of their settlements. If Warmow's figure of three hundred and fifty for the total population of Cumberland Sound and Margaret's figure of three hundred for the number living at Kekerten in June 1858 were both reasonably close to the truth, then Captain Penny had succeeded in attracting almost 90 per cent of the dispersed native residents of the region to one place – an island that suited his own objectives but was not closely related to the Eskimos' traditional migrations. Even if there were only one hundred and fifty Eskimos at Kekerten, as Warmow stated, Penny's winter harbour had still attracted almost half the population of Cumberland Sound. This suggests something of the seductive influence of the European presence in the Canadian Arctic.

Margaret's remarks during May and June are not entirely those of a detached observer. It is true that she often walked to the lookout position on the summit of the island to gaze out at the whaling activities beyond the floe edge, sometimes spending as long as four hours at this vantage point, which was so far removed from the whaling operations as to render the scene one of beauty and tranquillity rather than one of danger, death, and gore. At other times, she took pleasant walks on the land and rejoiced in the company of Eskimo women, who brought her berries, birds' eggs, and other gifts. Being curious about the whaling, she was not averse to walking a few miles to the floe edge, even at two in the morning, to watch the men tow a dead whale in for flensing. When Captain Quayle of the American whaler *Amaret* visited twice from Niantilik in late June, Margaret was on hand to act as hostess and hear his news. But in addition to enjoyable diversions such as these to occupy leisure hours, her activities included many tasks directly related to the busines of floe whaling. Margaret had become much more than a disinterested passenger or the privileged wife of a whaling master. She now had certain duties to perform, not only distributing food to the Eskimos but also serving as a "shipkeeper," responsible for the safety of the vessel when the captain and crew were away at the floe edge. In this, she apparently alternated with Brother Warmow; on 27 May, after watching the whaling from the summit, she returned "to allow Mr. Warmow to go up & have the pleasure of a look." Two days later, when a number of boats were reported adrift, Captain Penny dashed off with cooks, coopers, and cabin boy (the rest of the crews already being away at the whaling), but not before sending Warmow to the hilltop and placing Margaret "in charge of the ship." Given authority, Margaret was not shy about using it when the situation demanded action. When some boats were again reported in danger, she ran over to the *Sophia* and told the mate to go and help retrieve them. When he protested that he had no orders to do so, she told him to get moving – he would get the "orders" later – and off he went.

Floe whaling was an activity in which Scots and Eskimos, men, women, and children were all involved somehow. The success or failure of the operation could affect everyone; there were no disinterested parties. Any crisis threatened the welfare of the entire community and brought an immediate response from all individuals. When some boats were reported adrift on 29 May, Margaret recorded, "We sent word on shore to the females to see if they would help. They were no sooner told than they set off, old & young, to lend their aid." Later in the day, when another emergency arose, she saw "the floe covered with men, women & children flying towards" the boats. Although both Eskimos and Scots had strong traditions about the roles that women and men should and should not perform, these ideas were instantly relaxed in emergencies. Even in the day-to-day operations, the usual gender-related roles were modified according to need. Margaret took charge of the ship, a responsibility always carried out by men; Eskimo women dragged the produce of the hunt back from the floe edge on 7 June, work usually allotted to Eskimo men; and at the ships they sliced whale blubber up on 19 June, performing work normally carried out by European men.

Economically, spring whaling at the floe edge was highly significant. With the exception of the whale taken during the summer of 1857, the one captured on 29 June 1858 following the break-up of the fast ice, and the dead whale retrieved on 6 July, all the remaining twenty-five whales were taken by boats operating from the floe edge between late April and late June 1858. During the fourteen-month voyage, more than 90 per cent of the total catch of the two ships was obtained during two months, a mere 14 per cent of the time.

Made All Sail for Aberdeen

1–7 July

July 1st   Seven boats out, but no whales seen. Mr. Penny is to send the Sophia up to Kingua to see if they have taken refuge there, but he has not much hope as there is no land ice.

July 2nd   Mr. Warmow & William set out yesterday upon a shooting excursion with a boat round the island. They returned this morning about 4 A.M. bringing with them various kinds of birds & eggs. Mr. Penny sent off 6 boats with natives to go as far as Kingua to take a look if any whales have taken up in that direction. I had a long & pleasant walk on land today. The flowers are all in blossom again, so quick is vegetation in this country.

July 3rd   The wind has changed to the south & blows very strong with heavy rain. People all busy stowing away the bone in both ships.

July 4th. Sunday   Heavy rain all day with strong wind. Divine service as usual.

July 5th   All hands called at 4 A.M. Busy all day stowing bone & trimming the vessels for sea. A native has just come on board to say that he has seen a large dead fish on an island close by. Mr. Cheyne was dispatched with seven boats to bring her to the ship.

July 6th   The boats arrived this morning about 6 A.M. bringing the
dead fish with them. She is about 10 feet [bone] & newly dead.
Mr. Warmow & William have gone upon another shooting excursion.

July 7th   People all busy. Mr. Penny & some natives went to the hill.

Young William and Brother Warmow returned from a "shooting excursion" on 2 July laden with "various kinds of birds & eggs," and four
days later they were off shooting again. Birds were abundant in Cumberland Sound in early July as the continental flyways funnelled tens of
thousands of winged visitors into the tundra nesting grounds, but
Greenland whales were becoming fewer. Two months earlier they had
been moving eagerly up the sound, milling impatiently at the barrier
of the floe edge, and advancing farther by way of leads, bights, and
pools whenever ice ablation and disintegration provided the opportunity. The Scottish whalemen who had wintered at Kekerten and Nuvujen, and the Americans who had wintered at Niantilik, had sledged
their whaleboats over the landfast ice to hunt the whales congregating
in the expanding area of open water. But the steady reduction of ice
cover had gradually enabled the whales to disperse, removing most of
the whalemen's advantage. The crews operating from Kekerten killed
their last whale on 29 June and were not destined to catch another.
They did, however, recover a dead whale that had drifted ashore. Animals that died from natural causes or from wounds inflicted by harpoons were frequently found by whalers, either floating aimlessly at
sea like dismasted half-submerged hulks or cast up along the shore by
tides, waves, and currents. The rotting carcasses betrayed their location by a powerful aroma, attracting scavenging sea birds, foxes, and
polar bears, a phenomenon well known to Eskimo hunters. Unless putrefaction was too advanced, the whalemen flensed them and saved the
blubber and bone.

   With the two ships full and whaling prospects declining, it was time
to make preparations for the homeward voyage. Abruptly and inexpli-
cably, Margaret's journal ends on 7 July, but the ships' logbooks provide some details about the remainder of the voyage. About this time,
the *Sophia* appears to have set sail for Kingua and Nuvujen, but the
Lady Franklin remained at Kekerten for almost two more weeks. On

19 July her seamen took breakfast at four in the morning, and by five they had the anchor cable clattering rhythmically through the hawse-pipe. In order to gain some distance from a dangerous lee shore, Penny had set out a kedge anchor farther ahead. They hauled the ves-sel up to it, weighed anchor, and got under way some time after nine in the morning, arriving at Nuvujen, "our fishing station on the west side of the Inlet," next morning. The *Sophia* joined them in the afternoon.

During three days at Nuvujen the men worked at getting the two vessels in shape for the Atlantic crossing – stowing cargo, checking rig-ging, lashing boats down securely, topping up fresh-water tanks, and making everything shipshape. But in addition they had to put things in order ashore, because Penny intended to keep the stations at Nuvujen and Kekerten occupied through the winter and continually after that, using company whalers to bring in supplies and personnel replace-ments each summer and to take out staff, whale oil, and bone in the fall. The stations would employ Eskimos to catch and flense whales, to try out oil from the blubber, and to hunt game. Accordingly, the crews landed spare "stores, boats and other gear," and Penny sent Sur-geon Erskine Grant, Second Mate John Lucas, and Ordinary Seaman Gilbert Garster to live at the whaling station, where two of the *Sophia*'s crew – Cooper John Duncan and Ordinary Seaman William Leask – had already taken up residence. These men were to remain there un-der the authority of the doctor "until the Alibi arrives out," after which they would presumably be divided between the two stations. The *Alibi*, commanded by the refractory Captain Stewart, had left for home a year ago, but was expected to return to Cumberland Sound within the next month or so, bringing additional supplies for the men.

Normally, the Eskimos who came into contact with European whaling vessels encountered all-male crews unaccompanied by women. Yet the sexual appetite demonstrated by the sailors when they went ashore among Eskimo women revealed that they were susceptible to the usual biological urges. Logic suggested that there must be women back home, and the few individuals who had been taken to Britain or the United States confirmed that this was so. But why did the sailors not bring their women with them? Margaret's appearance in Cumberland Sound did nothing to explain the whalemen's curious practice of mak-ing voyages without their families, but it did at least serve to remove any lingering doubts about the existence of women in the whalers' world. The presence of Margaret and her son provided a more realistic model of European culture than the totally male crews of the whalers that had been seen up to that time, and the Eskimos must have surreptitiously observed with great interest the relationship between Margaret and her husband and son, the nature of child rearing in their family, the way Margaret interacted with the ships' personnel, the types of task she performed, and the way she dressed and behaved.

The Europeans sailed from Kekerten with a feeling of sadness at leaving their Eskimo acquaintances. Margaret was parting from friends with whom she had strolled, picked berries, ridden on dogsleds, and sipped tea, women who had entertained her in their tents and snow houses and shown her many facets of native culture. Brother Warmow was leaving people who had been his pupils in spiritual matters, his patients when sick, the recipients of his sympathy when bereaved. He had forged strong bonds with many of them and perhaps created a feeling of hope, some promise for the future. He wrote:

On the 19th, we left the harbour of Kekertak, where we had lain for three-quarters of a year. The Esquimaux came on board early in the morning, and there was no end of asking if I would not return in the ensuing year. I regretted that I could not promise this, for so attached to them did I feel, that I would gladly have lived and died with them, had the Lord's will been so. I also recollected, that it was at this place, that I had had the most opportunity to speak to them about our Saviour, and the prayer arose from my heart, that He would graciously forgive my mistakes and short-comings, and bless my feeble testimony. I would earnestly hope, that my residence here may not have been altogether in vain. For myself it has not been so, as I have had many proofs of my weakness, and of the Lord's mighty power, to the humbling of my proud heart. (*Periodical Accounts* 1858, 23:134–5)

His leave taking at Nuvujen on the twenty-third, like his departure from Kekerten four days earlier, was also a time of profound emotion:

At parting, many of the Esquimaux shed tears. Some begged that I would give their hands a hearty squeeze, so that they might feel it for a long time. Others asked me to scratch their faces, or cut their hands, that they might have something to remember me by. I omitted these latter ceremonies, but I squeezed their hands till the joints cracked.

At the last moment, I again felt strongly tempted, to express my determination to stay with the Esquimaux, and to live and die among them; but it happily occurred to me in time, that it was my immediate and bounden duty to return home, in order to furnish my superiors with the requisite oral information. I therefore entered on my homeward voyage, with sincere thankfulness to the Lord for the mercy and truth maniifested toward me. To Him be praise and glory! (*Periodical Accounts* 1858, 23:135)

The ships left Nuvujen on 23 July but called briefly at Niantilik on their way down the sound. Penny wanted to persuade Tessuin to work at the Nuvujen station over the winter. The renowned harpooner had been employed by ships of the Aberdeen Arctic Company for several seasons. The previous summer Penny had countermanded Captain Stewart's plan to take Tessuin to Scotland, because he wanted him to work at Nuvujen (as Margaret had noted on 19 August), but he had learned in December that Tessuin had been persuaded by Stewart to transfer his allegiance to Captain Reid of the Peterhead whaler *Arctic*. Now was the time to reclaim the expert harpooner for the company, and according to the ship's logbook, Tessuin "agreed to go up to the station." Whether Tessuin actually went to Nuvujen after Penny left for home is unknown, but he certainly did not remain there for the winter as Penny had expected; in early December the *Peterhead Sentinel* (1858) reported the arrival in that port of Captain Reid and the *Arctic* with two Eskimos from Niantilik on board – "Tesween" and his wife Pedleatu.

That there might be competition between different captains for the services of a skilful native harpooner is easy enough to understand. What inducement Stewart and Reid held out to Tessuin to go back on his promise to work for Penny is not recorded, but Reid was anxious to have the harpooner working for the *Arctic*, and Stewart seems to have sided with Reid. They achieved their objective and could triumphantly thumb their noses at Penny. Tessuin may have wanted to visit Scotland, but there was also a practical reason for taking him there. On 17 December he took the stand in Edinburgh to give evidence in the dispute over ownership of a whale he had lanced and killed two years earlier while working for the *Sophia*. Although at the time of the incident he had been employed by the Aberdeen Arctic Company, who were defenders in the case, he testified on behalf of the pursuers, Captain James H. Sutter and the other owners of the Peterhead brig *Clara*. It is a fair measure of Captain Stewart's antipathy towards the company for which he worked that he facilitated Tessuin's court appearance for rival interests, even though he himself had commanded the Aberdeen Arctic Company's ship *Alibi* at the time and had claimed possession of the whale.

Unfortunately, Tessuin's sojourn in Scotland was tinged with sadness at the illness and death of his wife Pedleatu less than two months after their arrival. The *Peterhead Sentinel* (1859) reported, "The female Esquimaux who ... was brought over by Captain Reid of the Arctic, along with her husband, died at her lodgings, Shiprow, on the morning of Wednesday last, having been very ill for a considerable times before."

On 25 July the *Lady Franklin* and *Sophia* weighed anchor and started for Scotland, two thousand miles away. After being immobilized at Kekerten for nine months, everyone must have been exhilarated to be under sail once again and starting on the final part of their adventure. Thoughts of home, loved ones, warm hearths, favourite food, green grass, leafy trees, and countless other long-denied delights must have compensated somewhat for the discomfort of the crowded quarters, the monotony of shipboard food, and overexposure to the irritating habits and repetitive conversation of their now tiresome shipmates.

Whaling captains plotting a course from Davis Strait across the North Atlantic to Scotland could take advantage of some of the same oceanic currents and prevailing winds that had hindered them on the outward voyage. Once outside the mouth of Cumberland Sound, they had to reduce their latitude by at least five degrees (about 350 miles) to clear the southern tip of Greenland. To do this, they could get some assistance from the southward-flowing Canadian Current. Going due south with it would add significantly to their overall distance, but by slanting across it in a southeasterly direction, they could strike an effective compromise. This course would take them into the North Atlantic Drift (Gulf Stream) and the prevailing southwesterly winds, which would help carry them eastward towards Scotland. Indeed, a ship disabled or abandoned in Davis Strait might in time make its own way back to the British Isles, propelled by winds and currents. A message bottle thrown overboard from one of John Ross's vessels off Cape Farewell in 1818 was washed ashore at Ireland a year later (*Aberdeen Journal* 1819), and pieces of wreckage from the whaler *William Torr,* lost with all hands in Davis Strait in 1835, were picked up at the Shetland Islands the next year (Lubbock 1955, 327).

When the *Lady Franklin* and *Sophia* emerged from Cumberland Sound, they headed due east, and while this course would seem to have sacrificed the influence of the Canadian Current, a few excerpts from the logbook of the *Sophia* reveal the reason:

25 July "Ice in sight from the mast head about ⅔ across the mouth of the sound ..."

26 July "The ship plying to windward amongst sailing ice. At 10 we got out side of what ice was in sight ... At 6 tacked ship for the ice ..."
28 July "Passed several ice bergs ... A great many ice bergs in sight ..."
29 July "Several ice bergs in sight ..."
30 July "Three ice bergs in sight."

Clearly, the ships were taking the most direct path through a belt of ice lying along the Baffin Island coast. July had not yet run its course, and the pack ice of Baffin Bay and Davis Strait was still in the process of disintegrating, dispersing, and melting. The drifting floes, carried southward by the current, tended to concentrate against the land. Icebergs, whose bulk resisted rapid ablation and whose depth made them especially susceptible to the force of currents, were also abundant near the coast and could be encountered in any month. Navigators therefore had to consider the occurrence of ice as well as the patterns of currents and winds in their homeward journey. Captains Penny and Cheyne wanted to get through the zone of coastal drift ice as quickly as possible.

When the ships reached clear water, they turned and followed a course trending southeast, roughly halfway between Greenland and Labrador, for about five days (450 miles). Passing approximately 200 miles south of Cape Farewell, they proceeded eastward between latitudes fifty-seven and fifty-nine degrees. The two ships did not manage to keep company throughout the voyage; they sailed together for only three stretches amounting to about eight days of the twenty-seven-day run from the mouth of Cumberland Sound to their landfall in northwest Scotland. On 9 August, after staying within sight of one another for more than two days, bad weather drove them apart. The *Lady Franklin* recorded a "strong breeze" from west-northwest. By four in the afternoon, the wind had freshened into a "strong gale." According to the Beaufort Scale, a "strong gale" means winds of 41 to 47 knots (47–54 mph), with seas up to 23 feet high, rolling over at the crest, and horizontal streaks of wind-blown spray (Kemp 1976, 72).

Captain Penny ordered one sail reduction after another as the wind velocity increased. Studding sails were taken in; royals were handed; topgallant sails were furled; topsails were double-reefed. Buffeted by a cross sea, the ship took a lot of water on deck. "Not a dry stich on any one on deck," the log reported. At noon they hove to and spent the next eight hours "lying too like a duck." Meanwhile, Captain Cheyne was also experiencing difficulties. After the *Sophia* had registered a speed of 9 knots (11 mph) for two successive hours (an impressive performance for a deeply laden whaler), he sent his crew scurrying aloft onto the swinging yards to take in sail, after which his ship also rode out the gale under a close-reefed main topsail. Next day, the wind moderated enough to set sail again, and the *Lady Franklin*'s carpenter set to work fixing the broken bentinck boom at the foot of a headsail and repairing other damage.

Except for the gale that pummelled then in mid-ocean, the crossing appears to have been pleasant. For much of the time light breezes drove the ships along leisurely at a few knots. Their average run of about 75 miles per day masks a wide variation from a low of 13 miles (picking their way through pack ice in fog on 27 July) to a high of 163 miles (as the gale began on 8 August). The *Aberdeen Journal* (1858), using information probably obtained from Captain Penny on arrival in the port, called it a voyage that "afforded matter for no special remark." Gales at sea were common enough in the experience of seafaring men, particularly those manning arctic whalers, who habitually sailed in the least hospitable of environments.

When the duty watches were not changing and trimming sail or performing other operations related to the ships' progress, they were put to work on maintenance jobs. The masters and mates, whose responsibility it was to make regular entries in the ships' logbooks, were evidently not inclined towards verbosity. On most days the logbook of the *Lady Franklin* does not mention the men's activity at all, while the logbook of the *Sophia*, although referring to the men's employment almost twice every day, often contains vague statements such as "People employed at Sundry jobs"; "People employed varisouly [variously]"; "People employed at various jobs"; "The wacth [watch] employed as yesterday"; "The wacth employed as before"; and "The wacth employed as usual." Tasks specifically mentioned in the logs include cleaning, painting below deck, painting masts and mastheads, setting up and tarring the standing rigging, scraping and oiling spars, and repairing storm damage. Doubtless, the men carried out a good many other jobs as well. Many of the tasks, such as overhauling rigging, were simply part of proficient seamanship; keeping the gear in good order was preventive medicine for the ship. But appearance counted for something too. Whaling captains liked to enter home port in style, with their ships looking smart, as if to say, "Yes, it was a long, hazardous voyage, and the ship took a terrible beating, but as you can see, we have managed to cope." One is reminded of the fur-trading brigades in the Canadian Subarctic which, after voyaging by canoe through the wilderness for hundreds if not thousands of miles, would stop just before reaching the trading post in order to wash, shave, cut hair, and put on clean clothes so that they could make a grand entrance at the fort.

On long sea voyages in the age of sail, encounters with other vessels were wonderful diversions. The sighting of a strange sail growing imperceptibly larger on the encompassing horizon did much to arouse curiosity and elevate spirits. Nowadays, little of interest transpires between passing ships – perhaps a brief greeting by way of the radio – for there is no longer any real need to exchange news or compare positions and chronometer time; radios, television sets, and facsimile machines keep sailors in close touch with weather patterns and global events, and satellite navigation systems provide instant and accurate latitude and longitude. In the mid-nineteenth century, however, information travelled much more slowly and not nearly as far, relying on signal flag, semaphore, unaided voice, or delivered written message. Out of sight of land was out of reach of news, so a ship coincidently encountered on the high seas was regarded as eagerly as a mobile library arriving at a remote atoll inhabited by shipwrecked Rhodes scholars. If the sea was calm enough to lower boats and the captains were not too pressed for time, they might meet on board one of the ships for a gam, during which news would be exchanged in a relaxed, convivial atmosphere. Otherwise they would heave to or sail on parallel courses, then shout a few choice bits of news from ship to ship across the intervening water, using speaking trumpets.

On 1 August the *Sophia* spoke two American whalers, the *Daniel Webster* and *Hannibal*, roughly midway between the mouth of Hudson Strait and Greenland. The former, a ship of 336 tons, owned by S. Thomas & Sons of New Bedford, Massachusetts, had left port under the command of Dexter Bellows on 11 June, giving her destination as Cumberland Sound. She had already captured three sperm whales – evidently small ones – somewhere in the Atlantic and had encountered the *Hannibal* quite by accident, probably in July (*Whalemen's Shipping List* 1858). The *Hannibal*, a ship of 441 tons owned by R. Brown's Sons and commanded by C.B. Chapel (sometimes spelled Chapell or Chappell), had started her voyage at New London, Connecticut, on 6 November 1856 with a declared destination of the Pacific Ocean (Starbuck 1878, 2:544–5); but Captain Chapel either had a change of heart or had been laying a smoke screen, for the ship seems to have remained in the Atlantic during the winter and is known to have spent the period from May to September 1857 in the "Spitzbergen Sea," following which she sailed south to the Azores with a scurvy-ridden crew that was badly in need of fresh vegetables and fruit. Chapel evidently cruised near the Azores during the second winter, intending to return to Spitsbergen in the spring of 1858 (*Whalemen's Shipping List* 1857b), but his chance meeting with the *Daniel Webster* persuaded him to sail with her, try his luck in Cumberland Sound, and perhaps pass the winter there. Did this man have difficulty sticking to a plan? Was he a victim of incurable wanderlust? Or, after a year and a half at sea, did he simply have a desperate craving for some intelligent conversation with another captain?

The two American ships reached Cumberland Sound a week or so after their encounter with the *Sophia*, wintered there, and apparently travelled homeward in company, for they both arrived at their respective ports on 23 November 1859. The *Daniel Webster* had 50 barrels of sperm oil, 1,316 barrels of whale oil, and 18,000 pounds of whalebone, while the *Hannibal*, which had been out much longer and had sent home some of its cargo, probably from the Azores, had obtained a total of 2,236 barrels of whale oil and 31,100 pounds of bone (Starbuck 1878, 2:558–9, 544–5).

The flexibility of Captain Chapel's itinerary and the impulsive marriage of convenience between the two ships suggest something of the freedom of whaling. Like the tramp steamers of a later age, many whalers wandered about the world's oceans without a fixed itinerary, their masters reacting to whaling news from other ships, playing hunches, sometimes acting on whim, and sending cargo home from remote ports on other vessels so that they could stay out longer. One vessel, the *Hope* of New Bedford, made a Pacific voyage lasting five years, five months, and eleven days (*Whalemen's Shipping List* 1857a). Another, the *Belle*, cleared from Fairhaven, Massachusetts, in December 1844 and arrived home seven years and nine months later (Starbuck 1878, 2:412–13). Long voyages and freedom of movement were characteristic of the sperm whale fishery, which took place in equatorial and temperate regions, unconstrained by the rigid timetable of winter (although many Pacific whalers included in their wanderings a summer cruise to cold regions such as the Sea of Okhotsk, the Bering Sea, and the Chukchi Sea). Captain Chapel appears to have replicated the casualness and opportunism of Pacific whaling in the North Atlantic and eastern Arctic, integrating the Azores, the Greenland Sea, and Cumberland Sound into an agreeable and profitable voyage of three years' duration.

Like William Penny, Christopher Chapel was an explorer as well as a whaler, a man who wanted to find out for himself what unknown regions were like, a true frontiersman of the oceans; and like Penny, he opened up a new whaling ground. A few years later, he and his brother Edward commanded the first two American whalers to winter in Hudson Bay, beginning a half-century of exploitation in that region. Doubtless, Chapel and Penny would have enjoyed a good gam together, but although Captain Cheyne on the *Sophia* exchanged information with the two American whalers on 1 August, Penny and the *Lady Franklin* missed them altogether. Margaret Penny might have enjoyed an encounter with the *Hannibal* too, because Mrs Chapel had sailed with her husband in 1856, although after a year at sea she had booked a passage home from the Azores (Druett 1992, 414).

Land was sighted from the *Lady Franklin* on 18 August, three and a half weeks after leaving Niantilik. It turned out to be the Flannan Islands, uninhabited rocky outcrops off the seaward flank of Lewis, the northernmost island of the Outer Hebrides. The islets were also known as the Seven Hunters, an appropriate name with which to salute men who had successfully pursued giant whales from small open boats in arctic waters. The next day, they encountered a fishing boat and went begging for some provisions. "Got some codfish and two pieces of beef, all our provisions being left at our fishing stations for fear any thing should have happened to the Alibi," the logbook noted. Having seen how Captain Stewart had flouted orders the previous summer, Penny was worried that the *Alibi* might fail to deliver the provisions needed by the five men left in Cumberland Sound, so he had dipped heavily into the remaining stores of his two ships to provide the wintering parties with some security.

The *Lady Franklin* passed the Butt of Lewis, continued towards the welcoming landmark of Cape Wrath on the mainland, followed the familiar east-trending coast, took on board a pilot for the passage through Pentland Firth, turned the corner at Duncansby Head, sighted the "South Land" – the west-east trending coast between Inverness and Fraserburgh – and began the final leg of the voyage. Meanwhile, the *Sophia* was making her way homeward on a slightly different course. She had made her landfall on the same day as Penny's ship – but almost a hundred miles farther south, at Barra, near the southern extremity of the Outer Hebrides. This put the ship almost on the same latitude as Aberdeen, but she had to circle the northern part of the Scottish mainland to get there and, in doing so, lost ground to her consort.

On the morning of 22 August, almost fourteen months after her departure on the arctic whaling voyage, the *Lady Franklin* reached her home port of Aberdeen. Captain Penny made the following brief entry in the log: "Moored ship at 11 AM in the harbour of Aberdeen. At

noon alowed the seamen to return to their homes." Another eleven
hours passed before the *Sophia* reached port. Captain Cheyne's logbook contains only marginally more information about the arrival: "At
10 [PM] got the pilot on board. The steam tug took hole of us and
towed us in to dock. Moored ship and cleared the decks up. So this
end the voyage of the Sophia."

Neither master took the trouble to record any overall judgment
about the voyage or to set down any details about the arrival itself,
accompanied as it must have been by joyous reunions with loved ones.
Such information would have been extraneous in an official document
compiled for the shipowners and the Board of Trade. In any case, a
ship's approach and entrance to port was a crucial operation demanding the total concentration of her captain. Together with the harbour
pilot, he had to reckon with a complexity of factors, including the
direction and velocity of wind, current, and tide, the depth of water,
the location of navigational hazards such as shoals and submerged
wrecks, and the presence of other ships under way or at anchor. The
phenomenon of arrival tended to receive little if any attention in journals or logs written by captains, because they were too busy with other
things. So, in fact, was almost everyone on board, for the crew had to
be on hand during the approach to make sail changes, clear anchors
and cables, rig mooring lines, heave to for a pilot to come on board,
pick up and secure a steam tug's hawser, lower and furl sails, and
tend docking lines. Once the ship was safely alongside, a host of other
duties occupied the captain and his officers. The men had to be paid
off and discharged; the unloading of oil and bone had to be supervised; stores had to be inventoried; customs declarations had to be
completed; and reports had to be made to the owners. In the excitement and bustle of homecoming, journal writing was far from anyone's mind.

To those in the port – family, friends, owners, newspaper reporters,
business people – the arrival of a ship after a long cruise was a noteworthy event, yet it was a scene so familiar that it required no description
in the local newspaper. Dozens of ships arrived in Aberdeen every day.
Accordingly, when the *Aberdeen Journal* (1858) published a summary of
the voyage three days later, it wasted no time describing the dockside
scene of reunion and celebration but stuck to the essential facts, beginning with this concise paragraph: "The Aberdeen Arctic Company's
vessels 'Lady Franklin,' Captain Penny, and 'Sophia,' Captain Cheyne
– the expedition being under Captain Penny's command – arrived in
our harbour on Sunday forenoon last. Both ships, we are glad to say,
are full."

Entrance to the port of Aberdeen in 1840
(City of Aberdeen, Art Gallery and Museums Collections)

When a ship's estimated time of arrival was known in advance, there was bound to be a crowd of well-wishers gathered at the docks looking anxiously for the faces of relatives and friends on board, while those on board the ship scanned the dockside figures just as intently. In many cases, the first news of the death of a husband, brother, father, or son during a voyage was received only after the returning ship had safely moored alongside the dock, and in many cases this was months after the man's death. Such unexpected news, secretely dreaded, was always especially shocking because it was received at a time of widespread celebration. No one had any illusions about the risks involved in the arctic fishery; there had been too many shipwrecks, besetments in the ice, and deaths from exposure and scurvy for anyone to feel confident about the arrival of a loved one, or even the return of the ship it-self. The families and friends waiting at the quayside therefore held their emotions in check until they were quite certain that the person they had come to welcome home was in fact alive. And it worked both ways. Some of those on board might return to find that a parent, wife, or child had died during their absence. So when the *Lady Franklin* approached her berth, people both on the dock and on the ship were experiencing intense anxiety as well as hope. The ship had in fact lost her cooper, John Falconer, to scurvy four months before. He had been married with nine children (*Missionsblatt* 1859, 9), and it seems very likely that his widow and some of his children were on the dock, waiting in vain for him to appear. On the deck of the ship, Margaret Penny waited for news of her family, probably still unaware that her mother had died more than a year before, shortly after she had sailed for the Arctic.

Lengthy periods away from home were a concomitant of whaling, a seasonal deprivation which whalemen simply accepted as part of the job. For many young unattached men, the prospect of an arctic voyage, with its attendant risks and adventures among ice floes and whales, was enormously seductive and certainly preferable to a humdrum existence in a Scottish town. Men with wives and children had more to miss when they went to sea and perhaps had a keener desire to embrace homeland and family once again at the end of the voyage. But whether young or old, single or married, most of them responded year after year to the lure of the arctic regions and shipped out on whalers bound for Greenland or Davis Strait. And most of them, after several months or even a year in the Arctic, were ready to admit that the familiar landscape of home was drawing them back with an irresistible intensity. At age fifty, Captain Penny had made more than two dozen voyages to Davis Strait and almost a dozen to the Greenland fishery. Since the age of twelve, he had spent roughly half of his life away at sea. One hopes that his sentiments on once again seeing the bold headlands of the Scottish coast had been sharpened by absence rather than dulled by repetition.

For Margaret and young William, the arctic voyage had been a novel experience in sharp contrast to their normal yearly round, a liberation from the confining grey stone streets and buildings of Aberdeen, a momentous expansion of geographical and cultural awareness. Margaret had enjoyed a year's respite from some of the burdens of rearing children and managing a household. In the Arctic, the task of looking after Billie had largely been transferred to Captain Penny, Brother Warmow, Dr Grant, the mates, and even some of the Eskimo hunters. Billie had managed quite nicely without school, living the dream of many a teenager – tramping across the tundra to hunt small game, stalking seals at the floe edge, travelling hundreds of miles by dogsled, living in snow houses with Eskimo companions, and learning in Eskimo fashion – by example, imitation, and experience – how to survive in the Arctic.

The presence of Margaret Penny on a returning whaler was not overlooked by the *Aberdeen Journal* (1858), which announced, "Captain Penny was accompanied by his wife, who not only successfully braved

Silver teaset presented to Margaret Penny by the shareholders
of the Aberdeen Arctic Company after her voyage of 1857–58
(City of Aberdeen, Art Gallery and Museums Collections)

the rigour of an Arctic winter, but, by intercourse with the natives and
otherwise, was of great service to the expedition." Evidently, the Aberdeen Arctic Company concurred with this last opinion, for it presented
her with an ornate silver tea service, inscribed as follows: "Presented
to Mrs. Penny by the Shareholders of the Aberdeen Arctic Company
on her return from Cumberland Inlet in the 'Lady Franklin,' August
1858." What more appropriate gift could they have selected for a
woman who had regularly entertained the Eskimo belles of Kekerten
at tea on board ship during the winter? Margaret had indeed "been of
great service to the expedition," not only by preparing food for the
ships' natives and acting as shipkeeper when the men were away, but
also by acting as foster mother to more than forty lonely men. She had
succeeded in enriching the harsh, somewhat barren life of the whalemen, and in providing companionship to her husband and son she
had reminded the men of the comforts and continuity of family life.
And perhaps she had managed to soften, just a bit, the rigid, authoritarian rule of Captain Penny, who often confided to her some of his
concerns about the ship's business. Margaret's presence had certainly
been appreciated by the officers and men. Even her husband, who was
rarely generous with compliments, went so far as to admit in the ship's
logbook, "What a blessing she has been for all on board."

Epilogue

WHALING

The *Lady Franklin* and *Sophia* were described as "full ships" when they arrived at Aberdeen. The expression "full ship" hardly needs explanation. When there was no more space in a vessel's hold for casks of blubber or oil and parcels of whalebone, that was the end of the whaling and it was time to start for home. A captain and crew could do nothing more to satisfy the owners, short of taking foolhardy measures such as stowing cargo on deck – or even heaving food stores overboard to make more room for oil, as one American captain did in the Pacific (Druett 1991, 88).

Many ships had returned full from the Davis Strait whale fishery during the boom years of the 1820s and early 1830s, after British whalers had added Lancaster Sound and the flank of Baffin Island to their whaling territory. Exploiting a previously unmolested segment of the whale population, they obtained catches that were never again equalled. British whaling interests took full advantage of the bonanza; but under the relentless hunting pressure, the whale population steadily declined, and captains found it harder and harder to fill their holds. By the 1850s the return of a full ship had become a remarkable event, and the arrival of a "clean" ship – one without a single whale – was not uncommon.

A comparison of 1858, the year of Penny's return, and 1833, a quarter-century earlier, shows the enormous fluctuations that could occur in whaling effort and yield, and suggests that a significant decline had taken place. The reduced catches explain why Penny and other whalemen of the 1850s were driven to experiment with wintering and with Eskimo labour. In 1833 more than seventy British vessels had secured over sixteen hundred whales at the Davis Strait fishery (the highest catch ever), making an astounding average of twenty-two whales per vessel. Six ships obtained more than thirty whales each, only five ships killed fewer than ten, and none returned clean. In 1858 the Davis Strait fleet was only one-third as large, and the total catch was less than seventy whales, a mere 5 per cent of that obtained in 1833. On the average, each vessel obtained only three whales. The highest catches in the fleet were obtained by three steam-auxiliary whalers, which had sailed first to the waters between Spitsbergen and Greenland, and then on to Davis Strait; these vessels, the *Diana* and *Chase* of Hull, and the *Tay* of Dundee, managed to kill thirteen, nine, and six whales, respectively. These catches, the best of the season, obtained by ships possessing the advantage of steam propulsion and exploiting two whaling grounds in turn, would have been among the worst among Davis Strait whalers in 1833. Three ships returned clean in 1858.

By continuing to apply maximum pressure on the resource without establishing any restrictions on the number of ships, the length of the whaling season, or the hunting methods used, the whaling industry had brought about its own decline. Falling yields led to ships being withdrawn from whaling and put into more profitable trades. Several ports abandoned whaling altogether. A dozen ports had sent ships to the arctic whale fisheries in the early thirties but only half of them were still outfitting whalers a quarter-century later.

Aberdeen was one of the survivors. Its arctic fleet, numbering fifteen ships in 1820, was reduced to ten by 1830 and to a single vessel a decade later. For three years the port sent out no whalers. Then, in 1844, a modest revival commenced, and by 1857 six ships, including the *Lady Franklin, Sophia,* and *Alibi,* were sailing from Aberdeen to Spitsbergen and Davis Strait. Despite the decline from the boom period, whaling was still one of Aberdeen's foremost industries, and the return of each whaler was eagerly awaited. Whaling success was bound to trickle down into many related economic activities in the city, not merely because the oil and bone delivered by the whaling ships supported various manufacturing industries, but also because the ships themselves, and the associated processing operations at dockside, created a demand for a diversity of equipment, foodstuffs, services, and labour. Boiling yards, manufactures for whalebone articles, shipbuilders, ship chandlers, sailmakers, ropemakers, ironmongers, food suppliers, the proprietors of boarding houses and taverns, and so on would all face a brighter future if the arctic whalers remained in business and achieved success. Not surprisingly, the return of Penny's full ships, as the *Aberdeen Journal* (1858) proclaimed, was "hailed with satisfaction at our port."

Margaret's journal records the capture of twenty-two whales and the retrieval of one dead whale, making a total of twenty-three (see appendix 3), but gaps in the journal make her record incomplete. The ships' logbooks add no information because they were not kept up during the spring whaling period. According to a newspaper summary of the voyage, the ships secured a total of twenty-eight whales, and this was corroborated by Warmow (*Missionsblatt* 1859, 12). These were expected to yield 240 tons of oil, and 16 tons of bone. The gauged amount of oil later reported in an annual summary of British whaling (Kinnes Lists) was slightly less, 218 tons, but discrepancies between a captain's estimate of oil and the final yield were quite normal, because the former was based on the number of casks of blubber stored in the hold, regardless of its oil saturation and without taking evaporation and leakage into account. Penny's ships probably carried a mixture of oil and blubber, complicating the calculations.

How did the catch of Penny's ships compare with those of other whalers that sailed to Davis Strait? Leaving aside vessels that were lost and those for which data are unavailable, the ships making one-season voyages in 1857 captured, on average, slightly under two whales each. The following year, the average was three. In contrast, Penny's ships, working together, captured a total of twenty-eight whales, an average of fourteen per vessel. Of course, this was a catch obtained in two seasons rather than one, but it still amounts to seven whales per ship per year – three times the average of summer voyages. A wintering voyage, however, incurred greater costs than two one-season voyages because the owners had to feed and pay the crew during half a dozen idle winter months when whaling was impossible, and during that time they could not dispatch the ship on profit-making merchant voyages in European or transatlantic trade, or on a late-winter sealing trip to the Greenland Sea. The superiority of a wintering voyage was therefore not as great as it first appears. Seen in this light, Penny's move towards year-round shore stations in Cumberland Sound was an attempt to eliminate the wasteful overwintering of ships and crews while continuing the productive spring whaling from the floe edge.

In 1840 Penny had been largely responsible for bringing Cumberland Sound within the range of one-season whaling voyages, and a dozen years later he had been among the first to winter on board ship.

Kekerten Harbour twenty-five years after Captain Penny established
the whaling station (American Philosophical Society)

Now he had initiated a third stage, in which ship-based whaling and
ship wintering were supplemented by permanent shore stations staffed
by a few resident Scottish managers but relying on Eskimo labour. In
part at least, it was a realization of the concept around which the Aberdeen Arctic Company had been built half a dozen years earlier. The
methods introduced by Penny outlasted the company, which sold off its
whalers *Alibi, Lady Franklin,* and *Sophia* in the 1860s (Pyper 1929, 104),
bringing down the curtain on Aberdeen whaling.

The Davis Strait whale fishery persisted for another half-century, but
the yields declined further, the ships became fewer, and the whales
dwindled towards the threshold of survival. The owners turned more
and more to steam power to achieve an advantage over ice and whales,
but this only hastened the end. In Cumberland Sound a few shore
stations operated. Two places, Kekerten and Blacklead Island, were
occupied by a few Scots and Americans, providing a year-round Euro-
American presence in the region and facilitating trade and employment. For two decades after Margaret's voyage, British and American
whaling ships visited Cumberland Sound as before and some wintered

Forty years after Captain Penny's men erected a house at Kekerten,
Aberdeen interests still operated a whaling station there
(photo by Graham Drinkwater during the Wakeham expedition of 1897,
National Archives of Canada, c-84687)

over, but after 1880 the main economic emphasis swung away from
whale oil and baleen to seal skins, and the whaling ships rarely wintered. The Eskimos, already dependent on the stations for imported
goods, continued to serve as hunters of the whales, seals, and other
animals desired by Euro-Americans, but they experienced a "shrinking
personal contact" with whites (Goldring 1986a, 163).

WARMOW

A few days after the return of the *Lady Franklin* and *Sophia*, the *Aberdeen Journal* (1858) remarked on the presence of the missionary
Matthäus Warmow. It reported a rising interest in the welfare of the
Eskimo people, who had been so helpful in the whaling operations,
and pointed out that the Moravian Church, interested in the possibility

Kekerten Harbour. Ships' try-pots for rendering blubber into oil
(photo by the author, August 1976)

of expanding its northern missionary endeavours, had sent a repre-
sentative with Captain Penny on a "visit of observation." Brother Warmow, the newspaper stated, had "made his report to his employers
at London," and it added, "It is probable that one or more agents
may be appointed by the Moravian Church for this hard but noble
service." This prediction, however, proved to be wrong.

When Warmow left Aberdeen, he travelled by way of Edinburgh and
Fulneck, Yorkshire, to Moravian House in London, and after deliver-
ing a preliminary report there he continued to Herrnhut, Germany,
to present a full report to the Mission Board and the elders of the
church. The ensuing discussions are not a matter of record, but the
Periodical Accounts (1858, 23:61) later announced, "With every desire
to enter upon this new field of Arctic labour, to which their attention
had been providentially directed, they could arrive at no other conclusion than that it would be inexpedient to do so, at the present time,
and under existing circumstances."

The decision not to establish a permanent mission seems surprising. The published excerpts from Warmow's letters reveal his concern for the welfare of the Eskimo people, his sympathy for the hungry, sick, and bereaved, and his eagerness to point the way to Christ. They lead one to expect that he would have campaigned with heart and soul for a mission. On departure, he had declared that he would "gladly have lived and died with them" if the Lord had willed it. On arrival in Aberdeen, he (or possibly Captain Penny) had given the newspaper reporter the impression that a mission would be set up. Yet it was clearly Warmow's own recommendation, subsequently endorsed by the church, that put an end to the idea. A dozen years after the voyage, a brief "Retrospect of the History of the Missions of the Brethren's Church in Labrador for the Past Hundred Years" stated categorically, "Br. Warmow's report was, however, not favourable to the commencement of a mission in that place" (*Periodical Accounts* 1871, 28:66).

The following reasons were given for the church's decision not to expand its missionary work into Cumberland Sound: the Eskimo population was small and evidently declining; the visits of British and American whalers presented "obstacles" to missionary work; and it would be difficult to supply and communicate with missionaries, especially if British whalers stopped visiting the region (*Periodical Accounts* 1858, 23:61). As the first and last of these factors must have been known to the Moravians when they originally agreed to send out a missionary, and as the account admitted that they might be overcome, it seems that the stumbling block must have been the "obstacles interposed in the way of Missionary labour" by the whalers. What were these obstacles?

In Greenland and Labrador the Moravian missions operated in a paternalistic socio-economic milieu in which the native population was protected from the perceived evils of foreign influence. The Danish government, through the Royal Greenland Trade Company, decided on the assortment, quantity, and price of imported goods to be sold to the Greenlanders. Similarly, within the lands allotted by the British government for Moravian missions in Labrador, the church enjoyed a trade monopoly. In proposing to set up missions there in the eighteenth century, it had demanded "the authority to keep other Europeans at a distance, considering it was better not to expose the Eskimos to Christianity at all than to allow converts to be contaminated by undesirable outside influences – whether in the form of other denominations or rum-toting merchants" (Hiller 1971, 842–3). In both these regions, restrictions on foreign commerce permitted the missions to exercise control over the material side of Eskimo life, which in their opinion was intimately connected with spiritual well-being. But in Cumberland Sound, no such control would be possible because the whaling masters were already accustomed to paying their native help with whaleboats, whaling gear, guns, and other manufactured articles, without any restrictions or supervision. Warmow, who at Kekerten had disappoved even of Eskimos wearing European clothes, pointed out to his superiors that "the frequent intercourse of the Esquimaux with Europeans had, to a considerable extent, weaned them from their original habits, and created artificial wants." His sentiments were in accord with the Moravian preference for a simple, unadorned life.

The *Periodical Accounts* (1858, 23:61) also noted that the whalers had attracted the people away from their usual places of residence and from their traditional pursuits, "for which they are rendered increasingly unfit." But was it really the concentration of Eskimos at whaling harbours and their use of manufactured articles that disturbed the Moravians? After all, they themselves encouraged converts to settle at their Labrador missions, where they sold them imported goods. Their basic strategy was virtually identical to that of the whalers in Cumberland Sound, namely, to attract the natives from their traditional dispersed, nomadic existence to a comparatively sedentary life near the Europeans, where they would be available for religious instruction, education, labour, and trade. The Moravians could not justifiably disapprove of the whaling approach, for they relied upon it themselves. The real problem was neither population centralization nor trade. It was the fact that control would be exercised by the whaling interests rather than the missionaries, making their religious objectives difficult if not impossible to achieve.

Two concomitants of whaling around the world were the introduction of alcoholic beverages to native societies and the sexual relationships between whalemen and native women. Both could create problems. Although Captain Penny was a stern master and well aware of the harmful aspects of whaling contact in Cumberland Sound, it would be naive to suppose that his crews had no access to alcohol or sex at Kekerten. The ships did carry some spirituous beverages, and in December the men were brewing beer ashore. During the winter, with so many Eskimos living at the harbour, the men must have had some opportunities for sexual liaisons. But the only reference to any unacceptable behaviour is Margaret's vague remark about the natives on 25 May: "I am sorry to say they have been taught much evil." Unfortunately, Victorian reticence, her relationship to the ship's captain, and the fact that he read her journal and sometimes added his own remarks may have discouraged her from elaborating, so we can only speculate about what evil things the Eskimos had learned. Although the Moravian newspapers were reluctant to criticize the whalers at the time of Warmow's voyage on the *Lady Franklin*, their 1871 review of missionary activities did mention British and American whalers, "whose influence – especially in the introduction of spirituous liquor among the poor natives, – was proving very injurious, and evidently leading to their rapid extermination" (*Periodical Accounts* 1871, 28:66).

One-third of a century after Brother Warmow's voyage with Captain Penny, when a permanent mission was at last established in Cumberland Sound by the Church Missionary Society, the Reverend E.J. Peck and his fellow Anglican missionaries had to confront the very problems which the Moravians had foreseen and shied away from in 1858.

In January 1859, at Herrnhut, Brother Warmow married Sister Maria Elisabeth Richter (née Beck), whose first husband, Friederich Valentin Richter, had died a few years earlier. Four months later, he and his bride sailed from Copenhagen to resume work in the Greenland missions. It was an eventful voyage, plagued by unfavourable ice conditions. After managing to reach the coast almost a hundred miles north of Lichtenau in early June, the ship was beset for a fortnight. When the ice opened a little, the captain obtained a pilot from a village and set off south, but pack ice closed in again and brought the ship to a halt. By this time, the mission at Lichtenau had become aware of their position and sent a boat, which collected the Warmows and several others. They took almost a week to cover the remaining sixty miles to the mission, during which time the party of eleven persons, soaked by heavy rain, crammed themselves into a small tent for three days to wait out the deluge. A few days after arriving, Warmow wrote to Herrnhut:

I am often, in spirit, at Cumberland Inlet, and most heartily desire that a day of grace may soon come, for the poor Esquimaux at that place. I know it would not be possible for Missionaries to go thither, under present circumstances, with the slightest prospect of success, even should they be willing to endanger life, and squander resources in an unjustifiable manner. Yet I cannot forget those poor Esquimaux. (*Periodical Accounts* 1858, 23:248–9)

The Warmows began work at the Lichtenfels mission and were later transferred to Neuherrnhut, where Elisabeth died in May 1862 at the age of only forty-two (*Periodical Accounts* 1861, 24:452). Within five weeks, Matthäus was engaged to Sister Emma Renata Halbeck, fifteen years his junior, who had gone out to Greenland to marry

The Reverend E.J. Peck, who established a mission at Blacklead Island
(near Niantilik) almost four decades after Brother Warmow's visit
(Anglican Church of Canada, General Synod Archives,
Peck Papers, P-7502-12C)

Brother Böhnisch but had learned on arrival that her fiancé had just
died. Matthäus and Emma were married in November 1862, and she
gave birth a year later to a stillborn son. For the next two decades the
couple worked in the missions at Igdlorpait, Lichtenfels, and Lichtenau, until 1883, when, after thirty-seven years of arctic missionary endeavour, Brother Matthäus Warmow returned in deteriorating health
to Germany with Emma. She died in Herrnhut in 1897 at the age of
sixty-four, and he passed away a year later, aged eighty-one.

M'CLINTOCK AND THE FRANKLIN SEARCH

When the *Lady Franklin* and *Sophia* returned to Aberdeen in August
1858, people were eager to hear if there was any news of Franklin's
missing expedition. Thirteen years had elapsed since Her Majesty's
Ships *Erebus* and *Terror* had left England, and although few dared to

believe that the men could still be alive, everyone – especially Lady Franklin – wanted a final answer, an explanation, a solution to the mystery. Francis Leopold M'Clintock had set out to complete the picture, leaving Aberdeen in the screw yacht *Fox* the morning after Penny's ships. During the summer of 1858, it was learned in Scotland that the *Fox* had been beset in Baffin Bay during the previous winter, drifting helplessly in the grip of the pack ice for eight months, quite unable to reach the supposed site of the tragedy. Despite this hazardous and uncomfortable experience, "the gallant M'Clintock," after emerging from the icy prison, had resumed his mission, pressing northward once again through Baffin Bay towards Lancaster Sound.

It was too early to expect M'Clintock in Aberdeen, so people looked to Penny for news. But their notions of arctic geography were somewhat vague, and few of them were probably aware that Lancaster Sound, Franklin's first destination, and King William Island, the supposed site of the tragedy, were farther from Cumberland Sound than London was from Nice – considerably more than hailing distance. The men of Penny's ships could add nothing significant to the Franklin story. None of them had attached much importance to the confusing bombast of Pakak about white men arriving by boat in Pond Inlet some years before. Penny (1858) later called the story "feasible" but thought that it probably referred to whalemen from a wrecked ship rather than Franklin survivors.

Before returning to Aberdeen in 1859, M'Clintock found plenty of grim evidence on King William Island to corroborate the stories told by Eskimos to John Rae about the starvation and death of many of Franklin's men as they stumbled southward towards fur trade posts an impossible thousand miles away. And he brought the final answer that Jane Franklin feared. A note found in a cairn revealed that Sir John had died on 11 June 1847. He had been dead and she a widow for more than eleven years.

WILLIAM PENNY, JR

Unlike his father and grandfather, young William Penny did not choose a life at sea. A decade after the whaling voyage he was in India, a young man of twenty-one years, working on a tea plantation and dreaming of establishing himself in the business. He was already making enough money to send some home to his mother to pay for the wedding of his sister Janet in August 1867. But he expressed a need to obtain capital to "lay out a tea garden" and set himself up as a grower.

William Penny, Jr, who, at the age of twelve, accompanied his parents
Captain and Mrs Penny on the 1857–58 voyage to the Arctic and
who later became a tea planter in India (private collection)

Margaret Penny (1867) suggested approaching "Osborn," who had worked in Bombay and was now the influential managing director of the Telegraph Construction and Maintenance Company. This was the same Sherard Osborn who had commanded HMS *Pioneer* in the Arctic during the Franklin search expeditions of 1850–51. After Osborn had criticized Captain Austin (under whom he served) and expressed admiration for the work of Penny, he had pointedly been overlooked in the promotion list. Penny had written to protest, and the two men had become good friends. But now, when Captain Penny approached him seeking a favour for his son in India, he was rebuffed. "Like many of my great designs, [it] fell to the ground," he later lamented to John Barrow (William Penny 1872).

Young William settled at Bisnath in the Darrang District of Assam Province and spent the rest of his life there. When he died in 1917 at the age of seventy-two, he was manager of the Shakomato (or Shako-matha) Tea Company Limited and evidently possessed tea plantations of his own, the income from which he was able to bequeath in equal shares to his children. The salubrious climate of the Himalayan foot-hills, augmented perhaps by the stimulating influence of tea, appear to have favoured family life and procreation. William had sired nine children by his first wife and two more by Radha Nepali when he was in his late sixties. The children's names reflected four generations of the Penny line; among them were James, John, Helen, Janet, Mary, and of course William and Margaret.

On 27 June 1917, the day before he died at Tezpur, Assam, William signed the last of four codicils modifying the will he had drawn up a dozen years before. He left a twentieth of his properties "to help the wounded in the War, and the dependants of those who are killed in the War," and another twentieth to a mission, "the Dufflas on the hills beyond Dhuba [Dhubia?]." Finally, he directed his executors to build a house for "the mother of my children now at Shakomatha Tea Estate" and to provide her with twenty head of cattle (William Penny, Jr 1917).

CAPTAIN WILLIAM PENNY

The voyage of 1857–58, during which "the whales were like to jump on board themselves" (William Penny 1859) and whose results Penny considered to be "equal to our most sanguine expectations" (William Penny 1858) capped two decades of important achievements. But what-ever satisfaction Penny derived from his accomplishments was over-whelmed by disappointment at not having done more. He had not secured a land grant or exclusive whaling rights in Cumberland Sound. The plan for a whaling colony on Baffin Island had fizzled out. His intention of taking a steam whaler past Novaya Zemlya into the Arctic Ocean north of Asia had not been realized. The goal of extending arctic whaling through the circumpolar region appeared more remote than ever. By this time, Penny may have begun to realize that when he drove himself relentlessly towards a lofty summit, some other men – less motivated, less ambitious, or simply less capable – would choose to turn back at lower elevations. His enthusiasm, optimism, determination, and success were widely admired from a distance, but many of those close to him became distinctly uneasy when he presented his bold and uncompromising ideas. Whaling was a risky enough venture for shipowners without their taking too seriously his talk about taking steamers into the unknown ice-bound Arctic Ocean.

To have played a strong role in the Franklin search, rediscovered Cumberland Sound, initiated the practice of wintering on board whaling ships, and established the first year-round whaling bases at the Davis Strait fishery was not enough for William Penny. He still dreamed of implementing the rest of the grand plan around which the Aberdeen Arctic Company had been built, a plan based on the assumption that to the north of the troublesome pack ice – with which whalers and explorers so often came into contact – lay a relatively ice-free polar sea. As we know today, this was nothing more than a seductive geographical myth, and it is sad to think that it became the El Dorado of a capable and well-meaning man who saw many other things with crystal clarity. Although by 1859 Penny hesitated to press his ideas forward with his previous persistence, having met with some scepticism and resistance during the preceding half-dozen years, he could at least outline them frankly to his confidant John Barrow, who never failed to give encouragement. Penny proposed that if a British dockyard were to be built on Vancouver Island – to be named Port Franklin in memory of Sir John – it would enable him "to start in the spring and fish home by Nova Zembla" (William Penny 1859; 1860a). Although his plan is not entirely clear, he appears to have envisioned taking one or more steam-auxiliary whalers past Novaya Zemlya to carry out whaling in the supposedly ice-free polar sea during the summer, then continuing across the roof of Asia and through Bering Strait to Vancouver Island in the autumn, and then, after wintering and outfitting there, retracing the route back to Scotland, pursuing whales again in the Arctic Ocean on the way. The idea was still very much on his mind sixteen years later, and he could confidently imagine what the polar region would be like.

A polynya (permanently ice-free area), he wrote, "will extend to a high latitude. The whales here will be so numerous that it baffles description and ... fine light floes to cross and recross the Pole" (William Penny 1875).

Penny remained in command of the *Lady Franklin* and *Sophia*. He sailed towards Greenland for seals early in 1859 and then to Davis Strait for whales in the summer. But he was somewhat disenchanted wih the Aberdeen Arctic Company; he wrote that he had received many offers to command steam whalers and it was only his attachment to his two ships that kept him from taking employment elsewhere (William Penny 1859). Although Penny had advocated steam propulsion for almost a decade and is said to have superintended the construction of Dundee's first steam whaler *Narwhal*, which was launched in 1859 (Holland 1970, 40), he had never commanded a whaler with an engine. Penny liked to be in the vanguard of new developments, and it was frustrating to see other masters given the opportunity to experiment with steam while he had only sail power at his disposal.

After another Davis Strait voyage on the *Lady Franklin* in 1860 he confessed, "I have been too long struggling with my two little favorite vessels but I must test the power of steam" (William Penny 1860b). The following winter he accepted an offer from a Dundee firm to command the new steam whaler *Polynia* on a voyage to the Greenland Sea and Davis Strait (*Dundee Advertiser* 1861). Working for Dundee owners was a novel experience. Except for one voyage with the *Advice* of Dundee a dozen years before, he had been sailing Aberdeen ships for a quarter-century. But his flirtation with Dundee led to divorce from Aberdeen. In March 1861 the directors of the Aberdeen Arctic Company, which Penny's initiative had helped found a decade earlier, wrote to advise their agent George Findlay at "Newboin, Cumberland Inlet," that Captain William Penny was no longer in the service of the company: "He cannot interfere with you, or with the natives in your employment; and you will take your orders either from Capt. Couldrey of the 'Lady Franklin,' Capt. McKinnon of the 'Alibi,' or Capt. Fraser of the 'Sophia'" (Wood 1861). It was not until a year and a half later (possibly because of an existing contract or of a need to ratify the decision at a general meeting of shareholders) that the directors notified Penny that his "services would not be required" after 30 September 1862 (Aberdeen Arctic Company 1862).

On 1 July 1863, accompanied again by Margaret, Penny set off on another wintering voyage, in command of the whaler *Queen* from his home town of Peterhead. Because the facilities at the stations he had established at Kekerten and Nuvujen were now denied to him, and because the Eskimos he had worked with for several years and tried so hard to Christianize were now employed by new captains in the Aberdeen Arctic Company, he decided to sail for Hudson Bay. After years of protesting against the presence of a few American whalers in Cumberland Sound, Penny was now in the awkward situation of intruding on a territory that had recently been opened up for whaling by the Americans, of whom he openly disapproved. And technically he was as much an interloper as they, because the west coast of Hudson Bay, where whaling was carried out, was within the vast region (ten times the size of the British Isles) over which the powerful Hudson's Bay Company had held broad administrative powers and a monopoly of trade for almost two centuries.

After traversing Hudson Strait, Penny attempted to reach Roes Welcome Sound, the principal whaling region, by rounding the northern tip of Southampton Island as William Edward Parry had done in 1821 on his second voyage in search of the Northwest Passage. But pack ice in Foxe Channel barred the way, so he turned back from Seahorse Point, skirted the island's south coast, and arrived at the continental mainland in the vicinity of Marble Island and Chesterfield Inlet. These were new waters for Penny. He was not familiar with any suitable winter harbours, the weather was foggy, his charts were "imperfect," and to make matters worse there "was no great appearance of fish" (*Buchan Observer* 1863). After a narrow escape in shoal water, he turned the ship eastward and made all sail for the familiar territory of Cumberland Sound, more than a thousand miles away. News of Penny's voyage reached Scotland in early November; a letter carried from Cumberland Sound by the American whaler *Georgiana* was delivered to St John's, Newfoundland, and transferred to a ship destined for Europe. Dated 8 October, the letter revealed that Penny was once again at Kekerten, preparing to winter on board the *Queen*. The reaction of the Aberdeen Arctic Company directors is not recorded.

After a voyage lasting fifteen months, the *Queen* reached Peterhead, Scotland, on 20 September 1864, having secured only one whale (*Buchan Observer* 1864). There was one curious outcome of this voyage: Penny's name was cited in connection with a case of plunder in Hudson Strait. The story begins with the wreck of the American whaler *George Henry*, which had departed from New London, Connecticut, for Hudson Bay under Captain Christopher B. Chapel in 1863. Only half a dozen American whaling masters had ever ventured into Hudson Bay, and although Chapel was one of them, he did not have the experience gained by repeated voyages to the region. The whalemen's knowledge of ice conditions there was still superficial. Hudson Strait is analogous to the neck of a huge tilted bottle, out of which flows the disintegrating pack ice of Hudson Bay, Foxe Channel, and Foxe Basin. Ships attempting to force their way westward against the disgorging ice too early in the season – as the *George Henry* did – were as effective as mosquitoes in a wind tunnel. They could hug the north coast to profit from a counter-current flowing into the strait, but the combination of currents and tides was tricky, and a ship could easily find itself beset by drifting floes.

The *George Henry* passed Resolution Island and entered Hudson Strait on 12 July but got immediately into heavy ice near the Lower Savage Islands. Captain Chapel moored to a floe one and a half miles in circumference, but its rotation carried the vessel towards the rocky shore. When he shifted the vessel to another floe, the lines parted. His description of the incident in a letter to his friend Captain Jackson half a year later illustrates the helplessness of the beset ship:

Tide done and turned, was swept back again so near the rocks that as she went along stern first partly head in, her jibboom nearly touched. A switch tide brought her back, and after being sent past it three times took a tide that set her off a little, and then whirled her round and round, and some single pieces of ice coming with great force against her sides as if determined to go through.

During the night drifted off some, but the next flood set us back, and at 9 o'clock on the morning of July 16 my ship was forced on to the rocks on a small isle at the top of high water, a bad time as you know, when the tide had fallen some 12 feet, the ship resting on a shelf of rock, she slid off sideways, and striking on to the rocks below with such force that her bilge was stove in. Saved all we could and made the hull fast. (Lubbock 1955, 380)

For ten days the crew camped on the rocky shore, lashed by winds and rain, while the victorious ice ground and spun past. They then took to their small open boats and started across Hudson Strait through the drifting floes, hoping to reach a Moravian mission settlement on the Labrador coast. After three days, the five boats became separated during rough weather; but just short of the Button Islands at the northern tip of Labrador, they all had the extraordinarily good luck to be picked up by the *Actor,* a New London whaling schooner heading for Hudson Bay. Her master, John Spicer, who later became well known for his whaling exploits in Hudson Strait, took the survivors to the site of the wreck so that they could collect the provisions and gear they had managed to save. But Captain Chapel "found that some one had been there and robbed everything away." As he later complained, "All the property I had saved was stolen; the man I have learned since was William Penny" (Lubbock 1955, 380–1).

How did Chapel connect Penny with the theft? As Spicer worked the *Actor* through the ice floes towards Hudson Bay in mid-August with the shipwrecked crew on board, he encountered the Hudson's Bay Company ship *Prince Arthur,* sailing from London to Moose Factory under Captain Smythe. Spicer asked if they had seen any ships about and was told that "they had seen the ship 'Queen' to the north of them about Savage Islands" (Wakeham 1898, 58). In fact, the *Prince Arthur* had done more than see the *Queen*; she had exchanged information with her, as the ships' logbook entry for 14 August reveals (*Prince Arthur* 1863): "At 1.p.m. spoke the vessel that was in company last night. They gave her name Queen of Peterhead going a whaling." But the *Prince Arthur* had not noticed anything that might connect the *Queen* with the place of the wreck, so it was purely circumstantial evidence that prompted Captains Spicer and Chapel to blame Captain Penny for the plunder of the *George Henry*'s stores. Ships passing through Hudson Strait in 1863 were few indeed – a few trading vessels, half a dozen American whalers, and the *Queen.* Captains Chapel and Spicer may have concluded that neither the American ships nor those of the honourable Hudson's Bay Company would have committed the theft. But a Scottish whaler? Highly suspicious!

In fact, Penny had visited the wreck site. In November 1863 the Scottish whaler *Sir Colin Campbell,* returning from Davis Strait, reported that the *Queen* had arrived in Cumberland Sound from Hudson Strait in early October. According to the article:

In coming down the [Hudson] Straits he [Penny] fell in with the wreck of the George Henry, an American whaler, on one of the Lower Savage Islands. Although dismasted, and on the rocks, the hull was in a state of considerable preservation. She had two anchors down, and a hawser out to the land. Part of her provisions, and most of her small stores, sails, lines, &c., were ashore. From some writing on a board on the wreck, Capt. Penny learned that the crew had taken to their boats intending to proceed to St. John's, Newfoundland. (*Buchan Observer* 1863)

The circumstantial evidence that Penny took the stores now appears much stronger, but it is still not conclusive. Even if he did take them, it is difficult to explain the incident satisfactorily. He was embittered because he had been dismissed from the whaling company he had founded; he was strongly opposed to the American presence in regions that he considered British; and he was unquestionably disappointed at his lack of success in whaling in Hudson Bay. Had his frustrations and his anti-American sentiments led him to remove the stores landed from the wreck? Or had he simply felt that he possessed legitimate rights of salvage over what had been taken off the disabled ship? We may never know.

The incident is reminscent of a similar event involving Penny off the coast of Greenland seventeen years earlier. The following details and quotations are from a journal written on board the Aberdeen whaling barque *Pacific* (1846) by her surgeon Andrew Hamilton. On 8 July, as the vessel approached Disco Island from the northward – all hopes of a passage through Melville Bay having been extinguished – they came upon a wreck. The following day, Hamilton wrote:

Had information concerning the wreck that was seen last night, that it was a brig from Denmark with provision for the settlements. It had been boarded by Mr. Penny, Master of the St. Andrew, when he plentifully helped himself to the stores designed for the helpless settlers in these inhospitable climes. What did not find its way to the St. Andrew, was left, to sink about 60 miles off the coast, without one effort made to save the cargo. If it was not sacrilege it must have been next to it as there is one settlement viz. Upernavick, which has got no supply since this time two years. The consequence to them must be lamentable. Such conduct on the part of the master of a British ship must impress the Danes & other inhabitants of the Greenland coast with any thing but a favourable view of the character of the whale-fishers who frequent the Straits, not a few of whom have been obliged to live among them in consequence of losing their ships.

A few days later he obtained more news when they encountered the *Chieftain* from Kirkcaldy, which had been at the wreck when Penny was there. Hamilton learned that

Capt. Todd had sent a boat alongside of it and offered his assistance to get it taken ashore when the Shark who commands the St. Andrew and who had then possession of the wreck, ordered the boat off, saying that the wreck and all in her was his. Praiseworthy philanthropy. There certainly ought to be erected to the worthy skipper of the barque St. Andrew a monument more lasting than brass for his gallant exploit in ransacking a sinking wreck appropriating to his own use the money found in her, destroying the dispatches and condoling with the governors and other officials over their loss. Villainous hypocrisy!

Surgeon Hamilton certainly sounds a high and self-righteous tone of disapproval. Whether or not his account is accurate we cannot know. He was, after all, not an eyewitness. He only repeated what he had heard from the captains, and it is worth mentioning that Captain Reid of the *Pacific* may have been antagonistic towards Penny. He was probably the same Reid who later, while commanding the *Arctic* in 1858, managed to attract the Eskimo workers of the *Alibi* away from Penny and the Aberdeen Arctic Company with Captain Stewart's connivance, and he was possibly the same Reid of whom Penny once remarked to Lady Franklin, "He is a man incapable of commanding himself" (William Penny 1850). One wonders whether, if Captain Reid had been the first to arrive at the wreck, he would have put his men to work extracting as much as possible and then sailed to the nearest settlement to present the cargo to the Danish authorities for the "helpless settlers" of the "inhospitable climes." In fact, Captain Reid did have the opportunity to perform just such a service a week later when the *Pacific* came on another Danish wreck off Rifkol. This is Surgeon Hamilton's description of the gallant way in which Reid and his crew rose to the occasion:

At 2 A.M. whilst racking off to the westward, we fell in with the wreck of the Danish brig off Reef-koll. Two of our boats boarded it with the two carpenters to break up her decks. She had got her bowsprit carried away, her foremast and main top mast, and the sea was passing right over her decks. Our men laboured away at her, to try if possible & save her cargo which might yet be found. After two hours work one boat came off with several articles among which was a naval officer's uniform, with shirts, towels and a good many fine handkerchiefs, all marked with the initials A.U. and numbered. Several parts of ladies apparrel & childrens dresses were also found. It was evident that all hands must have perished from the state their dresses were found in. A gentleman's coat with his gloves in the pocket, and such like undoubtedly was cast off only to turn in to bed. It was truly heart-rending to witness the state of several articles which we were led to believe, we[re] designed, for settlers as presents from some dear friends at home & no less so was it to find the remains of what might have been held most sacred by those who had perished with the wreck. Many papers & books were found among which was a volume of Sir W. Scott's (Quintin Durward) in the Danish tongue. It would be endless to enumerate all the stuff that was got. Suffice it to say that by 12 noon the most of our men on board of wreck were in a tremendous state of intoxication from what was got by way of drinkables out of the wreck. We however got them all aboard safely after not a few of them had been properly souced in the sea. After dinner they turned to and had an out & out boxing match at it till the one had completely mastered the other.

On the next day, 17 July, Captain Reid headed west across Davis Strait with whatever they had managed to save from the wreck. The party was still continuing; some of the men "could still muster a bason full of spirits." This, evidently, was the proper way to salvage a wreck. Surgeon Hamilton saw no fault in it. Nor did he see any "villainous hypocrisy" in his views about Penny.

It is reassuring to learn that a month later, when the *Pacific* stopped in at Holsteinborg, Greenland, they found the captain and crew of the wrecked Danish brig alive and well. After abandoning the ship, the crew had spent twenty-five hours on the ice and had then reached the coast after a twelve-hour pull in the boats. In fairness to Captain Reid, it must be said that he delivered to the Danes the articles saved from the wreck (with the exception of the spirituous beverages). Surgeon Hamilton handled the paper work of signing over the wreck property, and he made medical rounds in the settlement. So grateful were the inhabitants that when the ship departed a group of women made a valiant attempt at singing "God Save the Queen." The sailors replied with three cheers.

Hamilton's 1846 account lends more credence to Captain Chapel's accusation that Penny sailed away with the stores of the *George Henry* in 1863. Was Penny a cold-hearted pirate who capitalized on the losses suffered by others, as Captains Chapel, Reid, and Todd appear to have believed? Or was he simply an opportunist who made good use of the provisions and gear he could extract from wrecks and abandoned caches ashore? Unfortunately, there is not enough reliable evidence about the two incidents to know where the truth lies.

Penny's 1863 voyage to Hudson Bay and Cumberland Sound was almost certainly his last whaling venture. His name does not appear again as master in the annual lists of British whaling, and it seems highly unlikely that he would have sailed under anyone else. But he did not join the ranks of the unemployed voluntarily. He simply could not obtain a command. In 1867 his daughter Janet wrote, "Poor papa tried every way for a ship but all in vain. I only wish we could do something for ourselves" (Janet Penny 1867a). A few months later, when the family was hard pressed to find money for Janet's approaching wedding, she wrote, "We will try & get on as best we can & perhaps Papa will get a ship next year" (Janet Penny 1867b). It was a cruel twist that the services of Scotland's most famous whaling master were no longer required. During thirty years as master he had opened up new whaling grounds, implemented new methods, and secured above-average catches. Sailing repeatedly to the most dangerous whaling ground in the world, where one in seventeen voyages ended in ship-wreck, he had never lost a vessel. He had participated in the Franklin search and made strong efforts to have a Christian mission estab-lished for the Eskimos of Cumberland Sound. At fifty-nine, he was still younger than some whaling captains. Yet no one would give him a command.

The most likely explanation is that company directors and shipown-ers considered William Penny "too hot to handle." His initiative had become a liability. His ambitious plans, which had once promised sal-vation for a declining industry, now seemed an unecessary financial burden. His belief in an ice-free polar sea was becoming an embarrass-ing obsession. His desire to improve the condition of the Eskimos on Baffin Island was regarded as a costly extravagance.

In addition, there was the matter of Penny's personality. Possessing a strong conviction that his opinion on any issue was the correct one, he tended to be impatient when others disagreed. Disliking compromise, he preferred to impose his own policies on everyone else. The calibre of his reputation, the intensity of his arguments, and the force of his persuasion often enabled him to override the protestations of others, but usually at a cost. Their resentment sometimes simmered until they could turn against him at a later date.

Penny was an outspoken man who did not hesitate to unleash powerful invective against those whose ideas differed from his own or those whose performance failed to match his own high standards. His targets included people who had once been good friends or had done him great favours. Even Lady Franklin, whose influence had been largely responsible for his appointment to command the Admi-ralty search expedition in 1850, incurred his disapproval for seeking assistance from the Americans, whom Penny had always regarded with extreme antipathy. Discretion and tact were not in Penny's vocabulary, and there is no doubt that he hurt some people with his violent attacks. Those who granted him favours and were later wounded by his insensitive criticism quickly learned not to grant him favours again.

On occasion, there was a measure of hypocrisy in his comments about other individuals. He once wrote sarcastically of the "influence" that had "brought a N.W. traper and placed him on board an expedi-tion and called him Captn.," evidently referring to William Kennedy, a Canadian of Scottish and Cree parentage who had left the employ of the Hudson's Bay Company in 1851 and volunteered to help without remuneration in the search for Sir John Franklin (Holland 1970, 42). With a recommendation from John McLean, a former chief trader of the Hudson's Bay Company, he had secured command of an expedition on the *Prince Albert*, sponsored by Lady Franklin. Penny felt that Kennedy had obtained the position unfairly – by "influence" rather than by virtue of experience and qualifications – yet Penny himself never hesitated to use influence to promote his own interests. "I feel confident of having your aid in procuring a grant of land about Cumberland Strait," he wrote to Sir Francis Beaufort (William Penny nd.a). "I now ask your aid which I know is powerful," he wrote to Captain W.A.B. Hamilton (William Penny nd.b). "I feel sure when I made my appeal to Captn. Hamilton for his aid he would have given it had it been in his power," he confided to John Barrow (William Penny 1855). It is most unlikely that Penny would ever have obtained command of a government expedition in search of Sir John Franklin without the powerful influence of Lady Franklin and her friends in high places.

When William Penny became angry it showed! Captain Stewart, Captain Cheyne, and harpooner George Ross were on the receiving end of his outbursts during the voyage of 1857–58, and half a dozen years earlier Captain Horatio Austin had felt the sting of his invective. Sir John Ross, who had wintered near Penny's ships during the Franklin search expedition, later declared, "He knows that I acted as a peacemaker between him and those whom his virulent temper had offended" (John Ross 1852, 10). In a telling comment to her son William, Margaret Penny (1867) wrote, "Govern your temper think of what your Papa had lost by his."

Robert Brown, while serving as surgeon on the *Narwhal* during a Spitsbergen voyage in 1861, visited the steam whaler *Polynia* when Captain Penny was in command. Penny was adjusting a new chronometer at the time, and although his thermometer and Brown's both read thirty-one degrees, Penny insisted that the temperature was really lower. "This is nonsense," concluded Brown, adding,

Penny is occasionally subject to curious fits of temporary [insanity?] & on one occasion – when wintering in Cumberland Inlet with Mrs. Penny & part of the crew – he threatened to shoot the Doctor if he made the slightest resistance whilst he put [him] in heavy chains. He kept [him] in chains for three weeks, labouring under the idea that he was attempting to poison him while giving him medicine to allay the inflamation of the brain [causing it?]. He used during that time to stalk about, a cutlass on one side & a brace of pistols on the other. It must have been awful during that long winter night to have such a man controling entirely their destinies. (*Narwhal* 1861, 1:256)

Brown had probably heard this bizarre story from Captain Deuchars of the *Narwhal*, his main source of information during the voyage. If there is any truth to the account, it might help explain the gap in Margaret's journal from February to May 1858. Penny had had trouble with a surgeon before. On the voyage of 1853–54, his doctor became "a deserter from the expedition." According to the *Aberdeen Journal* (1854), "Captain Penny kindly gave the Americans the services of his medical officer, for the cure of several of their number who were suffering from disease and frost-bite; and in return they harboured the surgeon, and allowed him to take up his quarters with them, when he had betrayed the trust reposed in him, and deserted his duty."

On the other hand, the story about confining the doctor in chains may have been based on the events that had occurred on the *Alibi* during the winter of 1856–57, when Captain Stewart had found it necessary to restrain Dr Robertson forcibly after the man began showing signs of insanity. If so, it appears that in the frequent retelling of the story, the insanity had been transferred to Captain Penny and many fanciful details had been added.

Although little is known about Penny's personal life, there are indications that his propensity for harsh criticism was sometimes exhibited within the family. His brother John once reproached him: "I will give liberty to kiss some of them for me but only once. Remember my love for little Ellen [Helen] and [try?] and be kinder to her than I understand you are. Magt. [Margaret] has told me several times of the unmanly habit you have of correcting her. I only wish I was within reach when you were at those low tricks" (John Penny 1845).

After 1864 the man of action was a man of leisure. He lived on South Crown Street, within a few blocks of the port, during the 1860s and on Springbank Terrace from the mid-1870s until his death. Undoubtedly, he would often have been drawn to the scene of ceaseless activity around the docks. Like many an old sea captain, he must have enjoyed strolling about the port, watching the bustle of loading and unloading, and the drama of departure and arrival. He recorded an unfortunate experience during one such outing: "An old master asked me to take a look of his ship and from the bright sunshine to the dock he allowed me to walk into the hould [and fall] some 14 feet amongst stone ballast. I discolated [*sic*] my shoulder smashed the blade and [was] otherwise maimed but when I found my legs safe I held up my broken fin and ascended an upwright ladder 19 feet and down another on shore and would not allow any one to assist me, I was so angary" (William Penny 1872). Revealingly, his account is slightly accusatory. The mishap was not his fault; it was that of the ship's captain who "allowed" him to fall into the open hold. In recounting how he refused help and angrily made his own way home with a dislocated shoulder and broken shoulder blade, Penny unconsciously gives us a glimpse of his temper and pride.

If Penny could no longer sail to the Arctic, he could nonetheless keep abreast of ship movements, the fluctuating fortunes of the whaling industry, and the progress of arctic exploration by tapping into the network of dockside gossip and by reading the *Shipping Gazette* and the *Times*. "I amuse myself with arctic matters," he wrote (William Penny 1872) as he launched into one of his private diatribes against a handful of arctic worthies, including Kane, M'Clintock, M'Clure, Osborn, Rae, and James Ross.

At the age of seventy-three William Penny reminded his son of the "great whale" they had captured a quarter-century earlier in Cumberland Sound, and he added, "I have no doubt my progress in the seal & whale fishries is the most pleasent retrospect in your early carrier though you was to young to understand all the far seeing knowledge I was possest of." Then the old bitterness and sense of injustice surfaced as he continued: "All my wisdom, great energy, [unriviled?] activity has gone to enrich others who had no other idea but robbery – local rascals fit for any dishonourable [action?]." "The old whalers of my day are all gone," he lamented, "I am the last" (William Penny 1881).

The rest of Penny's life was spent quietly at home with Margaret. During his last ten years he suffered from what his death certificate termed general paralysis, possibly the result of a stroke. Although unable to take outdoor exercise, he could still "move about his room and take an active interest in what was occurring around him" (*Aberdeen Evening Express* 1892). He lived for half a year longer than Margaret and departed on his final voyage, after a cerebral haemorrhage, on the morning of 1 February 1892. A small private funeral was held three days later. The Reverend Mr Hutchison conducted a short service in the home, following which the coffin of polished oak with brass mountings, decorated with a floral anchor, was taken to St Nicholas Churchyard. It was borne to the grave by members of the Shore

Porters' Society, an ancient organization of "pynours" (stevedores and general carriers) whose Aberdeen roots were four centuries old and whose lorries are still seen around the port today.

MARGARET PENNY

Five years after returning from her winter in Cumberland Sound, Margaret went whaling again. She joined her husband on board the *Queen* for the 1863 voyage on which Captain Penny sailed all the way across Hudson Bay but then reversed direction and headed for Cumberland Sound to winter. Somewhere north of the mouth of Frobisher Bay, as Penny in the crow's nest was conning the ship gingerly through a field of icebergs and floes, a gale struck with sudden force. He recruited Margaret to relay orders to the helmsman and deck watch through the howling wind. John Tillotson, who probably heard the story from Penny himself when he interviewed him six years later, wrote, "Mrs. Penny stood all through that long and dreadful night, passing the word of command, when an instant's delay might have been hopeless destruction. It was seven in the morning before the captain left the mast-head" (Tillotson 1869, 86). The *Queen* reached Cumberland Sound safely and spent the winter at Kekerten, but no details about Margaret's second wintering experience there have come to light.

Margaret is not known to have made any more voyages. As she and William approached the relaxed, contemplative years of retirement, their children were on the threshold of adulthood, preparing to chart their own courses through life. Not all the paths of life are smooth, however, and in 1867 Margaret had to suffer the cruellest of blows, the death of a child. The youngest of the family – her own namesake – passed away sometime in the late winter or spring of 1867 at the age of eighteen. She had developed into "such a splendid looking girl that every body used to turn & look after her on the streets," Margaret wrote several months later to her son William in India. She added: "I used to look & wonder how our rough Maggie could have grown so lovely. You would not have known her. I have still the feeling that she is always near me. It was a dreadful blow to us all but we may rest assured that it is for some wise end therefore we must not reprimand God's will" (Margaret Penny 1867).

The sudden and unexpected loss was deeply felt by Maggie's sisters and brother. "I am just like you Bill," Janet Penny (1867b) wrote to her brother in India, "I fancy it is all a dream but when I see her empty room, Oh! it is too true – I can't write about her Bill. I must let some of the others do it." She advised him, "Don't look upon her as dead, only gone before us" (Janet Penny 1867a).

The same year brought some respite from grief when Janet became engaged to James Craik, a wealthy manufacturer in Forfar. She bubbled with fun as she wrote to brother William in May to give him the news. James Craik was not the first to propose, she confided. The Reverend Mr Stevenson, the parish minister in Forfar, had previously asked for her hand in marriage, "but every body said he was far too old so I said no to him." As for her fiancé, "Don't fancy him good looking for he is not that," she wrote, but "he seems rather fond of me." If Craik's gifts to her were any indication of his fondness, this was a major understatement: "I got a very handsome opal ring from him with six diamonds & a diamond rubbie [ruby] gaurd [gawd] also a very handsome watch chain, & a very pretty locket. So I think I have done not that bad." Janet had picked out furniture in Dundee for their house; everything was on "a grand scale," and they expected to be married in August. But what if he really did not intend to marry? she asked half jokingly before providing her own answer: "He would'nt be worth having if he drew back when he knew that I was poor" (Janet Penny 1867a).

James Craik, however, was true to his word, and on 22 August he and Janet were married in Aberdeen. After a reception at which cake and wine were served, they left by train for a month-long honeymoon in Edinburgh, London, and Paris. Margaret Penny (1867) described her son-in-law as a "very kind intelligent husband" who had given her daughter "every thing that she has expressed a wish for." Tragically, the happy marriage ended three years later when Janet died, allegedly from complications during the birth of her second child. Two years after this sad event, Captain Penny (1872) wrote, "My beautiful Janet who had married a manufactour died 1870, 23 years of age leaving two pretty children, a boy & girl, who have been with us for a week and left today for Forfar their home. Their father, poor fellow, is only beginning to be something rational."

With their daughters Maggie and Janet dead and their son William living in India, Captain and Mrs Penny had only Helen at home with them in Aberdeen. She kept house for her parents until at least 1872. They all lavished affection upon the grandchildren, William Penny Craik and Catherine ("Katie") Fyfe Craik. In 1882 Margaret wrote to her son William, "Penny is a real Penny. He came all the way from Forfar on a Trycicale along with another boy 60 miles & returned again the second day. I hope he will be spared to turn out a good & clever man. He is very fond of shooting & fishing & very expert at them. Papa taught him to shoot & he is very proud of his pupil" (Margaret Penny 1882). "Penny," as the boy was called, was then about thirteen years old, much the same age as his uncle William had been when he sailed on a whaler, spent a winter in the Arctic, and accompanied Eskimos on hunting trips.

Margaret Penny never ceased to think fondly of her son William in far-off Assam. At the age of thirty-seven he was still her "baby" who had to be reminded of precautions to be taken in a dangerous world. Death had claimed three of her children, and she wasn't taking any chances with him. When he thought of visiting Scotland, she wrote with motherly advice: "When you start for home be sure to be provided with under clothing for the change of climate. I have heard of so many people being laid up in consequence of that neglect." At the end of this letter, the woman who had spent two winters in the land of polar bears and had thought nothing of tramping a few miles over the arctic ice to watch boat crews pursuing fifty-ton whales among the drifting floes, appended a postscript: "Be careful when you go to shoot or fish. Some of those dreadful animals might pounce" (Margaret Penny 1882).

Margaret Penny died at home on 7 June 1891 at the age of seventy-eight.

Appendices

Appendix 1
Crew Lists

(Ages in parentheses)

LADY FRANKLIN, 1857–58 (PRO, BT 98/5177)

William Penny (49), master
James Birnie (48), mate
John Lucas (34), ice master
John Eddies (30), carpenter
Erskine B. Grant (21), surgeon
Andrew Lindsay (35), spectioneer
George Ross (23), boatswain & harpooner
John Donaldson (26), harpooner & skeeman
Peter Brown (37), cook
James [Findlay?] (25), second carpenter
George Smith (26), boatsteerer
George Masson (22), AB (able-bodied seaman)
John Falconer (41), cooper
John [Lowrie?] (31?), blacksmith
Alexander Calder (23), steward
Charles [Niddries?] (24), cooper
Alexander Grey (28), os (ordinary seaman)
Hugh Bain (37), os
Peter Hunter (20), AB
Gilbert Garster (20), os

Alexander Ross (34), OS
Francis Garison (18), OS
Charles Mowat (22), AB
Lawrence Jamieson (18), OS
George Gibson (17), apprentice
Total 25*

SOPHIA, 1857–58 (PRO, BT 98/5177)

John Cheyne (26), master
Alexander Smith (62), mate
George Findley (31), loose harpooner
William Birnie (18), carpenter
John Duncan (31), cooper
William Johnstone (54), boatsteerer
Henry Anderson (20), OS
Charles Robertson (18), OS
Charles Johnson (18), OS
John Lawrenson (18), OS
William Leask (18), OS
Robert Sinclair (18), OS
Thomas Anderson (17), OS
James Lamb (22), OS
Richard Sheldrake (33), cook
George Kerr (24), boatsteerer
Richard McGee (18), apprentice
Total 17

---

* In addition to those listed for the *Lady Franklin*, there evidently was a cabin
boy who (like Mrs Penny, her son William, and Brother Warmow) was not on
the official crew list. On 28 September 1857 and 29 May 1858 Margaret mentioned "two boys," one of whom was probably young William, and on 14 September she spoke of "the boy Dick." Warmow also mentioned a cabin boy
(*Periodical Accounts* 1858, 23:134).

Appendix 2
Instructions to Missionary

The document given below, verbatim and in full, is entitled "Extract from the letter of instruction addressed by the Mission Board of the Moravian Brethren at Herrnhut in Saxony, to the missionary accompanying the expedition of Capt. Penny" (La Trobe 1853). It relates to Penny's voyage of 1853, in which he had arranged to collect Brother Warmow at Lichtenfels, Greenland, on his way to Cumberland Sound, but failed to reach the place. The "Extract" appears to be a translation of most of the German instructions sent to the missionary, provided for the benefit of Captain Penny. As the objective of the Moravians remained the same in 1857, it is likely that Warmow received instructions that were similar if not identical to these. The extract, which begins with point no. 2, reads as follows:

2 Your present commission has as reference to the establishment of a permanent Missionary station, on the Shores of Northumberland inlet. The visit you are about to pay to those shores is to be considered merely as exploratory. – nor is its duration to exceed the period of a year, – it having been arranged between Capt. Penny and the Secretary of our Mission in London that an opportunity shall be afforded you by the former, for your return to Europe in the summer or autumn of 1854. You will proceed in the first place to England, whence you will probably receive directions to continue your journey to Germany, – for the purpose of communicating to our Board the results of your inquiries & observations.

3 During your voyage to & from Hogarth Sound (or Northumberland Inlet) and while resident upon its shores, you will be provided with whatever is needful to your support, by Capt. Penny.

4 With reference to the nature of the commission in which you are about to engage we would observe[:]

5 That you will be expected to make it your principal concern & endeavour to establish and maintain friendly relations with the natives. – Though the dialect of the Esquimaux language which prevails on the western shores of Davis' Straits, differs in all probability more or less from that in use among the Greenlanders, we have little doubt of you being able to converse with the people to whom you may have access, and to hold intercourse with them in [illegible word] ways. By your knowledge of their language, and your acquaintance with their habits of thought and action, and their mode of life in general you will be enabled not only to attain the more effectually the great object of your mission, but also to be of essential service to Capt. Penny and his officers, in their dealings with the natives[.] Any opportunity that may be afforded you for speaking to them of God their Saviour and giving them such instructions out of His Holy word as they are capable of understanding you will of course gladly embrace. You will also endeavour to ascertain, in how far they may be desirous or willing to have the benefit of Christian teaching, through the instrumentality of a resident missionary.

6 Any transactions with the Esquimaux, – unconnected with your proper calling, whereby their suspicions or even hostility might be aroused, – and your own safety be recklessly compromised, you will endeavour to avoid. – On the other hand you will not shew yourself too fearful, – but whenever duty seems to call and a suitable occasion offers, – go boldly among them in dependence on the gracious help & protection of the Lord, and seek by confidence to [give them?] confidence. – It will be your especial object during your winter sojourn among them to establish with them friendly and useful relations, and to turn these to the best account.

7 In your relations to Capt. Penny and the officers and men under his command you will endeavour so to demean yourself that it may be evident to all that you are a servant of Christ, and a labourer in the missionary field. – We regret that owing to your want of familiarity with the English language, – you will hardly be able to hold spiritual intercourse with them, or even to officiate at any religious service, which they may be disposed to attend. If however any opportunity should be afforded you, of being spiritually useful to the crew, by the reading of the holy scriptures to them, or by testifying to them however imperfectly, of the love of God and the grace of Christ our Saviour, – you will not be slow to avail yourself of it. – Above all, it will be your constant desire and aim to render it manifest by your whole walk and conversation, that you are a believer in Christ and that you live by faith in Him. – You will endeavour to set a good example to others in all things, – as becomes a child of God, to shew yourself humble, simple and unpretending, – to avoid,

as far as possible, giving trouble to those around you and to conciliate by your whole demeanour, their affection, esteem & confidence In matters which have reference to faith and a good conscience – and which concern the law of our God, – you will however seek for grace & display that firmness and fidelity, which the Lord requires from all his true disciples and servants. "Finally, whatsoever things are true whatsoever things are honest; whatsoever things are just; whatsoever things are pure; whatsoever things are lovely; whatsoever things are of good report: – if there be any virtue, and if there be any praise, think on these things; Those things which you have both learned and received & heard, – do; – and the God of peace shall be with you." Phil. IV. 8. 9.

Appendix 3
Whales Killed

Date	Harpooner	Remarks
28 Sept. 1857	Penny	11′11″ bone; length 56′
20 May 1858	Lucas	7′4″ bone
26 May	–	–
27 May	–	small
27 May	Cheyne	11′ bone; large
7 June	Tshatluta [*sic*]	–
7 June	Newbullygar	–
7 June	Lindsay	–
8 June	Ross	–
8 June	Lucas	large
9 June	Cheyne	–
9 June	Birnie	large
10 June	Newbullygar	large
11 June	Cheyne	large
14 June	Findley	
15 June	Birnie	large
16 June	Cheyne	11′ bone
16 June	Lucas	11′ bone
21 June	Tsiatlita [*sic*]	large
21 June	Cheyne	–
21 June	Findley	–
29 June	Tsialita [*sic*]	large
6 July	drift whale	10′ bone

The above table, compiled from Margaret's journal and the two ships' logbooks, does not include the whales (probably five) taken in April and the first half of May 1858. The total number secured was twenty-eight.

Appendix 4
Native Place-Names

Versions used by Margaret (1), Captain Penny (2), Captain Cheyne (3), Brother Warmow (4)	Official name in Gazetteer (Canada 1980)
Juictacktooovick (2) Juiqtouktovick (2) Juiytaktuik (2)	(Location unclear)
Kakertine Islands (1) Kickertain Islands (3) Kickertian group (3) Kickertian Islands (3)	Kikastan Islands
Kekertak (4) Kekertat (4) Kicertye (1) Kickertine (1) Kickertyne (1) Kicktine Harbour (2) Kikertine (1)	Kekerten Harbour; or Kekerten Island
Kemisoke Kemisoke Island Kimersok (4) Kimisoke (3)	Nimigen Island

Versions used by Margaret (1), Captain Penny (2), Captain Cheyne (3), Brother Warmow (4)	Official name in Gazetteer (Canada 1980)
Kingaite (3) Kingite (1,2,3)	Kingnait Fiord
Kingaite Harbour (3)	Kingnait Harbour
Kingawa (3) Kingua (1,2,4)	(Region surrounding Clearwater Fiord)
Kickertactooack (2) Kickertatooack (2)	Kekertukdjuak Island (Kekertuk Island on 1:500,000 maps)
Medleaktuak (1) Middleactoowick (2) Middleaktuak Islands (1) Middleeaktualik (1)	Miliakdjuin Island
Naujaktalik (1) Naujartalik (4) Naujartalik Harbour (1) Neouaktalik (1) Nouactlick (2) Noualaktalik (1) Nouiactalik (1) Nouwacktoolick Harbour (2) Nouwactolict (2) Nowiactolict (2)	(Harbour near Blacklead Island)
Neubuen (2) Neuvowen (2) Newbeanen (1) Newbeonen (1) Newbeuian (1) Newbuean (1) Newbuian (1) Newbuivan (2) Nubuwan Harbour (3) Nuvujat (4)	Nuvujen Island

Versions used by Margaret (1), Captain Penny (2), Captain Cheyne (3), Brother Warmow (4)	*Official name in Gazetteer (Canada 1980)*
Nuvujarschuit (3)	(Location unclear)
Saumia (4) Shoumea (1)	(Southeastern part of Cumberland Peninsula)
Tongite (1) Tornait (4)	Kingnait Harbour

Appendix 5
Margaret's Eskimo Glossary

a b d e f g ng h i j k X [q] l dl m n o p r r s sh t u v

am, ila = yes
uvanga = I
áka = no
ibit = you
taima = so
tauko = they
ima = so
ukua = they
tauna = he
taushuma = he, his
una = he
taukua = theirs, or they do
nuna = land
nunangat = lands, or your land
igdlo = house
igdlut = houses, or your house
igdlunga = his house
kamik = boot
kamingit = boots
kamíka = my boot
niaqoq = head
niaqut = heads
niaqunga = his head

puishe = seal
puishit = seals
natseq = small seal
qasigiaq = fresh water seal
natsiaq = young seal
natseqarpoq = there are seals
teriániaq = fox
teriániat = foxes
teriániaqarpoq = there are foxes
teriániaqángilaq = there are no foxes
imaq = salt water
imeq = fresh water
imeqarpoq = there is water
imeqangilaq = there is no water
imeqarane = without water
imeqarungnaerpoq = there is no more
    water
imerusugpoq = he is thirsty
imerpoq = he drinks
imigshaq = something to drink
imigshaerupunga = I have nothing to
    drink
agdlunaq = line or harpoon rope

areq, or aleq = harpoon line

saqo = harpoon for seals

kardlingit = trowsers [trousers], or
   your trowsers

atigaq = dress

nasa = cap

nasanga = his cap

ine = room

inigit = your room

atâtaq = father

anânaq = mother

NOTES

1 The handwriting in Margaret's list of Eskimo words is not her own. It is probably that of Brother Warmow, who may have been instructing her in the language.

2 According to Dr Louis-Jacques Dorais of l'Université Laval, the words are in the Greenlandic dialect, which supports the theory that Brother Warmow compiled the list.

3 The Greenlandic dialect differs only slightly from that of Baffin Island and other parts of the eastern Canadian Arctic.

4 Warmow used a symbol resembling an upper-case letter *X* for what Dr Dorais calls "an uvular stop, rendered in modern Inuktitut and Greenlandic by the letter *q*, which is pronounced as in lo*ch* when between two vowels, but somewhat harder (like *kr*) at the beginning of a word, when doubled, or at the end of the word (where it sounds more like *rk*)." In the above list I have replaced Warmow's *X* symbol by the letter *q*.

5 The symbol that resembles an acute accent indicates that the following consonant is genirate, or doubled.

6 The symbol resembling a circumflex indicates that the vowel is long.

References

This list includes only the works referred to in the text, and it includes both published and unpublished material. The works are listed under author's surname and year of publication, with the following exceptions: (1) official log-books and private journals written on board ships are listed under the name of the ship, and unless they are certainly one or the other they are described as "shipboard logs"; (2) newspaper articles without identifiable authors are listed under the name of the newspaper; (3) articles in the Moravian *Periodical Accounts*, which lack titles and have no identifiable authors, are not listed here; the references in the text are adequate to locate the material cited.

In the following references, long newspaper names have been shortened for convenience. The *Aberdeen Herald and General Advertiser* is called *Aberdeen Herald;* the *Buchan Observer, Peterhead, Fraserburgh & General Advertiser* (Peterhead) is called *Buchan Observer;* the *Hull and Eastern Counties Herald* is called *Eastern Counties Herald;* the *Fifeshire Advertiser, of News, Politics, and Local Occurrences* (Kirkcaldy) is called *Fifeshire Advertiser;* the *Missionsblatt aus der Brudergemeine* (Herrnhut, Germany) is called *Missionsblatt;* the *Periodical Accounts Relating to the Missions of the Church of the United Brethren Established among the Heathen* are called *Periodical Accounts;* the *Peterhead Sentinel and General Advertiser for Buchan District* is called *Peterhead Sentinel;* and the *Whalemen's Shipping List and Merchants' Transcript* (New Bedford, USA) is called *Whalemen's Shipping List.*

The following abbreviations are used for repositories of archival material:

BL   British Library (Manuscipt Collections)
CO   Colonial Office

DM   Dundee Museums and Art Galleries
HBC   Hudson's Bay Company Archives, Winnipeg, Manitoba
KWM   Kendall Whaling Museum, Sharon, Massachusetts
ODHS   Old Dartmouth Historical Society, New Bedford, Massachusetts
PPL   Providence Public Library, Rhode Island
PRO   Public Record Office, Kew, Richmond
RA   Royal Archives, Windsor Castle
SPRI   Scott Polar Research Institute, Cambridge
SRO   Scottish Record Office, Edinburgh

Abbie Bradford. 1884–85. Shipboard log. ODHS.
Aberdeen Arctic Company. 1862. Extract from minutes of meeting, 22 September. SPRI, MS 116/98/1:D.
Aberdeen Evening Express. 1892. 4 February. "Funeral of the late Captain William Penny."
Aberdeen Free Press. 1853. 20 May. "Arctic Company."
Aberdeen Herald. 1854. 4 November. "Sir John Franklin's expedition."
Aberdeen Journal. 1819. 9 June. "Northern expedition."
– 1853. 2 March. "The Arctic Company."
– 1854. 30 August. "Arctic whale fishery."
– 1856. 22 November. "Davis' Straits whale fishery."
– 1857a. 22 April. "Lady Franklin's expedition."
– 1857b. 13 May. "The search for Franklin."
– 1857c. 24 June. "Adventure of Lady Franklin's boat."
– 1857d. 1 July. "Arctic fishery."
– 1858. 25 August. "Arctic whale fishery."
Alibi. 1856–57. Ship's logbook. SRO, CS 96/4890.
Ansel Gibbs. 1860–61. Shipboard log kept by Stephen B. Bennett. ODHS.
– 1866–67. Shipboard log kept by Elnathan B. Fisher. ODHS.
Barron, William. 1890. *An apprentice's reminiscences of whaling in Davis's Straits … from 1848 to 1854.* Hull: Waller.
– 1895. *Old whaling days.* Hull: William Andrews.
Baynham, Henry. 1972. *Before the mast: Naval ratings of the 19th century.* London: Arrow Books.
Bellot, Joseph-René. 1853. Letter to William Penny, 24 May. SPRI, MS 116/10:D.
Berton, Pierre. 1988. *The arctic grail: The quest for the North West Passage and the North Pole, 1818–1909.* Toronto: McClelland and Stewart.
Blythe, Ronald, ed. 1989. *Each returning day: The pleasure of diaries.* London: Viking.
Boas, Franz. 1885. Baffin-Land. *Petermanns Mitteilungen* 80:1–100.

– 1888. *The Central Eskimo*. Washington: Bureau of American Ethnology, sixth annual report, 399–669. (Reprinted in facsimile by Coles Publishing, Toronto, 1974.)

Bockstoce, John. 1980. "The consumption of caribou by whalemen at Herschel Island, Yukon Territory, 1890 to 1908." *Journal of Arctic and Alpine Research* 12, no. 3:381–4.

Buchan Observer. 1863. 13 November. "News from the whaling."

– 1864. 23 September. "Arrivals from the Cumberland whale fishing."

Canada. 1959. *Pilot of arctic Canada*. Vol. 2. Canadian Hydrographic Service. Ottawa: Queen's Printer.

– 1980. *Gazetteer of Canada: Northwest Territories*. Canadian Permanent Committee on Geographic Names. Ottawa: Energy, Mines and Resources Canada.

Carpenter, Kenneth. 1988. *The history of scurvy and vitamin-c*. Cambridge: Cambridge University Press.

Colby, Barnard. 1936. "Old New London whaling captains," no. 18. *New London Day*, 8 February.

Cole, Douglas, and Ludger Müller-Wille. 1984. "Franz Boas' expedition to Baffin Island." *Etudes Inuit Studies* 8, no. 1:37–63.

Cooke, Alan, and Clive Holland. 1978. *The exploration of northern Canada 500 to 1920: A chronology*. Toronto: Arctic History Press.

Cooke, Alan, and W. Gillies Ross. 1969. "The drift of the whaler *Viewforth* in Davis Strait, 1835–36, from William Elder's journal." *Polar Record* 14, no. 92:581–91.

Corner, George W. 1972. *Doctor Kane of the arctic seas*. Philadelphia: Temple University Press.

Daniel Webster. 1860–62. Ship's logbook kept by Richard H. Fisher and F.H. Bailey. ODHS.

Davis, C.H., ed. 1876. *Narrative of the North Polar Expedition U.S. Ship Polaris*. Washington: Government Printing Office.

Druett, Joan. 1991. *Petticoat whalers: Whaling wives at sea 1820–1920*. Auckland: Collins.

– 1992. *"She was a sister sailor": The whaling journals of Mary Brewster 1845–1851*. American Maritime Library, vol. 13. Mystic, Conn.: Mystic Seaport Museum.

Dundee Advertiser. 1861. 26 February. "Our arctic fleet."

Eastern Counties Herald. 1848a. 23 March. "Departure of the Esquimaux."

– 1848b. 16 November. "The Esquimaux – death of Ukaluk."

– 1853a. 23 June. "Mr. Bowlby's new arctic fleet."

– 1853b. 6 October."Return of Mr. Bowlby from the arctic regions."

– 1853c. 27 October. "The Hull arctic expedition."

– 1854a. 9 February. "The Esquimaux family."

– 1854b. 2 March. "The Esquimaux family."

– 1854c. 30 March. "The Esquimaux family."

– 1854d. 8 June. "Zoological Gardens."

Fifeshire Advertiser. 1846a. 7 November. "Kookie-Ekie."

– 1846b. 5 December. "Acquatook, the Esquimaux."

Franklin, Jane. 1850. Letter to Margaret Penny, 2 August. SPRI, MS 116/24/7:D.

Gad, Finn. 1973. *The history of Greenland II, 1700–1782.* Montreal: McGill-Queen's University Press.

Garner, Stanton, ed. 1966. *The Captain's best mate: The journal of Mary Chipman Lawrence on the whaler Addison, 1856–1860.* Providence: Brown University Press.

Glacier. 1864–65. Ship's logbook. PPL.

Goldring, Philip. 1985. "Whaling-era toponymy of Cumberland Sound, Baffin Island." *Canoma* 1, no. 2:28–34.

– 1986a. "Inuit responses to Euro-American contacts: Southeast Baffin Island, 1824–1940." *Historical Papers* (Canadian Historical Association), 146–72.

– 1986b. "The last voyage of the *McLellan.*" *Beaver* 66, no. 1:39–44.

Goodsir, Robert Anstruther. 1850. *An arctic voyage to Baffin's Bay and Lancaster Sound, in search of friends with Sir John Franklin.* London: John Van Voorst.

Great Britain. 1853. Remarks by "A.B." appended to letter and memo from W.A.B. Hamilton (Admiralty) to T.F. Elliot (Colonial Office), 30 May. PRO, CO 42/591/2854/24.

– 1854. *An act to amend and consolidate the acts relating to merchant shipping.* Anno decimo & decimo octavo Victoriae Reginae, cap. 104.

Hall, Charles Francis. [1864] 1970. *Life with the Esquimaux …* Edmonton: Hurtig.

Hegarty, Reginald B. 1965. *The rope's end.* Boston: Houghton Mifflin.

Hiller, J.K. 1971. "The Moravians in Labrador, 1771–1805." *Polar Record* 15, no. 99:839–54.

Holland, Clive. 1970. "William Penny, 1809–92: Arctic whaling master." *Polar Record* 15, no. 94:25–43.

Hull Advertiser. 1848a. 2 June. "A new adventure."

– 1848b. 17 November. "Death of one of the 'Yacks.'"

– 1856a. 20 September. "Arrival of the Emma, from Davis' Straits."

– 1856b. 29 November. "The Emma's whaling voyage."

– 1857a. 17 October. "The Greenland fishery."

– 1857b. 5 December. "Diary of a voyage to Davis' Straits, in the whaling brig Anne."

– 1858a. 23 January. "Diary of a voyage to Davis' Straits, in the whaling brig Anne."

‒ 1858b. 6 March. "Diary of a voyage to Davis' Straits, in the whaling brig Anne."

Hull Packet. 1853. 14 October. "Return of the 'Bee' from the Cumberland Straits expedition."

Illustrated London News. 1854. 8 February. "The Esquimaux family."

Isabella. 1878‒79. Shipboard log. PPL.

Jackson, Gordon. 1978. *The British whaling trade.* Hamden, Conn.: Archon Books.

Jardine, William. 1837. *The naturalist's library, Mammalia.* Vol. 6, *On the ordinary Cetacea or whales.* Edinburgh: W.H. Lizars.

Keegan, John. 1990. *The price of Admiralty: The evolution of naval warfare.* New York: Viking Penguin.

Kemp, Peter, ed. 1976. *The Oxford companion to ships and the sea.* London: Oxford University Press.

Kenyon, Walter. 1975. *Tokens of possession: The northern voyages of Martin Frobisher.* Toronto: Royal Ontario Museum.

King, W.F. 1905. *Report upon the title of Canada to the islands north of the mainland of Canada.* Ottawa: Government Printing Bureau.

Kinnes Lists. Annual compilations of whaling returns, 1814‒1911. Dundee: Robert Kinnes & Sons.

Lady Franklin. 1857‒58. Ship's logbook kept by William Penny. PRO, BT 98/ 5177.

La Trobe, Peter. [1853] "Extract from the letter of introduction addressed by the Mission Board of the Moravian Brethren at Herrnhut in Saxony, to the missionary accompanying the expedition of Capt. Penny." SPRI, MS 116/ 43/16:D.

Literary Gazette. 1853. "Topics of the week." No. 1883 (19 February): 180‒1.

‒ 1854. "Topics of the week." No. 1966 (23 September): 828‒9.

Lloyd, Christopher. 1968. *The British seaman 1200‒1860: A social survey.* London: Collins.

‒ 1981. "Victualling of the fleet in the eighteenth and nineteenth centuries." In *Starving sailors: The influence of nutrition upon naval and maritime history,* ed. J. Watt, E.J. Freeman, and W.F. Bynum, 9‒15. Greenwich: National Maritime Museum.

Lubbock, Basil. 1955. *The arctic whalers.* Glasgow: Brown, Son & Ferguson.

Lytle, Thomas G. 1984. *Harpoons and other whalecraft.* New Bedford, Mass.: Old Dartmouth Historical Society.

M'Clintock, Francis Leopold. 1859. *The voyage of the 'Fox' in the arctic seas: A narrative of the discovery of the fate of Sir John Franklin and his companions.* London: John Murray.

– 1875. "On arctic sledge-travelling." *Proceedings of the Royal Geogaphical Society* 19, no. 7:464–79.

M'Donald, Alexander. 1841. *A narrative of some passages in the history of Eenoolooapik, a young Esquimaux* ... Edinburgh: Fraser.

Mackinnon, C.S. 1985. "The British man-hauled sledging tradition." In *The Franklin Era in Canadian arctic history 1845–1859*, ed. Patricia D. Sutherland, 129–40. Mercury Series. Archeological Survey of Canada Paper no. 131. Ottawa: National Museum of Man.

McLaren, Ian A. 1961. "Methods of determining the numbers and availability of ringed seals in the Eastern Canadian Arctic." *Arctic* 14, no. 3:162–75.

McOwat, W. John H. 1992. Personal communication, 17 November.

Milton-Thompson, G.J. 1981. "Two hundred years of the sailors' diet." In *Starving sailors: The influence of nutrition upon naval and maritime history*, ed. J. Watt, E.J. Freeman, and W.F. Bynum, 27–34. Greenwich: National Maritime Museum.

Missionsblatt. 1857. "Von Br. Warmow." No. 8 (August): 131–3.

– 1859. "Fortsetzung aus Br. Warmow's Tagebuch." No. 1 (January): 7–21.

Narwhal. 1861. Shipboard journal, kept by Robert Brown, surgeon. 2 vols. SPRI, MS 441/1/1.

Nelson, Richard K. 1969. *Hunters of the northern ice.* Chicago: University of Chicago Press.

Nourse, J.E., ed. 1879. *Narrative of the second arctic expedition made by Charles F. Hall* ... Washington: Government Printing Office.

Ocean Nymph. 1866–67a. Ship's logbook, kept by James Taylor, captain. HBC, C 1/617.

– 1866–67b. Ship's logbook, kept by Alexander Hay, whaling master. HBC, C 1/618.

Orray Taft. 1864–65. Shipboard log, kept by George Parker, captain. ODHS.

– 1866–67. Shipboard log, kept by George Parker, captain. ODHS.

– 1872–73. Shipboard log, kept by George Parker, captain. KWM.

Pacific. 1846. Shipboard journal, kept by Andrew Hamilton, surgeon. DM.

Parker, John. 1848. Memorial to Her Majesty the Queen, 14 February. PRO, CO 42/555/26.

Parry, William Edward. 1824. *Journal of a second voyage for the discovery of a North-West Passage from the Atlantic to the Pacific.* London: John Murray.

Pearce, Stephen. 1903. *Memories of the past.* Edinburgh: Riverside Press.

Penny, Janet. 1867a. Letter to William Penny, Jr, 17 May. Family papers.

– 1867b. Letter to William Penny, Jr, 18 July. Family papers.

Penny, John. 1845. Letter to William Penny, 24 August. SPRI, MS 116/62/9:D.

Penny, Margaret. 1856. Letter to Sophia Cracroft, 22 May. SPRI, MS 248/453:D.

– 1867. Letter to William Penny, Jr, 18 September. Family papers.

– 1882. Letter to William Penny, Jr, 1 February. Family papers.

Penny, William. 1855. Letter to John Barrow, 29 January. SPRI, MS 116/63/34:D.

– 1856a. Letter to Sophia Cracroft, 8 October 1856. SPRI, MS 248/454/2:D.

– 1856b. Deposition, 31 October. SPRI, MS 116/63/142:D.

– 1858. Letter to John Barrow, 3 September. BL, ADD 35306/137–8.

– 1859. Letter to John Barrow, 17 January. BL, ADD 35306/139–40.

– 1860a. Letter to John Barrow, 6 February. BL, ADD 35306/141–2.

– 1860b. Letter to John Barrow, 18 November. BL, ADD 35306/143.

– 1872. Letter to John Barrow, 2 January. BL, ADD 35306/151–5.

– 1875. Letter to John Barrow, 7 January. BL, ADD 35306/156–9.

– 1881. Letter to William Penny, Jr, 24 March. Family papers.

– Nd.a. Letter to Beaufort. SPRI, MS 116/63/52:D.

– Nd.b. Letter to W.A.B. Hamilton. SPRI, MS 116/63/96:D.

Penny, William, Jr. 1917. Last will and testament. Family papers.

Peterhead Sentinel. 1856. 21 November. "Davis' Straits whale fishery."

– 1857a. 11 September. "Davis' Straits whale fishery."

– 1857b. 25 September. "Wintering in Davis' Straits."

– 1858. 10 December. "The arrival of the last of our fleet from the arctic regions."

– 1859. 14 January. "Death of the female Esquimaux."

Polar Record. 1953. "Influenze virus epidemic at Victoria Island, Northwest Territories, 1949." *Polar Record* 6, no. 45:680–1.

Porsild, A.E. 1957. *Illustrated flora of the Canadian Arctic archipelago.* Bulletin no. 146. Ottawa: National Museum of Canada.

Prince Arthur. 1863. Ship's logbook, kept by George Savage, second officer. HBC, C 1/729.

Pyper, James. 1929. "The history of the whale and seal fisheries of the port of Aberdeen." *Scottish Naturalist* 176:39–50, 177:69–80, and 178:103–8.

Rodger, N.A.M. 1988. *The wooden world: An anatomy of the Georgian Navy.* Glasgow: Fontana Press.

Ross, John. 1852. Letter to *Nautical Standard.* Published in *Further Correspondence Respecting the Expedition under Sir John Franklin,* 8–10. Great Britain. Parliament. Return to an Order of the Honourable the House of Commons, dated 6 April 1852.

Ross, W. Gillies. 1975. *Whalers and Eskimos: Hudson Bay 1860–1915.* Publications in Ethnology no. 10. Ottawa: National Museum of Man.

– 1979. "The annual catch of Greenland (bowhead) whales in waters north of Canada 1719–1915: A preliminary compilation." *Arctic* 32, no. 2:91–121.

– 1985. *Arctic whalers, icy seas: Narratives of the Davis Strait whale fishery.* Toronto: Irwin.

Savours, Ann, and Margaret Deacon. 1981. "Nutritional aspects of the British Arctic (Nares) expedition of 1875–76 and its predecessors." In *Starving sailors: The influence of nutrition upon naval and maritime history*, ed. J. Watt, E.J. Freeman, and W.F. Bynum, 131–62. Greenwich: National Maritime Museum.

Scoresby, William, Jr. 1820. *An account of the arctic regions, with a history and description of the northern whale-fishery.* 2 vols. Edinburgh: Constable. (Reprinted in facsimile by David & Charles, Newton Abbot, Devon, 1969.)

Scotland. 1859–60. Reclaiming note and closed record, Sutter and others against Aberdeen Arctic Company and others. Court of Session. SRO, CS 246/1756.

Sharman, Ivan M. 1981. "Vitamin requirements of the human body." In *Starving sailors: The influence of nutrition upon naval and maritime history*, ed. J. Watt, E.J. Freeman, and W.F. Bynum, 17–26. Greenwich: National Maritime Museum.

Shuldham-Shaw, Patrick, and Emily B. Lyle, eds. 1981. *The Greig-Duncan folk song collection.* Vol. 1. Aberdeen: Aberdeen University Press.

Sophia. 1857–58. Ship's logbook kept by John Cheyne. PRO, BT 98/5177.

Stackpole, Edouard A. 1965. *The long arctic seach: The narrative of Lieutenant Frederick Schwatka, U.S.A., 1878–1880 ...* Mystic, Conn.: Marine Historical Association.

Stamp, Tom, and Cordelia Stamp. 1976. *William Scoresby, arctic scientist.* Whitby: Caedmon of Whitby Press.

– 1983. *Greenland voyager.* Whitby: Caedmon of Whitby Press.

Starbuck, Alexander. 1878. *History of the American whale fishery from its earliest inception to the year 1876.* 2 vols. Washington: Government Printing Office. (Reprinted in facsimile by Argosy-Antiquarian, New York, 1964.)

Stefansson, Vilhjalmur. 1918. "Observations on three cases of scurvy." *Journal of the American Medical Association* 71, no. 21:1715–18.

Stevenson, Marc G. 1984. "Kekerten: Preliminary archeology of an arctic whaling station. Yellowknife, Northwest Territories." Unpublished report for Prince of Wales Northern Heritage Centre, Government of the Northwest Territories.

– 1993. "Central Inuit social structure: The view from Cumberland Sound, Baffin Island, Northwest Territories." PHD thesis, University of Alberta.

[Stuart, John] 1850–51. Journal of an unknown officer on Penny's ship Lady Franklin, 1850–51. Unpublished manuscript 119.8, J 826, University of Illinois.

Sutherland, Peter Cormack. 1852. *Journal of a voyage in Baffin's Bay and Barrow Straits, in the years 1850–51 ...* 2 vols. London: Longman, Brown, Green, and Longmans.

Syren Queen. 1860–61. Shipboard log. KWM.

Tillotson, John. 1869. *Adventures in the ice: A comprehensive summary of arctic exploration, discovery, and adventure, including experiences of Captain Penny, the veteran whaler, now first published.* London: James Hogg.

Times. 1848a. 7 January. "Visit of two Esquimaux to England."

– 1848b. 20 March. "The Esquimaux."

Tower, Walter S. 1907. *A history of the American whale fishery.* Series in Political Economy and Public Law. Philadelphia: University of Pennsylvania.

Townsend, Charles Haskins. 1925. "The Galapagos tortoises in their relation to the whaling industry." *Zoologica* 4, no. 3:55–135.

Troup, James A., ed. 1987. *The ice-bound whalers: The story of the Dee and the Grenville Bay, 1836–37.* Stromness: Orkney Press and Stromness Museum.

Tuttle, Charles R. 1885. *Our North Land, with a narrative of the Hudson's Bay Expedition of 1884.* Toronto: Blackett Robinson.

Victoria. 1854. Journal of Her Majesty, Queen Victoria. RA.

Wakeham, William. 1898. *Report of the expedition to Hudson Bay and Cumberland Gulf in the steamship "Diana" under the command of William Wakeham in the year 1897.* Ottawa: Queen's Printer.

Walder, David. 1978. *Nelson.* New York: Dial Press/James Wade.

Weyer, Edward Moffat, Jr. 1932. *The Eskimos: Their environment and folkways.* New Haven: Yale University Press. (Reprinted in facsimile by Archon Books, Hamden, Connecticut, 1969.)

Whalemen's Shipping List. 1853. 1 February. "Lady whalers."

– 1857a. 14 April. "A long voyage."

– 1857b. 3 November. "From Spitzbergen Sea."

– 1858. 5 October. "From Cumberland Inlet."

Wood, Joseph. 1861. Letter to George Findlay, 5 March. SPRI, MS 116/88/1:D.

Woodward, F.J. 1953. "William Penny, 1809–92." *Polar Record* 6, no. 46:808–11.

Yorkshire Gazette. 1854. 15 April. "The Esquimaux family."

Index

Page numbers in italics refer to illustrations

Abbie Bradford: scurvy on, 157

Aberdeen: port of, 9–10; and arctic whaling, 200–1

Aberdeen Arctic Company: formation of, xxxiii, xxxvi; and steam power, 43; and Penny, 46, 73–4, 213; ships of, 73, 74; and Miliakdjuin Island, 116; and whale dispute, 124–7; presents Margaret with teaset, *198;* plan for circumpolar whaling, 212; dismissal of Penny, 213

Actor: and shipwrecked crew, 215–16

Addison, 14

Advice: and Franklin search, xxxi; scurvy deaths on, 149; antiscorbutics of, 158

Aggamiut, 89

Akulagok Island, *94–5,* 95

alcohol: on whalers, 119, 206–7

Alert, xxix

Alibi: scurvy deaths on, 19, 30, 160; and whale dispute, 124–7; taken over by Capt. McKinnon, 213

Allan, George (seaman on *Alibi*): death from scurvy, 160

Amaret: winters at Niantilik, 182

Angekok. *See* shaman

Anne. *See* Tackritow

Anne, 16

antiscorbutics. *See* scurvy

Arctic, 37, 41, 75, 124

Arctic Academy, 158

Arctic Ocean: whaling in, 212–13

Athenaeum: declares Eskimos liars, 7

Aukutook Zininnuck (Eskimo man), 49

Austin, Horatio Thomas, 41

Bachstrom, John, 147

Baffin, 72

Baffin Bay: and whaling routine, xxi, xxxv, 43, 66, 149

Baffin Island: "distant and unsurveyed," xvi–xvii; political status, xvii; topography, 27; exploration of, 27

Balaena mysticetus. See whales, bowhead

baleen: uses of, xiv; length, 85

Barron, William (whaling captain), 57, 108

Barrow, John (Sr), 128

Barrow, John (Jr), 128, 212

Bates (police inspector), 8

Beaufort, Francis: Penny asks help from, 221

Bee, 54

beer: brewed at Kekerten, 119

Belcher, Edward, 42

Belle: long voyage of, 193

Bellot, Joseph-René, xxvii

Bellows, Dexter (whaling captain), 192

bergy bits, 15, 17

billet-head, 60, 67, 68, 69

Birnie, James (mate of *Lady Franklin*), 23, 63, 173; harpoons whale, 174

Blacklead Island: whaling station at, 202
blubber, rendered at Kekerten, 86, 103, 115, 116, 117, 118, 123, 132
Boas, Franz: records Eskimo place-names, 91
Böhnisch (Moravian missionary), 208
Bon Accord, xxix, 49
Bowlby, John: and Davis Strait, 54; takes Eskimos to England, 54–7
Bowser (agent for Bowlby), 55
Brown (whaling captain), xxxiii
Brown, John (cooper on *Alibi*): death from scurvy, 106, 107, 160; clothing, 106–7
Brown, Robert (whaling surgeon and naturalist): on Penny's character, 221–2
Buckingham, Leicester (lecturer for Bowlby), 55
Bullygar. *See* Newbullygar

Caledonia, 49
Cape Farewell, 15, 190
cape ice, 17
Cape Wrath: on outward voyage, 10; on homeward voyage, 194
caribou: consumed by whalers, 152
Cash, Azubah (whaling wife), xxiv
Chapel, Christopher B. (whaling captain), 192–4, 214–16
Chapel, Edward (whaling captain), 194
Chase, 200
Cheyne, John, 61, 62, 64; commands *Sophia*, xxxiii; erects house at Kekerten, 59; surveys harbour at Kekerten, 59, 93; harpoons whales, 61, 169, 170, 171, 173, 174; reproved by Penny, 62,

80; a "most active man," 118; explores by dogsled, 134
Chieftain, 217
Church Missionary Society: mission in Cumberland Sound, 207
Clara, 30; and whale dispute, 124–7
clothing. *See* Eskimos; Gardiner; Penny, Margaret; whalemen
cold, 114, 127–8, 144–5
Cook, James: and scurvy, 148, 155
Couldrey (whaling captain): at Kingaite, 37; takes over *Lady Franklin*, 213
Cracroft, Sophia: on Margaret's character, xxvi; at departure of M'Clintock, 8
Craik, Catherine Fyfe ("Katie," daughter of James and Janet), 225
Craik, James (husband of Janet Penny), 225
Craik, William Penny ("Penny," son of James and Janet), 225
crews. *See* whalemen
Cumberland Sound: exploration of, xxix, xxx, 27; confusion of names for, xxx–xxxi
currents: and outward voyage, 10; and Marble Island, 121; and homeward voyage, 189, 190

Daniel Webster: scurvy deaths on, 161–2; 1858–59 voyage, 192–4
Davidson, Alexander D. (clergyman), xxiv
Davidson, Fraser (seaman on *Alibi*): death from scurvy, 160
Davis, John, xxx, 27
Davis Strait whale fishery. *See* whaling
Deblois, Henrietta (whaling wife), 15

Dee: scurvy on, 149
De Haven, Edwin Jesse, xxxi
Deuchars, G. (whaling captain), 222
Deuchars, Mrs (whaling wife), xxvi
Diana: and steam propulsion, 42; brings highest catch, 200
Dick (cabin boy), 63
Dickens, Charles: declares Eskimos "treacherous," 7
disease. *See* Eskimos; scurvy
dogs: on Nuvujen Island, 34; transported from Nuvujen, 91; eat refuse from blubber boiler, 115, 116, 122; reach Kekerten over ice, 122
dogsleds, xxxiii, *180*
Donaldson, John (harpooner on *Lady Franklin*), 39; saved from drowning, 72
Druett, Joan, xxv
Duncan, John (cooper on *Sophia*): to remain in Arctic, 186
Dunnet, John (seaman on *Alibi*): death from scurvy, 160

Ebierbing (Eskimo man), 57, 140. *See also* Hackboch
Eclipse, xxix
Eenoolooapik (Eskimo man): visits Scotland, xxix, *xxx*, 28, 49, 138
Eenoolooapik (nephew of above; son of Mary), 62
Emily, xxv
Emma: winters at Disco, xxvi; at Kingaite, 41; in Melville Bay, 43–6
Erebus, HMS: equipped with steam engine, 41
Eskimos: visit Britain, xxix, 28, 48–58; at Niantilik, 19, 20; at Nuvujen, 20–2 passim, 187–8; gender-related roles of, 29, 183;

attracted to whaling harbours, 29, 88, 181–2; arrive at ships, 37, 39, 64, 77, 80, 82, 87; starvation among, 50; and origin of earth, 78; respect sabbath, 79, 109; kayak and umiak of, 80, 81; obtain whaleboats, 81; population, 96, 113, 180–2; play tottem on ship, 97; igloos and tents of, 98, 101, 111, 167; ill at Kekerten, 98, 99, 111–13, 120; better off in Greenland, 108–10; susceptible to diseases, 112–13; short of food, 114, 116, 120–3, 143; hunting cycle, 120–2, 136; sealing methods, 122, 135, 141–3, *142*, *143;* whaling methods, 125–7; nicknames, 128–9; orphan boys employed, 134; prepare seal skins, 135; adopt European-style clothing, 138, 140; burial practices and beliefs, 163–6; suicide among, 172

Esquimaux. *See* Eskimos

Explorers: bound by traditions, 107

Falconer, John (cooper on *Lady Franklin*): death from scurvy, 160–1

"fast fish," 124–7

fast ice. *See* landfast ice

Felix: scurvy on, 158

Fife (ice master of HMS *Hecla*): death from scurvy, 155

Findlay, George (agent at Kekerten), 213

Findley, George (harpooner on *Sophia*): harpoons whale, 175

Flannan Islands: landfall at, 194

floe edge: importance in whaling, 183. *See also* landfast ice; whaling, methods

Fox: purchase and refit of, 8; leaves Aberdeen, 8, 9; beset in Baffin Bay, 209

Franklin, Jane: and *Fox* expedition, 7, 8; finds Inglefield's "ice-boat," 8; and Penny, 8, 220–1; learns of husband's fate, 209

Franklin, John: final expedition of, xvii, xviii; search for, xxxi–xxxiii, 7–9, 208–9; Pakak's story, 88–90

Fraser (whaling captain): takes over *Sophia*, 213

Frobisher, Martin, 27

frostbite: among whalemen, 114, 134; and death of Eskimo man, 115, 118, 121, 129, 132, 163–4

gams, 14

Gardiner, Alexander (seaman on *Alibi*): death, 105; clothing, 105–6

Garster, Gilbert (seaman on *Lady Franklin*): to remain in Arctic, 186

Gedney, G. William, 51, 54; vaccinates Eskimos, 51

Gem: at Kingaite, 37, 41

George Henry: winters at Niantilik, 40; carries Eskimo home, 52; wrecked in Hudson Strait, 215–16

Georgiana: scurvy deaths on, 161; takes mail from Arctic, 214

Gibson, George (apprentice on *Lady Franklin*), 23

Gifford, Harriet (whaling wife), xxiv

Glacier: carries pigs, 150

Goldring, Philip, xxx–xxxi

Goodsir, Robert: directs cultural activities, 159

Grant, Erskine (surgeon on *Lady Franklin*): reaches crow's nest, 18, 26; tends

Eskimos, 19, 98, 99, 116, 129; goes shooting, 21, 22; officiates in church services, 21, 26; collects specimens, 22; accompanies Penny in pursuit of Stewart, 61, 74, 75; joins whaleboat crew, 79; on boat trip to Kingua, 171; compliments Margaret, 116–17, 128; on sledge trip to Niantilik, 131, 133; and cultural events, 159; to remain in Arctic, 186

Greener, William: and gun harpoon, 70

Greenland: missions, xxxiv, xxxv, 205–6, 207, 208; Danish administration of, 50, 51, 54

Gipsy, 45; crushed by ice, 37, 44–6

Hackaluckjoe (Eskimo boy), 54

Hackboch (Eskimo man): in England, 54, 57. *See also* Ebierbing

Hadlow (Eskimo man): baby named after Warmow, 100

Halbeck, Emma Renata (Moravian missionary): marries Warmow, 207–8

Hall, Charles Francis: meets Tookoolitoo (Tackritow), 57

Hall & Company: and *Fox*, 53

Hamilton, Andrew (whaling surgeon): and Penny's alleged plunder, 217–18

Hamilton, W.A.B.: Penny asks help from, 221

Hannah. *See* Tackritow

Hannibal: 1858–59 voyage, 192–3

harpoon guns: 20, 69, 70; as life-saving apparatus, 72, 79; as signal, 81

harpoons, hand, 69–70

Hawkins, John: and "scourge of the sea," 146, 147

Hayden, Mary Russell (whaling wife), xxv

Hegarty, Reginald: his youth on whaler, 26

Herbrich (Moravian missionary): to go to Cumberland Sound, xxxv

Hogarth Sound. *See* Cumberland Sound

Hope: five-year voyage of, 193

housing cloths, 102

Hudson Bay: whaling and scurvy in, 150, 152, 154, 156–7

Hudson Bay Minstrels, 154

Hudson's Bay Company: territorial limits of, xvi; scurvy on ships of, 157; encounters Penny in Hudson Strait, 216

Hudson Strait: bottleneck for ice, 215

Hutchison (clergyman): at Penny's funeral, 223

ice: types of, 5; and whales, 6, 66, 67; and ships, 15–17, 44–6, 149, 189–90, 224; and Eskimo hunting, 96, 121–2, 140–3; for water supply, 134. *See also* bergy bits; cape ice; floe edge; icebergs; ice streams; landfast ice; Middle Ice; pack ice; sailing ice; whaling, methods

icebergs, 15, 17; appearance of, 18, 26; disintegration of, 19

ice streams, 5, 15

igloos: built at Kekerten, 98; melt in spring, 167

Inglefield, Edward Augustus, 8

Innuit, 30; and steam propulsion, 42

Intrepid, HMS: and steam propulsion, 41, 42

Irvine, Catharine (sister of Margaret), xxiv

Irvine, George (father of Margaret), xxii–xxiv

Irvine, Helen (mother of Margaret), xxii, 197

Irvine, Margaret. *See* Penny, Margaret

Isabel (Franklin search ship), 8

Isabel (steam tender to *Emma*): at Kingaite, 37, 41, 43

Isabella, scurvy on, 156

Jackal (steam tender to *Traveller*): at Kingaite, 37, 41, 43

Joe. *See* Ebierbing

John Barrow (Eskimo baby), 119, 128

Kekerten: confusing names for, 90–2; sledge trips from Niantilik to, 119, 124, 133, 175, 176

Kekerten Harbour, *93, 94–5, 202;* characteristics, 92, 93–5

Kekerten Island, *93;* house erected on, 59; characteristics, 95–6; cut off during freeze-up, 121–2; shore station on, *203. See also* Kikastan Islands

Kennedy, William: and Franklin search, 220–1

Kidd (clergyman), xxiv

Kikastan Islands, 90

Kingaite (Kingite), 40–1

Kingmiksok, *33*

Kingnait Fiord. *See* Kingaite

Kingnait Harbour (also called Tornait). *See* Sophia Harbour

Kingua: voyage to, 65

Kinnear (whaling captain): takes Eskimo to Scotland, 49

Kinnear, Mrs, 49

Kleinschmidt, Samuel (Moravian missionary): attempts to reach Cum-

berland Sound, xxxv, xxxvi

Kudlago (Eskimo man): dies on homeward voyage, 52

Lady Franklin, 11, 103; outward voyage, 3–17; size and rig of, 12; accommodation on, 15; crew, 23, 24, 25; aground while under tow, 37; captures first whale, 77, 82–3; flenses first whale, 78, 85; takes up winter quarters, 82; homeward voyage, 189–95; taken over by Capt. Couldrey, 213. *See also* whalemen; whaling

landfast ice, 15, 17, 140; freeze-up of, 66, 81, 82, 92, 95, 96, 97, 101–2, 121–2, 123–4; break-up of (and spring whaling), 96, 167, 168, 170, 171, 172, 175, 177, 178, 185; and sledge travel, 116, 118, 130; and seal hunting, 140–3

Lawrence, Mary Chipman (whaling wife), 14

Lawrence, Minnie (daughter of Samuel and Mary), 14

Lawrence, Samuel (whaling captain), 14

Leask, William (seaman on *Sophia*): to remain in Arctic, 186

Leopold Island: depot vandalized, 89

Lichtenau, Greenland: mission at, xxxvii, 207

Lichtenfels, Greenland: mission at, xxxv, *xxxvi,* xxxvii, 207

Lind, James, 147. *See also* scurvy

Lindsay, Andrew (spectioneer on *Lady Franklin*), 34, 160, 173

loggerhead. *See* billet-head

"loose fish," 124–7
Lord Gambier, xxx
Lucas, John (ice master of
  Lady Franklin): makes
  boat trip to Kingua, 65;
  harpoons whales, 173,
  174; to remain in Arctic,
  186

M'Clintock, Francis
  Leopold: prepares for
  Franklin search, 7, 8, 9;
  beset in Baffin Bay for
  winter, 209; finds site of
  Franklin tragedy, 209
McKinnon (whaling cap-
  tain): leaves gear at
  Miliakdjuin, 116
Mackitow (Eskimo
  woman), 22
McLaren, Ian A., 143
McLellan: and wintering of
  crew, xxxiii
Manby, William George:
  life-saving apparatus of,
  72, 79
Marble Island: scurvy at,
  150, 154
Marble Island Theatre, 154
Margaret's Island, 91
Maria. *See* Mary
Martin (whaling captain),
  xxxiii, 62; leaves gear at
  Miliakdjuin, 116
Mary (sister of Eenoo-
  looapik): to keep house
  at Nuvujen, 39; clothing,
  138
Melville Bay hazards, 44–6
Memiadluk (Eskimo man):
  visits England, 49–52
Merlin, 15
Middle Ice, 43
missionaries: in Arctic,
  xxxiv. *See also* Moravians;
  Warmow, Matthäus
Moir, James (seaman on
  Alibi): death from
  scurvy, 160
Moravians: in Greenland
  and Labrador, xxxiv,
  xxxv; attempts to get mis-
  sionaries to Cumberland

Sound, xxxv, xxxvi; at
  Fairfield (near Manchester), xxxv; at Fulneck
  (Yorkshire), xxxvii; at
  Herrnhut (Germany),
  204; decide against mission, 204–5, 206, 207

Narwhal: xxvi, 213, 221, 222
Naujartalik. *See* Niantilik
Nelson, Horatio: went to
  sea young, 129
Nelson, Richard K.: and Es-
  kimo hunting methods,
  141
Nepali, Radha (second wife
  of William "Billie"
  Penny), 211
Neptune: first command of
  Penny, xxix
Neuherrnhut, Greenland:
  mission at, 207
Neu Terralie (Eskimo
  man): visits Scotland, 57
Newbullygar (Bullygar):
  visits Scotland, 58;
  reaches Kekerten from
  Niantilik, 119, 124; and
  whale dispute, 124–7;
  harpoons whales, 172,
  173
Niantilik, 19–22, 28–31,
  31, 32; sledge trip from
  Kekerten to, 131, 133
Noodlook (Eskimo man),
  77; son born to, 128
Northumberland Inlet. *See*
  Cumberland Sound
North Water, 43
Northwest Passage: search
  for, xxxi, 148
Novaya Zemlya, 256
Nuvujen: station established
  at, 33–5; dogs from, 91;
  death at, 160–1; men to
  remain at, 186; and
  Tessuin, 188

Ocean Nymph: and scurvy,
  150, 153, 156–7
open polar sea, xxxii, 212,
  213
Orray Taft: and scurvy, 157

Osborn, Sherard: and
  Penny, 211
Oshallee (Eskimo man),
  39, 64

Pacific: takes stores from
  wreck, 218–19
pack ice, 15, 16; and ships,
  43–6; and winds, 177;
  on homeward voyage,
  189–90
Pakak: reports white men
  in boats, 80, 88–90, 100
Parker, John (whaling
  captain), *38;* winters at
  Disco, xxvi; leaves depot
  for Franklin, xxxi; at-
  tempts to take missionary
  to Cumberland Sound,
  xxxv–xxxvi; takes Eski-
  mos to England, xxxv,
  49–52; at Kingaite, 37;
  narrow escape in Melville
  Bay, 44–6; petitions
  Queen Victoria, 50; and
  scurvy, 154
Parker, Mrs (whaling wife):
  winters in Davis Strait,
  xxvi
Parry, William Edward:
  and scurvy, 148, 155
Pearce, Stephen: paints
  Penny's portrait, xxxii–
  xxxiii
Peck E.J. (clergyman):
  mission in Cumberland
  Sound, 207, *208*
Pedleatu (wife of Tessuin):
  dies in Scotland, 189
Penny, Charles (grandfa-
  ther of William), xxviii
Penny, Helen Eliza (daugh-
  ter of William and Marg-
  aret), xxiv, xxvii, 225
Penny, James (uncle of
  William), xxviii
Penny, Janet, née Robertson
  (mother of William), xxix
Penny, Janet Robertson
  (daughter of William
  and Margaret), xxiv, 225
Penny, John (uncle of
  William), xxviii

Penny, John (brother of William), 222

Penny, Margaret, née Irvine (wife of William): journal of, xv–xvi, xxxvii–xli, 144, 185; early years, xxii–xxiv; marriage and children, xxiv; forcefulness of, xxvi; and whaling voyages, xxvi–xxvii, 224; on ship, 15, 25, 73, 128; and Eskimo women, 20, 21, 22, 28–9, 37, 136, 137, 138, 140, 168, 175, 187; and Eskimos in Britain, 28, 49, 53, 57, 58; scolds Warmow, 63; eats maktak, 78, 117, 133, 162; wears fur clothing, 98, 107; rides dogsled, 115, 168; birthday, 116–17, 128; worries about Billie, 118; ill from fumes, 119; entertains at tea, 119, 128, 130, 133, 134, 137–8; distributes food, 173, 181; responsibilities, 181–3; "great service to the expedition," 198; winters again in Arctic, 224; loses daughter Maggie, 224–5; marriage of daughter Janet, 225; loses Janet, 225; and grandchildren, 225–6; gives advice to Billie, 226; death, 226

Penny, Margaret Irvine (daughter of William and Margaret), xxiv, 225

Penny, William (father of William): whaling career, xxix

Penny, William, *xxviii;* early years, xxvii–xxix; whaling voyages before 1857, xxix–xxxiv; marriage, xxix; brings Eskimos to Scotland, xxix, 57–8; finds Tenudiakbeek (Cumberland Sound), xxix–xxx; and Franklin search, xxxi–xxxiii, 41,

75–6; and Royal Arctic Company, xxxiii; wintering voyages, xxxiii, 46, 179–81; attempts to take missionaries to Cumberland Sound, xxxvi; contributes to Margaret's journal, xxxviii; releases carrier pigeons, 13; tends Eskimos, 19, 98, 134; skilled in ice navigation, 31, 32, 33, 224; and whaling station concept, 33, 67, 201, 202; proposes steam power, 43; finds harbour at Kekerten, 46; reproves Stewart, 47, 74–6; instructs harpooners and boatsteerers, 60, 66–71; uses harpoon guns, 69, 70; authority of on whaling grounds, 73, 74; lectures crew about winter hazards, 98–9, 104; and Eskimo funeral, 163, 164, 166; not satisfied with achievements, 211–12; proposes "Port Franklin" on Vancouver Island, 212; proposes whaling in Arctic Ocean, 212–13; commands steam whaler, 213, 221; leaves Aberdeen Arctic Company, 213; winters again in Arctic, 213–14; blamed for plunder, 214–19; fails to obtain a command, 219–20; personality, 220–3; and Lady Franklin, 220, 221; and Austin, 221; and Barrow, 221; and Beaufort, 221; and Robert Brown, 221; and W.A.B. Hamilton, 221; and John Ross, 221; retirement, 222–3; death, 223–4

Penny, William ("Billie," son of William and Margaret): birth, xxiv; on ship, 26, 129; at Kek-

erten, 29–30, 97, 117, 148, 152; travels with Eskimos by dogsled, 115, 117–18, 129–30, 131, 133; saves doctor, 133; in India, 209–11, *210;* death, 211

Penny, William Kennedy (son of William and Margaret), xxiv

pigeons: released by Penny, 13

Pillouseak (Eskimo man), 134

Pioneer, HMS: and steam propulsion, 41, 42

Place-names: of Eskimos, 91; of whalemen, xxx, xxxi, 90, 91, 92

Polynia (steam whaler): commanded by Penny, 213

"Port Franklin," BC, 212

Prince Albert: and Franklin search, 221

Prince Arthur: encounters Penny in Hudson Strait, 216

Pyola media, 159

Quayle (whaling captain): arrives from Niantilik, 175, 176

Queen: wintering voyage of, 213–14, 224; and alleged plunder of depot, 214–17

Rae, John: brings news of Franklin disaster, 7

Reid (captain of *Arctic*): takes Tessuin to Scotland, 188

Reid (captain of *Pacific*): and Danish wreck, 218–19

Resolution Island: landfall at, 18, 26–7

Richter, Friederich Valentin (Moravian missionary), 207

Richter, Maria Elisabeth (Moravian missionary): marries Warmow, 207

Robertson (surgeon of *Alibi*): mental derangement and suicide, 36, 46–8

Ross, Alex (seaman on *Lady Franklin*): explores by dogsled, 134

Ross, George (harpooner on *Lady Franklin*): reproved by Penny, 63

Ross, John: use of steam in 1829, 41

Royal Arctic Company, xxxiii

Royal Cornwallis Theatre, 158

Royal Navy: and Northwest Passage, xxxi, xxxii; and scurvy, 146–9 passim

sabbath: observed on ships, 26; respected by Eskimos, 79, 109, 166

sailing ice, 16

Saint Andrew: commanded by Penny, xxxi

Saumia: Eskimos from, 88

Schwatka, Frederick: observation on scurvy, 156–7

Scoresby, William, Jr: takes Manby on voyage, 72; and whaling law, 124–5; and antiscorbutic foods, 149, 151–2

scurvy: kills five men on *Alibi*, 30, 46; Penny's measures against, 100, 104, 157–62; symptoms of, 146–7; history of, 146–62; on voyages of discovery, 146, 147; and the Royal Navy, 147, 148, 149, 152; on Cook's expeditions, 148, 155; on Parry's expeditions, 148, 155; on whalers, 149–62; earth treatment for, 154–5; and food prejudice, 155–7; Schwatka's observation on, 156–7; Stefansson's views on, 156; on John Ross's expedition, 158; death

from at Nuvujen station, 160–1; on *Lady Franklin*, 161

Seaflower, 54

seals:
– bearded, 168
– ringed: winter in Arctic, 41; hunted by Eskimos, 122, 135, 141–3, *142*, *143*

shaman: opposed by missionary, 163–5

Shore Porters' Society, 223–4

Sir Colin Campbell: brings news of Penny, 216

Skelton (mate of *Alibi*), 36

Smythe (Hudson's Bay Company captain), 216

Sophia, 11, 103; characteristics of, 12; crew, 23; homeward voyage, 189–95; taken over by Capt. Fraser, 213

Sophia Harbour: location and name, 41, 91

Souter (whaling captain). *See* Sutter

Southwest Ice, xxxv

Spicer, John (whaling captain): and shipwrecked crew, 215–16

steam propulsion for ships: early experiments in Arctic, 41, 42; in whaling fleet, 42; proposed by Penny, 43, 213

Stefansson, Vilhjalmur: and scurvy prevention, 156

Stevenson, Marc, 94–5

Stevenson (clergyman): proposes to Janet Penny, 225

Stewart, Alexander: ignores Penny's orders, 19, 46, 60–1, 62, 74–5, 119, 124; on Franklin search expedition, 75–6; identity of, 76n; and whale dispute, 124–6

Sturrock, Mrs (whaling wife): sails to Davis Strait, xxvi

Sutherland, Peter Cormack: and cultural activities, 152, 159; and antiscorbutics, 157, 159

Sutter (whaling captain), 19, 30; and whale dispute, 124–7

Syren Queen: and scurvy, 154

Tackritow (Tookoolitoo; Eskimo woman): visits Britain, 28, 48, 52–72, 138; at Kingaite, 37, 39; and European fashion, 138–40, *139;* and C.F. Hall, 140; death, 140

Tay: and steam propulsion, 42; high catch of, 200

teetottem. *See* tottem

Tenudiakbeek. *See* Cumberland Sound

Terror, HMS: equipped with steam engine, 41

Tessuin (Eskimo man): anxious to visit Britain, 37; persuaded to work for *Arctic,* 119, 124; and whale dispute, 124–5, 188–9; "poisoned by falsehoods," 131; at Niantilik, 133; visits Scotland, 188–9; wife dies in Scotland, 189

thrashers. *See* whales, killer

Tillotson, John, 224

Todd (whaling captain): and Penny's alleged plunder, 217

Tongite (Kingnait Harbour). *See* Sophia Harbour

Tookoolitoo. *See* Tackritow

Tornait (Kingnait Harbour). *See* Sophia Harbour

tottem, 97, 113

Towlow (Eskimo man), 63, 64, 65

Townsend, Charles Haskins, 150

Traveller, xxix, 36, 37, 41, 43

Truelove: and Franklin search, xxxi; takes Eskimos to England, xxxv

try pots, 86, *204*

Tshatluta (Eskimo man): harpoons whales, 172, 173, 175

Uckaluk (Eskimo woman), 53; visits England, 49–52; death, 52

Undaunted: crushed by ice, 37, 44–6

United Brethren. *See* Moravians

Victoria, Queen: petitioned for Eskimo welfare, 41, 50; and Eskimo visitors, 55, 57

Victory (discovery ship), 41

Victory (steam tug), 9

vitamin c, 146, 148

Ward, Thomas (shipowner), xxxv

Wareham (whaling captain), xxx

Warmow (Eskimo baby): birth, 100; death, 163

Warmow, Matthäus: ready to go to Cumberland Sound, xxxvi, xxxvii; background, xxxvii; on ship, 4, 13, 26, 65; and Lady Franklin, 8; instructs Eskimos, 19, 20, 21, 78, 100, 110–11, 116, 162–3; conducts church services, 21, 65; goes hunting, 21, 22, 40, 63, 172, 184, 185; dredges for specimens, 22; on boat trips, 65, 81; and Pakak, 89; and names for Kekerten, 92;

name given to baby, 100, 163; views on European impact, 108, 109, 110; shocked at Eskimo "poverty," 109, 111; describes igloo interior, 111; birthday, 133; feels arctic cold, 144–5; and confrontation with shaman, 163–6; helps during spring whaling, 169, 170; summoned after Eskimo suicide, 171; sadness at parting, 187–8; recommends against mission, 204–5; marriages of 207–8; death, 208

Warmow Haven. *See* Kekerten

Wellington, 54

whaleboats, 25, 60, 66–73 passim, *68, 70, 71,* 77–81 passim, 83–4, *84,* 87–8, 167–76 passim, 178, *179,* 180, 183

whalebone. *See* baleen

whalemen: jobs on ship, xxii, 3–6, 13, 20, 25, 186, 191; erect house at Nuvujen, 20, 33, 34; characteristics, 23, 24; ranks and functions, 24, 25; and Eskimo culture, 29–30; erect house at Kekerten, 59; play music and dance, 61; cut road through rough ice, 98, 99, 101–2; sick at Kekerten, 99, 112; house ship in for winter, 99, 102; and exercise, 104; clothing, 104–8; cut ice for water supply, 134; winter routine, 136; attracted to Arctic, 197

whales:
– bowhead: characteristics, xx; migration, 66, 67, 177; size, 67, 78, 83–5; carcasses, 87; depletion, 199–200
– Greenland. *See* whales, bowhead
– killer, 72, 85
– sperm, xix

whaling: products, xix; itinerary, xx–xxi, 10, 43, 44, 193; influence on Eskimos, xxi, 29, 30, 87–8, 108–10, 112–13, 120–1, 136, 180–1; ships, xxii, 12, 14, 15, 43–6; crews, xxii, 23–5; shore stations, 33–5, 186, 202–3, *203, 204;* methods, 66–72, 83, 85–7, 167–83 passim; laws, 124–7; decline after 1820s, 199–200, 202. *See also* blubber; Eskimos; harpoon guns; harpoons, hand; *Lady Franklin;* scurvy; *Sophia;* whaleboats; whaling wives; wintering

whaling wives, xxiv–xxvii, 14

William Torr: wreckage drifts to Britain, 189

winter: perception of, xxi, 136; hazards, 104, 107–8, 145–6; "period of hardship" for Eskimos, 141

wintering (of whalers), xxi–xxii; advantages, 16, 17; selecting a harbour for, 95–6; preparing for, 101–3; economics of, 201. *See also* frostbite; Penny, William

women: on whaling ships. *See* whaling wives

DATE DUE